BIRTH OF A TRAGEDY
KASHMIR 1947

Also by Alastair Lamb and published by Roxford Books

Tibet, China & India. A History of Imperial Diplomacy
Kashmir. A Disputed Legacy 1846–1990

By Alastair and Venice Lamb

Au Cameroun: Weaving – Tissage
Sierra Leone Weaving

BIRTH OF A TRAGEDY
KASHMIR 1947

Alastair Lamb

Roxford Books
Hertingfordbury
1994

© Alastair Lamb, 1994

The right of Alastair Lamb to be identified as the Author of the Work has been asserted by him in accordance with the Copyright, Designs and Patents Act 1988.

First published in 1994 by Roxford Books,
Hertingfordbury, Hertfordshire, U.K.

All rights reserved. No part of this publication may be reproduced, stored in a retrieval system or transmitted in any form or by any means, electronic, mechanical, photocopying, recording or otherwise, without the prior permission in writing of the publishers.

ISBN 0 907129 07 2

Printed in England by Redwood Books, Trowbridge, Wiltshire
Typeset by Create Publishing Services Ltd, Bath, Avon

Contents

	Acknowledgements	vii
I	Paramountcy and Partition, March to August 1947	1
	1. Introductory	1
	2. Paramountcy	4
	3. Partition: its origins	13
	4. Partition: the Radcliffe Commission	24
	5. Jammu & Kashmir and the lapse of Paramountcy	42
II	The Poonch Revolt, origins to 24 October 1947	54
III	The Accession Crisis, 24–27 October 1947	81
IV	The War in Kashmir, October to December 1947	104
V	To the United Nations, October 1947 to 1 January 1948	126
VI	The Birth of a Tragedy	165

Maps
1. The State of Jammu & Kashmir in relation to its neighbours. — ix
2. The State of Jammu & Kashmir. — x
3. Stages in the creation of the State of Jammu and Kashmir. — xi
4. The Vale of Kashmir. — xii
5. Partition boundaries in the Punjab, 1947. — xiii

Acknowledgements

Since the publication of my *Kashmir. A Disputed Legacy 1846–1990* in 1991, I have been able to carry out further research into the minutiae of those events of 1947 which resulted in the end of the British Indian Empire, the Partition of the Punjab and Bengal and the creation of Pakistan, and the opening stages of the Kashmir dispute the consequences of which are with us still. While in no significant respect altering the conclusions which I had reached in 1991, yet this new work has illuminated more brightly a number of topics including the process by which the Punjab was partitioned, the alleged signing of the Instrument of Accession by the Maharaja of Jammu & Kashmir on 26 October 1947, and the negotiations and discussions which finally resulted in the Indian reference of the Kashmir question to the Security Council of the United Nations on 1 January 1948. Such additional data, much of it amplifying and clarifying what was outlined in my 1991 book, seems to me to justify a further publication.

My research since 1991 has been based on many sources. I had the good fortune to be able to talk with several individuals who still remember what happened in 1947, and I have availed myself of their recollections here. There are also some extremely valuable papers, hitherto unexplored, preserved in the India Office Library and Records of the British Library, where the staff gave me their unstinting assistance which I have much appreciated. I must thank the Controller of Her Majesty's Stationary Office for permission to quote from Crown copyright material. I would also like to acknowledge the kindness of Athar Ali in securing for me all four volumes of *The Partition of the Punjab 1947*, an invaluable set of documents compiled by Mian Muhammad Sadullah and published in Lahore in 1983. These volumes are the essential companion to the final volumes of *The Transfer of Power 1942–7*; and without them it would have been much more difficult for me to work out how and why Punjab was partitioned.

ACKNOWLEDGEMENTS

I hope that the fresh matter contained in this book will eventually be incorporated into a revised edition of *Kashmir. A Disputed Legacy*, when it will be accompanied by all the appropriate references and explanatory footnotes. In the present book, bearing in mind some cogent criticism of my predilection for an elaborate critical apparatus, I have kept references to the absolute minimum, and those within the body of the text. The policy has been to mention only secondary works which have seemed to me for one reason or another to be of exceptional importance or interest. I have not given specific references for documentary material in the India Office Records though I have endeavoured to indicate their general whereabouts. For a variety of reasons the individuals whose memories have been drawn upon in this book are not named here though some of them will be acknowledged in the revised edition of *Kashmir. A Disputed Legacy*. Among the scholars to whom reference has not been made in the text I would particularly like to mention Ian Copland whose writings on so much of the background to the Kashmir dispute I have found exceptionally stimulating.

Kashmir. A Disputed Legacy received some extremely hostile reviews from Indian critics. Some of these were frivolous and just what one would expect in a situation so dominated by national polemic; but some have merited serious attention, coming as they have from writers who know a great deal about the recent history of the Subcontinent. I have, in any case, looked into all criticisms to see if behind the occasionally offensive language there might lurk a nugget of truth. As a result of such comment from the Indian side, for example, I re-examined very carefully the journal and other papers of Sir George Cunningham to see what light they might cast upon the events which immediately preceded the formal Indian intervention in Kashmir on 27 October 1947.

I must acknowledge my debt to Julia Allen whose skilled editorial eye spotted a number of infelicities in the earlier versions of the typescript which, I hope, I have managed to eliminate. My wife, as has been her wont for many years now, supported me during the preparation of this book in too many ways to list here. As in the case of *Kashmir. A Disputed Legacy*, she prepared the maps; and she also helped see the book through the press.

Alastair Lamb,
Hertford and St. Andéol de Clerguemort,
October 1993.

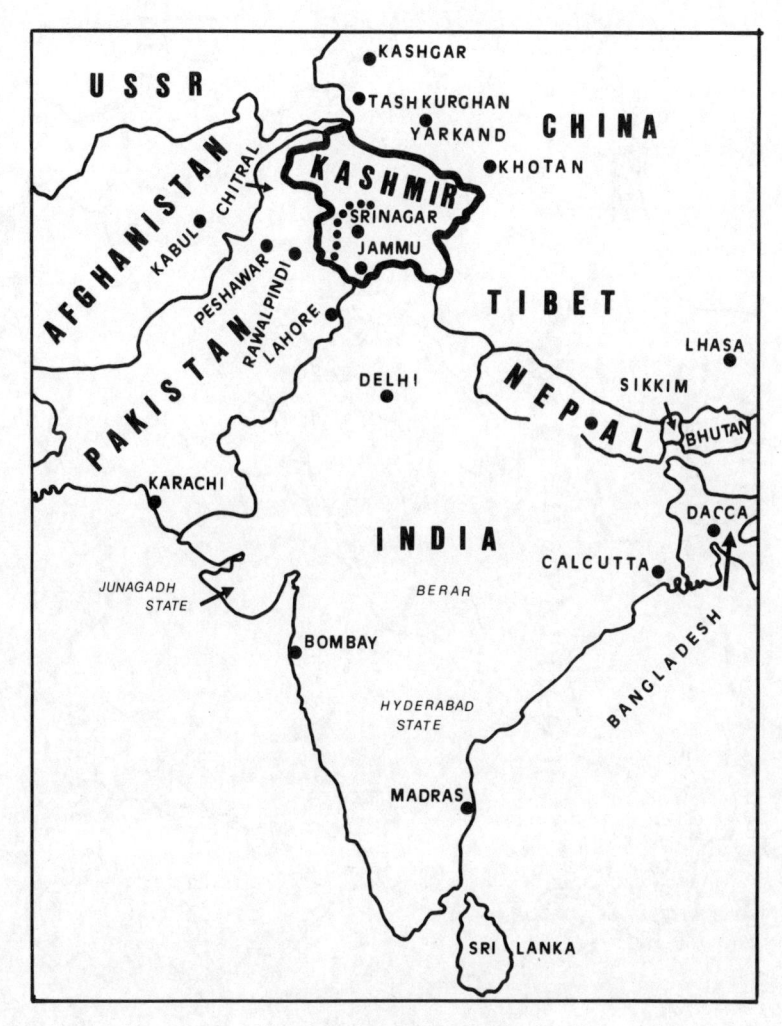

Map 1. The State of Jammu & Kashmir in relation to its neighbours.

Map 2. The State of Jammu & Kashmir.

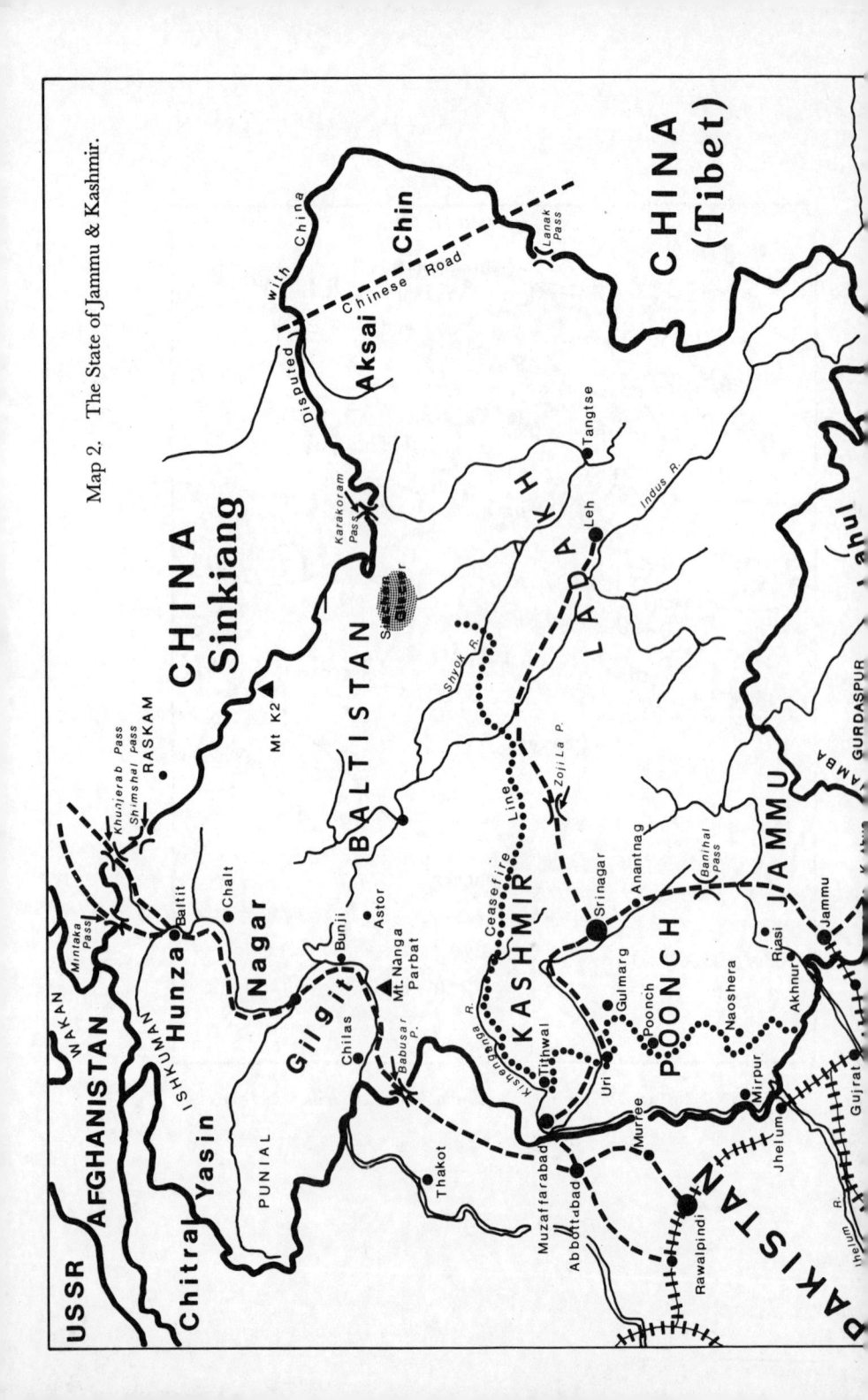

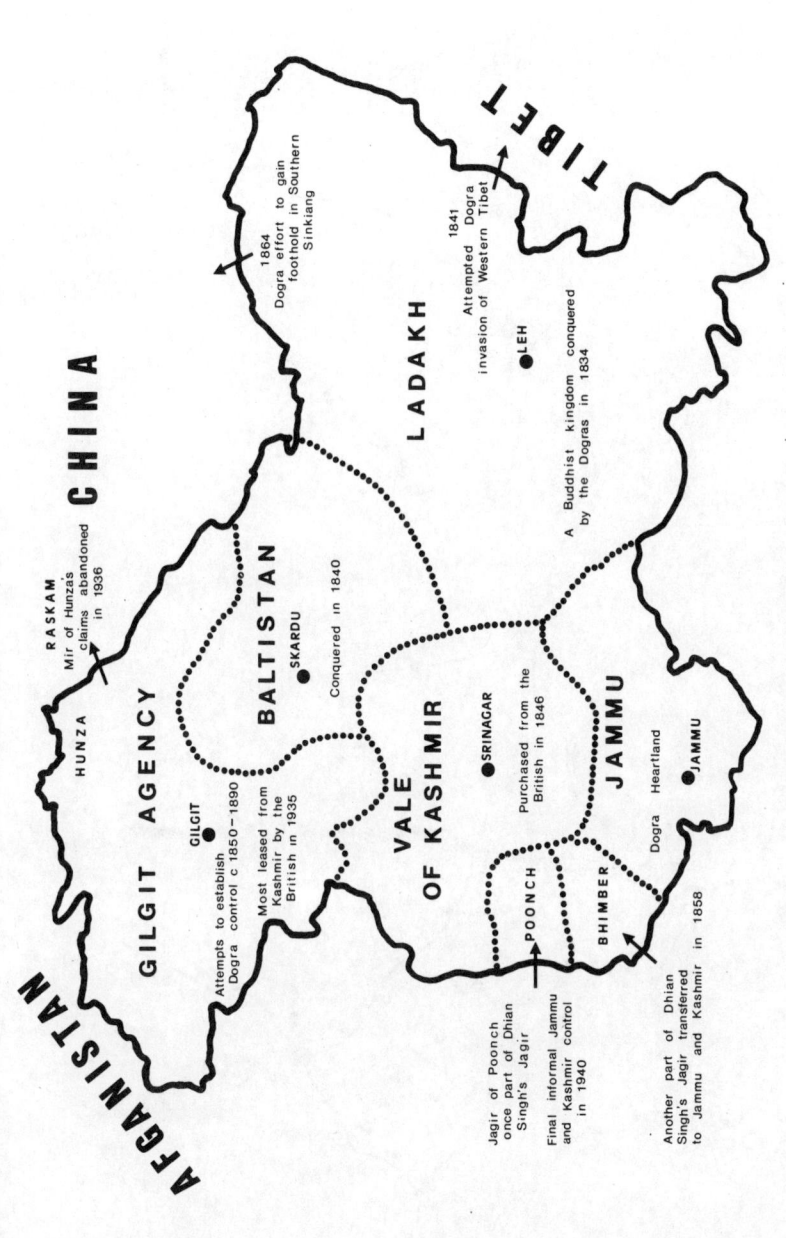

Map 3. Stages in the creation of the State of Jammu and Kashmir.

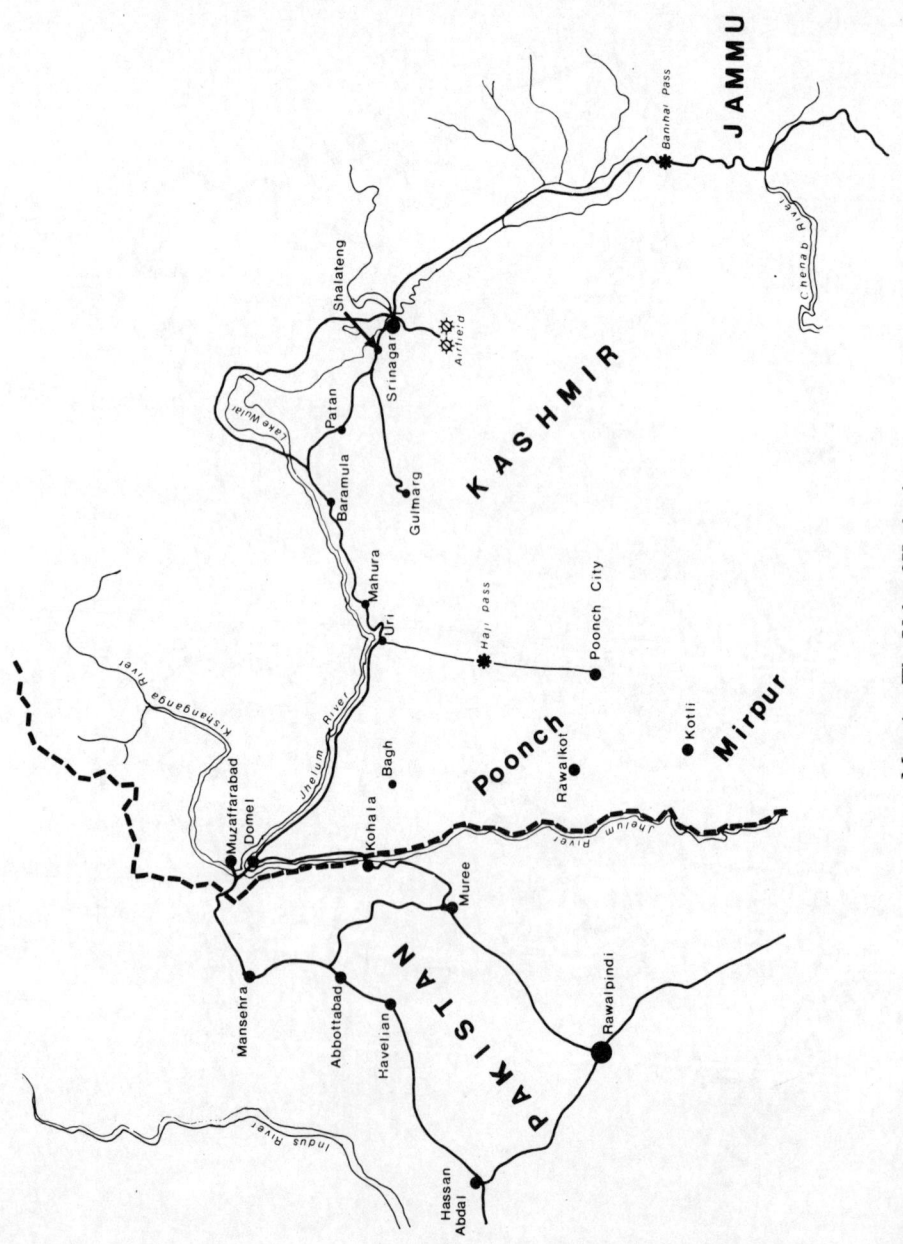

Map 4. The Vale of Kashmir.

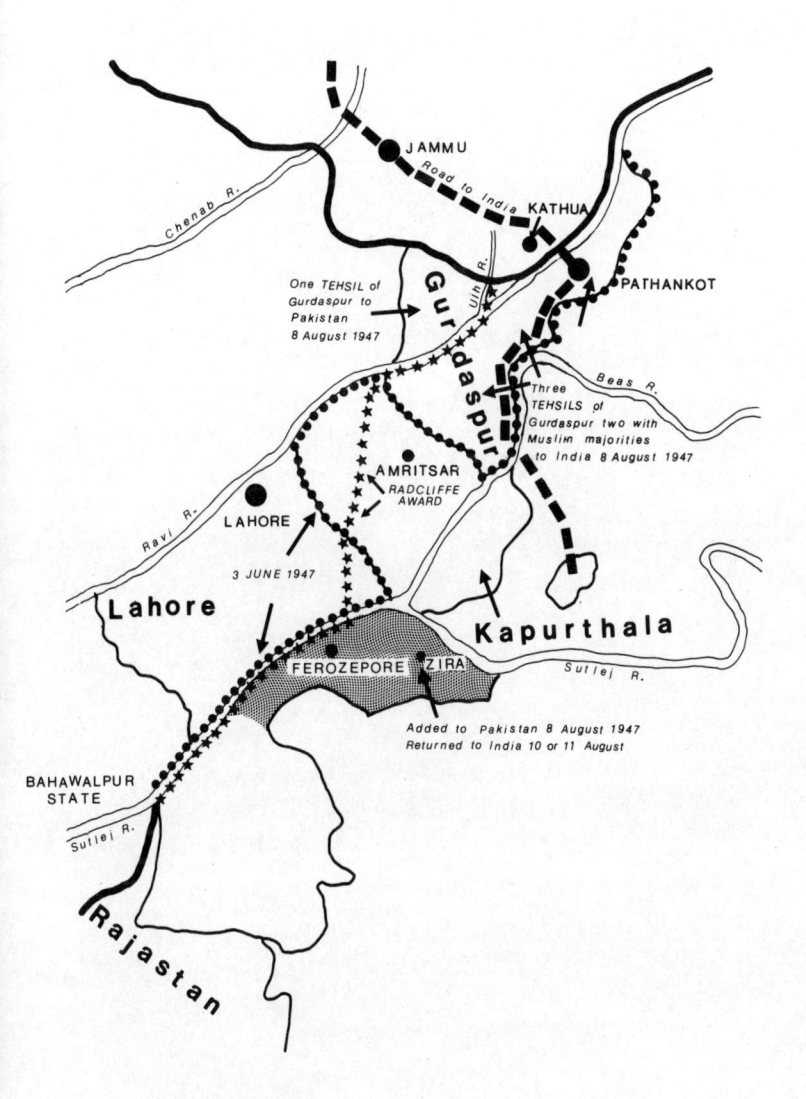

Map 5. Partition boundaries in the Punjab, 1947.

I

Paramountcy and Partition, March to August 1947

1. Introductory

At about 9 o'clock on the morning of 27 October 1947 units of the Indian Army started landing at Srinagar airfield. Thus began what many still today remember as Kashmir's Black Day, the formal commencement of the Indo-Pakistani Kashmir dispute which, despite the involvement of the United Nations as would-be mediator, has now persisted unresolved for some forty-five years. What provoked the Indian arrival? Did the Indians have any right to be there at all? What was the international status of the State of Jammu & Kashmir before, during and after the Indians came? What did the Kashmiri people think about it all? Three Indo-Pakistani wars, in 1947–48, 1965 and 1971, over Kashmir (in 1971, perhaps, as a secondary issue), have provided no final answers to any of these, and many other questions. The Indian-occupied portion of what was once the former Princely State is now held by at least 400,000 men who have spared no brutality in an attempt to suppress all traces of popular resistance to the oppressive rule of New Delhi.

The problem of the State of Jammu & Kashmir has it roots in two of the great political questions which dominated the final years of the British Indian Empire.

First: did those parts of British India with viable Muslim majorities have the right to look forward to an independent future free from Hindu domination, be it institutional or merely demographic? It was not a question which the Indian National Congress, the largest political grouping to confront the British, relished. Congress maintained then, as it still does, that it was in essence a secular organisation which (despite the fact that the great majority of its supporters were Hindus) represented all Indians regardless of religion. Congress was opposed by the Muslim

League, a body based upon an essentially communal view of Indian politics, that Muslim India possessed a national validity in its own right. By 1946 it was clear beyond doubt that some kind of division of power between the two organisations would be crucial to any orderly process of Transfer of Power from the British to Indian successors: hence the resort to the drastic measure of Partition, the Great Divide. In that the State of Jammu & Kashmir possessed an overwhelming Muslim majority (over 75% out of a total 4,000,000 – and more than 90% Muslim in the Vale of Kashmir – according to the 1941 figures) situated adjacent to that concentration of Muslim majorities in the Punjab and the North-West Frontier Province which was bound to be a core of Muslim political power, be it in an Indian federation or as a separate Pakistan, it simply was not possible in practice to insulate the State of Jammu & Kashmir from the great communal crisis which Partition brought about in neighbouring Punjab.

But, and this leads to the second question, Jammu & Kashmir was a Princely State, not an Indian Province. How were the Princely States to fit in with the process of Transfer of Power as it was to be applied to directly administered British India? Had Jammu & Kashmir been an integral part of British India, there can be no doubt that it would have automatically been embraced within the Muslim side, Pakistan, by the operations of the process of Partition. However, as a Princely State, despite its Muslim-majority population the future of Jammu & Kashmir was to be decided by its Ruler, who was a Hindu.

In 1947 the key phrase concerning the status of Princely States was "lapse of Paramountcy" (the meaning of which will be explored below). With Paramountcy lapsed, so constitutional specialists argued, once the British had left the Subcontinent, the State Rulers could make up their own minds what they now wished to do. Thus the Hindu Ruler of overwhelmingly Muslim Jammu & Kashmir was perfectly entitled to join India, should that be his wish.

Here was the immediate theoretical background to the Kashmir dispute, arising from those accidents of history which made an overwhelmingly Muslim population subject to a Hindu Maharaja. It was a conflict between one particular category of interpretation of Partition and one particular category of interpretation of Paramountcy. Other interpretations could well have produced totally different results. The significance of these two terms, Paramountcy and Partition, is the underlying subject of this chapter. It is the essential background to the outbreak of the Kashmir crisis in the latter part of 1947.

Had the State of Jammu & Kashmir been situated almost anywhere else in the Subcontinent, and had it embraced a lesser area, Indo-Pakistani argument over its future might not have been conducted with particular intensity. The State, however, lay not only adjacent to both India and Pakistan but also on a key frontier region which gave access to Central Asia, a part of the world which had for more than a century attracted the attention of British strategists whose attitudes were to great degree inherited by their successors. The State, moreover, was large, embracing over 80,000 square miles (comparable in magnitude to the United Kingdom), and title to such an extensive (and physically pleasing) territory, therefore, was not to be abandoned lightly.

The State of Jammu & Kashmir also possessed particularly powerful emotional associations with some of the leaders of the new Dominions of India and Pakistan. Jawaharlal Nehru was the scion of a line of Kashmiri Brahmins (Pandits). In many ways the product of an English education, the first Prime Minister of independent India felt deeply that his Indian roots, so vital for his current political position, required for their credibility an access to the soil of the Vale of Kashmir. Many leading Pakistanis possessed family ties with one or other part of the State, and all remembered that one of the major sources of their national inspiration, Sir Muhammad Iqbal, was profoundly concerned with all that had to do with Kashmir.

All this being so, however, the Indo-Pakistani Kashmir dispute was not inevitable. Had the process of the departure of the British from their Indian Empire followed a slightly different course, had the relations between those immediately responsible for the execution of that departure been more or less amicable, and had the implications of certain political decisions made during the course of 1947 been better understood, then the State of Jammu & Kashmir in general, and the Vale of Kashmir in particular, might indeed have enjoyed a happier future. Of course, there were to be other turning points and moments of truth in the four decades and more after 1947. The events of 1947, however, established the pattern for all that followed. 1947 did indeed see the birth of a tragedy, the full extent of which is still being revealed today (1993).

2. Paramountcy

[The key document collections are: Mian Muhammad Sadullah, *The Partition of the Punjab 1947. A Compilation of Official Documents*, 4 vols., Lahore 1983, hereafter *PP*; N. Mansergh, *The Transfer of Power 1942–7*, Vols. IX, X, XI, XII, London 1980–83, hereafter *TP*. See also: Kirpal Singh, ed., *The Partition of Punjab 1947*, New Delhi 1991].

The British Indian Empire, superficially until its abrupt termination in 1947 the most impressive of all the colonial structures of modern times, was no monolith. The Governor-General, who after 1858 was also Viceroy, presided in great pomp and circumstance over two distinct categories of territory.

The bulk of the Empire, roughly two thirds of it, consisted of tracts directly administered by the British. There were Provinces (under Governors or Chief Commissioners), Bengal, Assam, Bihar, Orissa, United Provinces, Punjab, North-West Frontier Province, Sind, Baluchistan, Central Provinces, Bombay and Madras, to which must be added a number of territories, tribal areas and some tracts leased from Princely States.

But at least a third of the total area of this subcontinental empire was made up of Princely States, well over 560 of them, some like Jammu & Kashmir, Kalat, Hyderabad, as extensive (though by no means as populous) as the British Isles (Jammu & Kashmir, with a population of some 4,000,000, and Hyderabad, with a population of over 16,000,000, each occupied more than 80,000 square miles), some stretching to a few thousand acres only, and some so small that it was open to argument whether they were States at all (which is why there is no definitive figure for the number of Princely States). The Princely States were separate polities which had in differing ways entered into their own treaty relations with the British. By 1947 it was widely argued by constitutional lawyers that their relationship was not to the Government of India, presided over by the Governor-General, but to the British Monarch through his Crown Representative in India (who happened, of course, also to be Governor-General and Viceroy). What the Rulers recognised was not the authority of the Governor-General as such but, rather, the Paramountcy of the British Crown, whose views the Governor-General expressed in his capacity as Crown Agent. Take away Paramountcy, and the Princely

States would be as independent and sovereign as they had been before they made the original treaty arrangements with the British Crown.

This was the theory. It was not based on particularly firm foundations. Before the great crisis of 1857, when the East India Company's Bengal Army had rebelled against British authority, the Governor-General of India was often quite happy to deal with Indian Princes in an extremely autocratic and arbitrary manner. Many of the treaties upon which the structure of Princely India was laid were definitely not negotiated with the British Monarch but with the East India Company, in whose name so much British oriental diplomacy was conducted; and it was not uncommon for a State-Company relationship to have developed through usage without the formality of any document at all. In the majority of cases, moreover, the Princes who dealt with the East India Company were already subject to somebody else (such as the Moghul Emperor in Delhi), so usually what was involved was not the surrender of sovereignty but the transfer of allegiance. Up to 1857 Governors-General, when it suited them, annexed States with great aplomb. Indeed, with a few small exceptions, Provincial India was no more than the product of past annexations or acquisitions backed by force. After 1857, however, when it was thought by many British students of Indian affairs that the Empire had been saved very largely by the loyalty of some of the Princes, prudence dictated that every effort ought to be made to avoid annexations. The doctrine of Paramountcy then started to emerge, though right up to the end of British rule in India there were many constitutional experts who doubted whether it had much merit.

The concept of Paramountcy was at first of little but symbolic import, and, despite such extravaganzas as the Great Delhi Durbar of 1911 when King George V was crowned Emperor of India and received in person the homage of the Princes, it is probable that at the end of World War I the Princes on the whole still looked on themselves as individual and diverse parts of the structure of a British Indian administration with the Viceroy at its head. After the War, however, one can detect major changes in attitude on the part both of the Princes and of the British.

During the War the Princes had contributed greatly, in money, men and loyalty, to the British effort. In 1919, in the Government of India Act of that year which set out the Montagu-Chelmsford reforms, to some extent as a gesture of gratitude, the British established in India a Chamber of Princes, an assembly dedicated to the identification, discussion and promotion of the States' collective interests, and which emphasised their separateness from the rest of the British Indian Empire. The Chamber could be interpreted as a special kind of Princely Parliament, an Indian version of a very superior House of Lords, directly responsible to the King-Emperor. It was formally inaugurated in 1921.

With the approach of the 1935 Government of India Act, the problem of the future of Princely India became a subject of increasingly concentrated study. How would these polities, some of them bizarre and nearly all autocratic to a degree that would have seemed out of place in eighteenth century Europe, fit in with the political liberalisation of British India? Some influential constitutional lawyers now began to argue that the Princes as a class or category had a right of choice as to their future. There was, indeed, in their status under British Paramountcy the latent possibility of their reverting, in the event of the termination of British rule in the Subcontinent, to total independence (which, in fact, they may never have enjoyed before the arrival of the English East India Company).

As the British appeared to weaken, so did the doctrine of Paramountcy acquire additional force. One of its practical virtues was that it provided a good legal way, in a Subcontinent dominated by lawyers, to separate entirely the States with their highly restricted internal political life from what might be called British Indian "democracy", be it represented by Congress or the Muslim League. Thus the British were able to explore the question of Indian independence for many years without having to consider the future position of the States in the post-British era. What they were talking about was British India. The attempted answer to the question of the international status of the Princes and their dominions, which involved apparently extremely abstruse legal concepts, could best be left until later.

In reality, of course, the idea of Paramountcy and all that flowed from it was little more than fantasy. The vast majority of the Princely States were not situated geographically, or constituted demographically, so that they could turn, or be turned, overnight into viable sovereign States even if they possessed the legal entitlement to do so. Jammu & Kashmir, our subject, and a few others like Hyderabad, were rare exceptions, and even they lacked certain essentials for that independent statehood which was in the end to be denied to them. Moreover, the indigenous opponents of British rule in India did not have the slightest desire to see the British Empire replaced by a divided Subcontinent filled with autocracies which acknowledged the authority of neither Congress nor the Muslim League. The British might find the Rulers of the States useful as a check on the Indian nationalists. The Indian nationalists saw them as, at best, anachronistic nuisances and, at worst, as traitors in the service of the British imperial power. With the departure of the British the States were doomed, and most of their Rulers went willingly enough, and by no means as paupers, to meet their fate. Today in the Subcontinent one can still find Maharajas, Nawabs and the rest; but the Princely States have gone.

While the British in the last days of the Indian Empire talked much about Paramountcy, in practice most of their leaders (in Britain at least), too, found the idea of the Princely States a trifle peculiar. The Attlee Labour Government was not in the business of preserving Ruritanias as allies of the New Jerusalem it wished to build in Britain. On the whole, the British pushed the Princes into positions which could only lead to their total absorbtion, sooner or later, by either India or Pakistan. Where a Prince and his people shared the same religion, there was, in theory at least, a sporting chance that, given a helping hand by the British, such a State might survive as an independent sovereignty. Where this communal harmony did not exist, in a theoretically democratic world a Prince would of necessity have to give way to the wishes of his majority population, which in Indian practice would inevitably mean the termination of rule of his dynasty.

When the last British Viceroy, Lord Mountbatten, made public in June 1947 his plan for the end of the British Indian Empire (which we will examine in greater detail below), he made it clear enough that the British were not going to help the Princes preserve their powers. Indeed, he made it no secret that those who recognised British Paramountcy had to all intents and purposes been abandoned by their liege lord to the mercies of the successor regimes of India or Pakistan. As the Chancellor of the Chamber of Princes, the Nawab of Bhopal (a Muslim Ruler with a Hindu majority population) put it on 15 June 1947:

> the Mountbatten Plan recognises the political division of India into Muslim India and Hindu India. This cuts right across the principles to which the States have throughout adhered. As soon as His [Britannic] Majesty's Government found themselves compelled to accord their recognition, however, reluctantly, to the division of India on a religious basis, they should have called the representatives of the States in consultation to discover how

the proposed division of India would effect them and whether it would be possible for all or any of them to find a place in the future Indian political and constitutional set up. This was not done, and the omission to do so has resulted in the States being placed in a very grave and delicate predicament. Many of the States view this default on the part of His Majesty's Government as a virtual repudiation of the guarantees and assurances which have been given to the States at various times by and on behalf of the British Crown. [Nawab Hamidulla of Bhopal to Mountbatten, 15 June 1947, India Office Records].

The Nawab just could not understand how the constitutional rights of his peers could be dismissed so cavalierly by the British Crown. He concluded, charitably, that:

the treatment accorded by His Majesty's Government to the States under the Mountbatten Plan is so incomprehensible that the only assumption that can be made in His Majesty's Government's favour is that this consequence of the Mountbatten Plan was not sufficiently appreciated during the hurried consideration of the Plan by His Majesty's Government, and that it was not deliberately devised or intended. ... Nobody appears to have paid any attention to what the reaction of the States might be. In fact the States have in this connection been completely ignored as if they formed no part of India at all. His Majesty's Government appear to have been concerned only in devising a scheme for British India and have as a post-script to that scheme added that the States might enter the Constituent Assembly of one section or the other as they chose.

In the light of the great emphasis that has been placed subsequently upon the strict legalities of Paramountcy, particularly in the context of the Kashmir dispute, the Nawab of Bhopal's words are instructive. As he pointed out, the decision to partition India carried with it a tacit resolution to jettison the entire structure of Princely India including the doctrine of Paramountcy.

At best, Paramountcy was a nebulous doctrine. In practice it was not easy to separate in the interrelationship of Princely State with British India that which was a matter of Paramountcy (involving only Ruler and British Monarch) from that which emerged out of the day to day running of the general Indian body politic. Roads, railways and telegraph lines ran from British India to the States and back again. There existed bits of States as enclaves in British India and portions of British India lay entirely within

States. The two Indias, British and Princely, could only with the greatest difficulty be divided one from the other; they were both parts of a greater whole. It might have been possible to keep them separate in the late eighteenth century, in the age of Warren Hastings; it simply could not be done, with a very few potential exceptions, in the middle of the twentieth century. It was inevitable that the very concept of Paramountcy would be disposed of by both India and Pakistan very soon after the Transfer of Power.

With the best will in the world, in 1947 it was not always easy to see quite what followed logically from the lapse of Paramountcy. For instance (and this is an issue which had considerable significance for the evolution of the Kashmir dispute), what, after the British departure, would be the status of a tract of territory which the British Government of India had leased from the Ruler of a Princely State? Would the lease automatically lapse along with Paramountcy, and the territory revert to the Ruler, or would the lease be transferred from the British Government of India to the Government of its successor Dominion? One could argue convincingly either way, and, in practice, as the following example demonstrates, one did.

British India in 1947 contained two large tracts which had been leased from Princes whose residual sovereignty over the land in question was explicitly recognised by treaty. Berar, some 17,000 square miles in area, which had been part of the State of Hyderabad, in 1903 was leased by the British from the Ruler of Hyderabad, the Nizam, in perpetuity. In 1935 the Government of India leased from the Maharaja of Jammu & Kashmir the Gilgit Agency and dependent territories, of comparable area to Berar, for a period of 60 years. In both Berar and Gilgit the ultimate, or residual, sovereignty of the Ruler was acknowledged in the lease agreement. Had there been any effectively systematic doctrine of Paramountcy, it might be thought that these two leases would have been treated in precisely the same way by the Government of India on the eve of the Transfer of Power.

In practice, no such thing happened. Gilgit, on the grounds that the lease had lapsed along with Paramountcy, was returned by the British to the Maharaja of Jammu & Kashmir two weeks before the Transfer of Power in August 1947 (but, as we shall see, the local population, whose wishes were never consulted, refused in the end to go along with this arrangement made on their behalf). Berar, on the other hand, was retained within India; indeed, on 13 August, just before the Transfer of Power, it was virtually annexed unilaterally by the Indian leadership on behalf of the Indian Dominion about to be born [*TP*, XII, No. 455]. There was never any serious consideration of handing it back to the Nizam of Hyderabad, though the Prime Minister designate of the Indian Dominion, Jawaharlal Nehru, did give some slight thought to the possibility of a plebiscite to determine the wishes of the Beraris. These two diametrically opposed interpretations of the implications of Paramountcy were not based on that doctrine, rather on other practical considerations which it might perhaps be used to justify. Mountbatten, for reasons which appeared sound to him, was anxious that Gilgit form part of Jammu & Kashmir State at the actual moment of the Transfer of Power (as, interestingly enough, Nehru was not). Neither Mountbatten nor Nehru had the slightest wish to strengthen the Nizam of Hyderabad's pretensions to independence after the British departure, and to give him back Berar would do just this.

Such a confusion of expediency with elaborate constitutional theory contributed greatly to the various crises which arose over the fate of the Indian Princely States, of which Jammu & Kashmir and Hyderabad have a special importance here; virtually all the others were resolved somehow before the actual Transfer of Power.

Hyderabad, which had evolved from the State of Golkonda (once considered to be the source of fabulous riches) in the Deccan, was one of the oldest surviving polities in the Subcontinent. An offshoot of the Tughluqid Delhi Sultanate, it had been there before the arrival of the Portuguese at the very end of the fifteenth century, and before the foundation of the Moghul Empire in the sixteenth (which it had outlived), let alone before the rise of the British Raj in the latter part of the eighteenth century. Its ruling dynasty in 1947 had been founded in 1713. Why should it not now revert to its former condition of independence (its original Tughluqid masters having disappeared centuries ago, and the Moghul Empire, to which it had once been a tributary, having been formally ended in 1858)? Perhaps Hyderabad did lack a port, but so did many other members of the community of nations. The real reason why, in the end, its elaborate treaty relationship with the British Crown and the Government of India was to prove worthless lay in the difference in religion between its Ruler and his subjects; the Nizam was Muslim, the vast majority of his State's population were Hindus surrounded by other

Hindu majorities. As the Nawab of Bhopal pointed out in the passage already quoted, this was an inescapable consequence of the arbitrary division of the British Indian Empire on communal grounds. Hindu politicians would not tolerate enclaves, great or small, within India where Hindu majority populations were ruled by Muslim aristocracies.

Those same Hindu politicians of course, did not experience such difficulties with the reverse situation since, it was argued vehemently by Congress apologists, in reality the new rulers of independent India were secularists, neither Hindu nor Muslim but truly Indian. Thus Nehru, who could not bring himself to accept independence for Hyderabad on the terms implied by the concept of Paramountcy, was quite happy to see the Hindu Maharaja of Jammu & Kashmir deciding the fate of his overwhelmingly Muslim subjects. In secular terms this was entirely proper.

Jammu & Kashmir was, apart from the religion of Ruler and subjects, in a number of other ways the reverse of Hyderabad. It was not an ancient State but a collection of territories which had been assembled by the State's founder, the Hindu Dogra Gulab Singh, since 1820. A large part of the State, the Vale of Kashmir, had in fact been acquired by purchase from the East India Company in 1846, and subsequent expansion by the Dogra Dynasty took place with British encouragement and, at times, active participation. There was a long period, from 1889 to 1925, when the State had virtually been annexed by the Government of India. In 1935 the Gilgit area, as we have seen, was hived off by lease to become a British frontier Political Agency. Jammu & Kashmir was no ancient Golkonda; it was rather a British geopolitical artefact. There was no reason whatsoever why in 1947 it should not have been radically redefined to meet the requirements of the new order in the Subcontinent.

An analysis on communal lines of the State of Jammu & Kashmir as it existed in 1947 demonstrates the potentially fissionable properties of the State. The core of the State was Jammu, which at its heart possessed a Hindu majority (though Jammu Province as a whole did not). To the north of Jammu lay Ladakh and Baltistan which had been conquered by the Dogras not long before 1846. Ladakh was inhabited by people closely related to Tibet who practised Buddhism of the Tibetan variety. Adjacent Baltistan had people of Tibetan ethnic affiliations who were Shia (Twelver) Muslim. The Vale of Kashmir, which as we have seen Gulab Singh bought from the East India Company in 1846, was overwhelmingly Sunni Muslim. In the Gilgit area and its neighbourhood, into which the Dogras penetrated with considerable British help during the second half of the nineteenth century, scarcely a Hindu was to be found; the people were all Shia (Twelver) Muslims except in Hunza where the Ismaili sect prevailed. Poonch, also with an overwhelming Sunni Muslim population, was (as we shall see in the next Chapter) not really part of the State at all and had been brought under its control by questionable methods within the final seven years of the British Indian Empire. Given the will, and without an obsession with the rigid application of a particular interpretation of Paramountcy, it would not have called for great administrative skills to devise ways to divide up the State of Jammu & Kashmir into two or more segments. It is interesting that Mountbatten did not pursue this particular line of thought during his viceroyalty which brought down the final curtain on the melodrama of the British Raj.

Hyderabad was deep in the heart of what, by the process of partition, would be India. Jammu & Kashmir, in contrast, once partition of the British Indian Empire into Muslim and non-Muslim Dominions had been decided upon, was inescapably provided with a common external border with both Muslim and non-Muslim majority territories. By virtue of its population, overwhelmingly Muslim, it could well incline towards what was going to become Pakistan. Its Hindu Ruler, following the logic of the lapse of Paramountcy, could exercise his right to join India if he so wished. On the other hand, following the same rules, he could remain independent, in which case not only would his lands be in direct contact with both India and Pakistan, but also (and this was almost unique among Indian Princely States) with the world outside the limits of the old British Indian Empire, Afghanistan, China, and Tibet (with Russia but a few miles away).

A final feature of the State of Jammu & Kashmir, extremely rare among Princely States and of great importance for the future shape of the Kashmir dispute, must be noted. In the vast majority of Princely States (Mysore being a notable exception) political activity on the part of the general population had been so limited as to be virtually invisible. Not so in the State of Jammu & Kashmir, where by the time of the Transfer of Power a quite sophisticated opposition to the Maharaja had been developed. Following a crisis in 1931, when it looked as if the Muslims of the Vale of Kashmir would rebel against Dogra rule, two political organisations had emerged, the National Conference under the charismatic

Sheikh M. Abdullah, and the Muslim Conference (the two had a common origin, the detailed history of which need not concern us here).

Sheikh Abdullah was a figure of more than local importance. He had close links with the Congress, particularly one of its leading figures, his fellow Kashmiri Jawaharlal Nehru. He was widely known in India beyond the borders of his State, and in 1947 it was generally believed that he stood for some kind of association between his National Conference and the Indian National Congress beneath, as it were, an Indian umbrella. His views, or what they were thought to be, performed a powerful role in the story of how India actually intervened openly and with military force in the affairs of Jammu & Kashmir, as we shall see. The Muslim Conference had none of the Congress-like secular pretensions of Sheikh Abdullah's National Conference. By 1947 many of its members had established links with the Muslim League and looked to a future in or alongside Pakistan. We do not really know who commanded the majority support in the State of Jammu & Kashmir in 1947, the National Conference or the Muslim Conference, and it would be futile to speculate. What is important in the present context is that Jammu & Kashmir not only had clear ethnic and communal divisions, but also there was what might be termed a political fault line somewhere within the State to further undermine the value of any doctrine of Paramountcy which empowered a single Ruler to decide on his own the future for all his subjects.

3. Partition: its origins

There is a widely believed myth that had it not been for M.A. Jinnah's obsession with the idea of Pakistan, India would have emerged from under the British yoke as a united nation. This book is not a treatise on the history of Hindu-Muslim relations; one can only declare it as an axiom that by 1946 some form of Indian partition was inevitable, given the history, nature and distribution of Islam in the Subcontinent. The large concentrated Muslim populations of the Punjab, Sind and along the edges of Afghanistan in the north-west, and of Bengal in the north-east, simply could not be ignored. What was not inevitable was the particular plan which the last Viceroy, Mountbatten, adopted in May 1947. This brought about a partition of British India so drastic and so rapid that the resulting wounds in the Subcontinent still fester. How, and why, did such unhappy measures come to adopted?

By 1946 the British Cabinet in London, already totally committed to the idea of Indian independence, had accepted that there was no way of reconciling the two major players in the Indian political game, Congress (ostensibly secular but representing Hindu interests) and the Muslim League, so that they would both accept a unitary independent Indian state where a parity in power was accorded by Hindus to Muslims and vice versa. Such a recognition of the great Hindu-Muslim divide did not, of course, mean that in any scheme for a post-British India all Hindus would only be ruled by Hindus and all Muslims by Muslims; it was unavoidable, as a consequence of some twelve hundred years of history, that there would be Muslim pockets all over the Subcontinent (in the United Provinces, for example). By the same token, even in those two major areas of Muslim majorities in the north-west and north-east there would be some Hindus (not to mention other communities and ethno-cultural groups like Sikhs and various pagan hill tribes) governed by a Muslim majority. The underlying principle, however, was clear. Any independent India would have to make special provisions to deal at least with the two great Muslim concentrations. A simple unitary constitution would not do; a federal arrangement of sorts was essential as the only hope for the preservation of any measure of political unity.

A mission from the Cabinet visited India in the early summer of 1946, headed by Lord Pethick-Lawrence and containing Sir Stafford Cripps and A.V. Alexander. Its detailed plan, released in May, was for a federal structure in which the highest level, the Centre, would control defence, foreign relations and communications. Below this would be three groups of Provinces, A, B and C. Group A would possess what was called a General (that is to say Hindu plus anyone else who was not Muslim) majority; Groups B and C would contain the great Muslim concentrations, on the one hand, in Punjab, North-West Frontier Province and Sind (Group B) and, on the other, in Bengal and Assam (Group C), where the seats to the Provincial Assemblies would be assigned on an appropriate communal basis to ensure Muslim majorities (as well, in the Punjab in Group B, as providing for Sikh representation). The Provinces, in this scheme of things, would possess considerable power. They could form, for example, their own regional associations. There was no question of dividing up existing Provinces into smaller units on communal or any other grounds. Eventually, it was hoped, the Princely States would be brought into the plan by giving the Rulers the right to choose with which Provincial Group they wished to be associated in ways which had yet to be defined with any precision.

This proposal of the Attlee Cabinet, albeit complex and cumbersome (it involved three distinct tiers, Central or Federal, Provincial Group and Provincial), had much in its favour. It may well be a cause for regret that, in the end, neither Congress nor the Muslim League could bring themselves to accept it for reasons which have been intensively investigated over the years; there is a vast literature on the subject. The balance of opinion used at one time to incline towards awarding the greater blame to the Muslim side in general and M.A. Jinnah in particular. Of late much research, notably that of Ayesha Jalal [*Sole Spokesman. Jinnah, the Muslim League and the Demand for Pakistan*, Cambridge 1985] and H.M. Seervai [*Partition of India. Legend and Reality*, Bombay 1989], has shown that the matter is not so simple. The Congress leadership had much to answer for, and, perhaps, with a bit of good will it could have helped Jinnah come to terms with what was on offer. Generosity towards the opposition, however, has never been the strong point of Congress. What modern research has tended to reveal is that the Muslim League under Jinnah was seeking *parity* with Congress, and would accept any constitutional device which would offer prospect of this, while Congress really wanted a system which did not recognise that the Muslims had any need for, let alone right to, separate representation at all.

In the event, after the departure from India of the Cabinet Mission, the communal situation in the subcontinent began to deteriorate very rapidly. In August 1946 Hindu-Muslim tensions unexpectedly produced an explosion of communal hatred in Calcutta of extraordinarily lethal violence. This was followed, notably during October, by outbursts of killing elsewhere in Bengal in what is today Bangladesh. One conclusion was inescapable; it was unlikely that in a united Bengal, either as a Province or, even, as a nation, the Muslim majority would find it easy to establish an equitable symbiosis with the Hindu minority. It was already possible by the end of August 1946 to detect the logic of establishing some kind of permanent international barrier between the two Bengali communities (the Muslims with their majority in the east and the Hindus with theirs in the west) in the post-independence era such as was not provided for in the Cabinet Mission plan.

Bengal does not directly concern us. Punjab, however, does; and here precisely the same lesson was learnt in early 1947.

Faced with the failure of the Cabinet Mission plan, the Attlee Government eventually resolved to free itself from its Indian responsibilities come what may. On 20 February 1947 it announced that the British would be leaving India in June 1948, at about the same time, indeed, as they would be giving up for good their old League of Nations Mandate in Palestine. No doubt the Indian decision, along with drastic changes of policy towards Palestine, Greece and Turkey, was to a great extent dictated by financial crisis in Britain; but it probably also reflected well enough the gut feeling of the British liberal classes, that the Indian Empire had gone on long enough. To implement the new policy there would be a new Viceroy to take over from Lord Wavell. The last of a line of British proconsuls, whose office (at least as Governor-General) stretched back to Warren Hastings in the latter part of the eighteenth century, was to be Lord Mountbatten, successful in war, with royal connections and believed to be sympathetic to the post-imperial aims of the Labour Government. The new Viceroy arrived in India on 22 March 1947.

By this time the communal situation in the Subcontinent had taken a turn for the worse following an outbreak of violence in the Punjab between Hindus and Sikhs on the one side and Muslims on the other. On 2 March 1947, in the face of a variety of pressures including intense agitation by the Muslim League, the elected Provincial Government of the Punjab headed by Sir Khizar Hyat Khan Tiwana, a coalition of Muslim, Hindu and Sikh interests, collapsed. There seemed no alternative to the Governor's direct intervention, which was duly undertaken by Sir Evan Jenkins. A succession of communal riots then broke out in Lahore, Amritsar, Multan, Rawalpindi and elsewhere, and it was only by the extensive use of the military that law and order were restored. What these events seemed to indicate, apart from the extreme volatility of the Indian political climate, was that it would indeed be difficult to devise a form of government which would ensure tranquillity in a region where large Muslim, Hindu and Sikh populations co-existed. This, at any rate, was the fateful conclusion drawn by a Working Committee of the Indian National Congress which was then, in the context of the Attlee Cabinet's announcement of 20 February, considering the detailed constitutional shape of an India without the British.

On 8 March 1947 the Congress Working Committee produced a resolution, the final version drafted by Jawaharlal Nehru, which argued as follows. Since the Calcutta riots of 1946 all attempts at communal reconciliation in those key areas of the Cabinet Mission plan, Groups B and C Provinces, centred on Punjab and Bengal, had failed. As far as the Punjab was concerned, in the light of what had just been happening there, the Congress view was that it would be better to excise the communal cancer than try to go on living with it. This meant the division of the old Province into two parts, one predominantly Muslim which would go one way, and one predominantly non-Muslim, which would go another. There was still a question mark over the North-West Frontier Province which had a Congress Ministry even though, perhaps because, its population contained virtually no Hindus; but events were soon to show that in the final analysis the North-West Frontier Province was as unlikely to settle down in a Hindu-majority Congress India as Sind or the Muslim-majority parts of the Punjab. The actual words of the Congress Working Committee merit quotation:

> during the past seven months India has witnessed many horrors and tragedies which have been enacted in the attempt to gain political ends by brutal violence, murder and coercion. These attempts have all failed, as all such attempts must fail, and have only led to greater violence and carnage.
>
> The Punjab, which had thus far escaped this contagion, became six weeks ago the scene of an agitation, supported by some people in high authority, to coerce and break a popular Ministry which could not be attacked by constitutional methods ... [This view of events is not shared by most Pakistani writers. A.L.] ... A measure of success attended this, and an attempt was made to form a Ministry dominated by the group that led the agitation. This was bitterly resented and has resulted in increased and widespread violence. There has been an orgy of murder and arson, and Amritsar and Multan have been scenes of horror and devastation.
>
> These tragic events have demonstrated that there can be no settlement of the problem in the Punjab by violence and coercion, and that no arrangement based on coercion can last. Therefore it is necessary to find a way out which involves the least amount of compulsion. This would necessitate the division of the Punjab into two Provinces, so that the predominantly Muslim part may be separated from the predominantly non-Muslim part. [*PP*, Vol. I, Appendix IV].

Here was the real seed whence sprang Partition, a proposal with inescapable practical consequences. Once the Punjab was so divided into Muslim and non-Muslim parts, given the communal demography of the north-western corner of the Subcontinent there was really no alternative to the emergence side by side with India of a totally separate Muslim State free of the three-tier federal trappings of the Cabinet Mission plan, in other words a sovereign Pakistan. The same logic applied to Bengal, but that is beyond our present scope. This crucial piece of realism emanated not from Jinnah's Muslim League but from Congress, and it was to determine in many vital ways the subsequent course of events.

Just two weeks after the passage of the Congress Working Committee resolution of 8 March 1947, Mountbatten took over from Wavell as Viceroy, furnished by the Attlee Cabinet with what he maintained were plenary powers to hack through the Gordian knot of Hindu-Muslim politics and extricate the British from the greatest of their imperial entanglements. His first priority was to devise a practicable plan which he could sell to both Congress and the Muslim League.

Given his relative inexperience of Indian affairs, it was inevitable that Mountbatten should depend heavily upon the knowledge and wisdom of the Government of India Reforms Commissioner, his adviser on constitutional matters, Vapal Pangunni Menon, who had been wrestling in this capacity with the technical problems of Indian independence since 1942 and, in the process, had acquired a unique understanding of all aspects of this complex subject. V.P. Menon was perhaps at this moment the most influential of all Indians in the shaping of his country's future. Unlike most of the leaders of both Congress and the Muslim League, Menon did not have a legal training; he was a practical and pragmatic man. An official in the service of the Government of India, not a politician, yet he was a close associate and devoted follower of Sardar Vallabhbhai Patel, who was second only to Nehru in the Congress hierarchy (and, so many would argue, a man of far greater stature). In everything which Menon did during the Mountbatten viceroyalty there is high degree of probability that his real loyalty lay with the Patel faction of Congress rather than the last Government of British India. What is certain is that the essentials of Government of India thinking, particularly on matters which related to Partition and the creation of Pakistan, which came to Menon's notice were transmitted to Patel soon enough; and whatever Patel thought essential for the future of India under Congress rule was appreciated by

Menon. Menon, at all events, was fully aware of the implications of Congress Working Committee Resolution of 8 March, and he no doubt made sure that it was not forgotten during the gestation of Mountbatten's plan.

Mountbatten's first step was to look closely at the cumbersome structure of the Cabinet Mission plan of 1946, to see if it could somehow be converted into the framework for a scheme of communal separation which went beyond federal bounds. As the preamble to his own first draft plan put it:

> they ... [the British Government] ... had hoped it would be possible to transfer power to Governments within a single Union. ... The Viceroy has however reported that leaders of main political parties in India have been unable to reach agreement on any form of united Government. His Majesty's Government have therefore decided ... that arrangements must now be made to ensure that power can be transferred by due date ... [June 1948] ... to more than one authority. [*TP*, X, No. 379].

The problem, of course, was to determine what bits of India went to which of the more than one authorities now under consideration.

Mountbatten's initial plan was ready on 2 May 1947, when his Chief-of-staff, Lord Ismay, and his Private Secretary, George Abell, took it off to London. Drafted largely by V.P. Menon, it was a most complex arrangement for the convening of a number of Constituent Assemblies. The idea of the separate treatment of the Cabinet plan Group B and C Provinces was retained; but in the Constituent Assembly or Assemblies for those Provinces there was provision for a further subdivision into Muslim and General (still the euphemism for Hindu) groups, with the implied possibility of some kind of partition. The whole process would involve a reference to the people in each Province; and here Mountbatten included those Group A Provinces with a General (Hindu) majority. It was the best that could be done with the skeleton of the old Cabinet Mission plan (largely, one suspects, thanks to the skills of V.P. Menon, who, however, had his private doubts about its viability). The Attlee Cabinet were greatly impressed. The Indian problem, they thought had, if not been solved, at least moved onward to a more comfortable stage. A Cabinet Committee approved a final revision of the first draft on 8 May.

On 10 May the first Mountbatten plan met a sudden death. It had, of course, pending Cabinet approval, not been shown either to M.A. Jinnah or Jawaharlal Nehru (though it is extremely unlikely that Nehru from one source or another did not know what was afoot). Now, with Cabinet approval to hand, Mountbatten decided, at a moment when he and Nehru happened to be together in the congenial climate of Simla, to let the Congress leader have a look at the plan. Nehru effectively rejected it outright. Congress, he said, would never go along with it. What he objected to in particular was the need to hold some form of Group A Provincial elections of an essentially plebiscitary nature, with the implied possibility either of the total fragmentation of British India into a mess of independent Provinces, or the partition of Provinces *other* than those in the Cabinet Mission plan Groups B and C. The plan, Nehru told the Viceroy, must be completely redrafted. Nehru refused to contemplate the slightest trace of those Balkanisation projects (in which, typically, the British would withdraw to two or three secure ports, leaving the hinterland to whomsoever was able to seize the reins of power) which the British had hinted at during the Wavell viceroyalty, perhaps seriously, or perhaps merely as goads to Congress and the Muslim League to force them to make up their minds.

On the morning of 11 May, with Nehru still obdurate, the task of devising a new plan began. Inevitably, the main burden fell on V.P. Menon. Meanwhile, the Attlee Cabinet in London had been told rather mysteriously that the old plan had been cancelled and a replacement was in the post. It would appear that Jinnah never did see the original draft plan, and Mountbatten, whose dislike for Jinnah was both profound and mutual, managed to avoid the stress of trying to explain its details to the Muslim leader.

The new plan, ready by 17 May, and confusingly just called the Mountbatten plan (like the previous plan of 2 May), provided an electoral mechanism whereby two Constituent Assemblies would be set up in the Subcontinent, one for India and one for what would become a Pakistan consisting of Sind, North-West Frontier Province, Baluchistan and a partitioned Punjab, plus a partitioned Bengal plus Sylhet (in Assam) provided that the electorate in the last place decided by plebiscite to join Pakistan.

Neither plan, old or revised, was particularly specific about the future of the Princely States in the post-British Subcontinent. Paramountcy would lapse and the Rulers would, as the Cabinet Mission had already set out in a memorandum to the Chamber of Princes on 12 May 1946, have to make up their minds whether they would join one of the new Dominions or endeavour to establish their own independence. Mechanisms had yet to be worked out in detail to give practical effect to these possibilities.

As far as the Kashmir dispute is concerned, the real matter of importance in the Mountbatten plan was that section dealing with the partition of the Punjab, because the new boundary here would determine the theoretical access of India to Jammu & Kashmir, without which the State's options would in practice be severely limited. The key, as will be discussed again below, was what happened to the various *tehsils* (sub-districts) of Gurdaspur District (with a very small Muslim majority according to the 1941 census). If those three *tehsils* to the east of the Ravi (of which one, Pathankot, had a modest Hindu majority) went to India, then that Dominion would possess a passable road link with Jammu & Kashmir which could be balanced against the established Jhelum Valley Road from Pakistan to Srinagar. With both these routes open, in theory the State could join either India or Pakistan, but it did not mean, of course, that it *had* to join either. With Gurdaspur east of the Ravi in Pakistan, so at least conventional wisdom had it in 1947 (ignoring the possibility of constructing an Indian road through the Himalayan foothills of the Kangra District and, perhaps, Chamba State), the State of Jammu & Kashmir *could not*, as a practicable proposition, join India. This did not, of course, mean that it *had* to join Pakistan, but it was certainly a strong pressure in that direction.

Here is what the revised plan suggested for the actual mechanics of Partition:

> for the immediate purpose of deciding the issue of Partition, the members of the Legislative Assemblies of Bengal and the Punjab will sit in two parts according to Muslim majority districts ... and non-Muslim majority districts. This is only a preliminary step of a purely temporary nature as it is evident that for the purposes of a definitive partition of these provinces a detailed investigation of boundary questions will be needed; and, as soon as a decision involving partition has been taken for either province ... [Punjab or Bengal] ... a Boundary Commission will be set up by the Governor-General, the membership and terms of reference of which will be settled in consultation with those concerned. It will be instructed to demarcate the boundaries of the two parts of the Punjab on the basis of ascertaining the contiguous majority areas of Muslims and non-Muslims. It will also be instructed to take into account other factors. [*TP*, X, No. 476].

All this was far more detailed than before, and in some respects significantly different from the original plan (which Nehru may have seen and Jinnah had not). In the 2 May plan it was specified that "until the report of a Boundary Commission has been adopted", that is to say voted for, "by both parts of a Province" (in other words, what would be India and Pakistan), the "provisional boundaries" would be based on a line separating Muslim-majority Districts from those without such a majority without taking any other factors into consideration (in other words, with a division on a strict District by District basis). Had this form of words survived, the Gurdaspur District in its entirety would have gone initially to Pakistan from which it would not have been easily dislodged. With this formula either the key access to the State of Jammu & Kashmir via Gurdaspur would have been retained by Pakistan or its eventual transfer to India would have been debated in the two parts of the Punjab Provincial Assembly before a final boundary line was agreed. It is difficult to see how in these circumstances the question of the future of the State of Jammu & Kashmir would not have been subjected to considerable scrutiny before the shape of Partition had been set in a solid mould.

On 18 May Mountbatten, with his new plan on paper and accompanied by V.P. Menon, set out by air for London to explain his proposed changes to the British Cabinet. A few days later the revised plan was approved after the briefest discussion by the Attlee (Labour) Government; and the unity of the Subcontinent, which it had taken the British three centuries to achieve, was broken for ever.

About the same time Mountbatten underwent yet another conversion. Hitherto it had been accepted that the target date (which probably would not be achieved in practice) was June 1948. Now Mountbatten began to speculate whether it might not be a good idea to set a new, and closer, deadline. By the end of May he had fixed upon 15 August 1947 as the day upon which the British Indian Empire would come to its formal end (perhaps to coincide with the second anniversary of the official end of the War with Japan – it is not easy to find any other special significance for this particular day). Whether V.P. Menon, and through him the leaders of Congress, had any part in this decision is not known; it is not improbable. They well appreciated that haste favoured the established Indian institutions over those of Pakistan which in nearly every case were having to be built up from scratch. What is certain is that, once the time limit of 15 August had been settled, the options possible for the actual work of partitioning the Punjab became extremely limited. Surgery had not only to be drastic but also fast.

The Attlee Cabinet had detected serious dangers in the proposed rush. Mountbatten's reply was that unless the whole business were done quickly it might bog down in protracted debate and never get done at all. The Cabinet were reluctant to overrule their own Viceroy, so Mountbatten got his way. In order to ensure that there would be no second thoughts on this point, Mountbatten insisted that the 15 August deadline was actually written into the Independence of India Act of 18 July 1947: "as from the fifteenth day of August, nineteen hundred and forty-seven, two independent Dominions shall be set up, to be known respectively as India and Pakistan". [*TP*, XII, No. 164].

If V.P. Menon did play a major part in all these proceedings – as seems highly probable – then there is an intriguing whiff of Mountbatten-Congress collusion about it all (in which, of course, Mountbatten could just possibly have been an unwitting party). Congress decided that Partition was called for. V.P. Menon, having helped Mountbatten with a plan which could be argued to represent a hopeless last ditch stand against Partition, then, when Nehru had rejected it, quickly produced from his pocket a new plan with contained the essentials of the Congress decision for Partition of 8 March. Mountbatten thereupon persuaded an apparently reluctant Nehru to accept the new plan, and Jinnah, probably failing to appreciate the significance of V.P. Menon's part in its drafting, duly followed suit in the belief that, if he did not, Mountbatten and Congress might do something rather more harmful for the idea of Pakistan. The new plan, possibly again at Nehru's instigation or with his approval, contained a deadline which guaranteed that there would be a very limited number of options for the actual mechanics of Partition, which in any case were already dominated by the provisions in the plan relating to Boundary Commissions and other procedural matters (drafted by or with V.P. Menon).

It was as if the final shape was already set out in some kind of genetic code in the plan, a code which the Pakistan side did not devise and were quite unable to modify even though they increasingly detected within it defects which could cripple them. Here, it may be, is one of the foundations for that suspicion with which all Pakistani observers have regarded the process of Partition in the Punjab. Such mistrust has been particularly apparent in their interpretation of the history of the Radcliffe

Commission which, officially, defined the line separating India from Pakistan in the Punjab. The real story of this Commission we must now try to extract from the available evidence.

4. Partition: the Radcliffe Commission

The revised Mountbatten plan was announced in India on 3 June 1947, and on the following day the Viceroy made it clear that the whole exercise would terminate on 15 August 1947, by which date the British Raj would be over for good. The magnitude and quantity of problems which had either to be solved or ignored by that date defied the imagination. We will confine ourselves here to a single example. How precisely could it be arranged for a Province of the extensive area and ethnic and communal complexity of the Punjab to be bisected in ten weeks?

The revised Mountbatten plan contained a mass of detail about electoral procedures (as one would expect in something largely drafted by that constitutional expert V.P. Menon). It was rather vague, however, on the practical details of how the Boundary Commissions for Bengal and the Punjab would be constituted, let alone on the geopolitical principals underlying the borders which they were supposed to delineate; it merely established the basic doctrine of separation of Muslims from non-Muslims.

It was clear from the outset that the Punjab boundary would have to run somewhere through a stretch of territory about 250 miles in length from Bahawalpur State in the south to the State of Jammu & Kashmir in the north, neither State being within the proposed Commission's brief. In one way, by running a line between Muslim-majority Districts and Districts without such majorities a technically correct boundary could be derived through no more labour than the consulting of the appropriate administrative map. Unfortunately, the matter was not so easy in the real world. Basically, there were three immediate problems.

First: the country through which the new boundary was to run was also the heartland of the world of the Sikhs. This community was a minority even in the Punjab, but its importance to the life of India could not be overestimated. An international boundary, passing perilously close to the Sikh Holy of Holies at Amritsar, had to be drawn which did not so disturb their traditions as to result in the permanent alienation of these martial people from the Dominion with which they had decided finally to throw in their lot, India. The Sikhs are another story, but it must be noted that the terrible consequences of the failure in this respect of the 1947 Partition of the Punjab are still with us.

Second: the Punjab, through which the line of proposed partition would have to run, was the land of the "five rivers" which in the British period had been exploited to create an extremely complex system of dams, barrages and canals. To divide the Punjab was to cut across irrigation works of one kind or other upon which the agriculture of the region depended. Was it possible to execute such drastic surgery without fatal damage to the economies of East and West Punjab, and particularly the latter? Certainly, something more subtle than the rigid adherence to District boundaries would be called for.

Finally: the boundary had to be practicable. It had both to be delimited and to be administered. The traditional British Indian view had always been that "natural" boundaries, along the thalwegs of rivers or mountain watersheds, were best. The closest to a "natural" boundary here would have been a line which followed the Montgomery and Lahore District borders along the Sutlej from Bahawalpur State north-eastward to a point near Ferozepore, whence it would swing due north to the Ravi, passing to the west of Amritsar, and then follow the Ravi upstream (and again north-eastward) all the way to the border of Jammu & Kashmir State. There would, with this line, be virtually no Pakistan to the east of the Sutlej below Ferozepore or east of the Ravi north of Lahore (though there would be *some* small pockets of Pakistani territory on the east bank of the Sutlej since the boundaries of Lahore and Montgomery Districts meandered in a perplexing manner from one bank of the Sutlej to the other, and, by the same token, there would also be Indian pockets on the west bank; and District and *tehsil* boundaries along the Ravi likewise frequently crossed and recrossed the river).

In the discussion which follows we will deal mainly with the Punjab Boundary Commission and rather ignore the parallel Commission for Bengal. The terms India and Pakistan are used here for convenience to represent the two parties. Strictly speaking, of course, this is an anachronism since the two Dominions did not come into existence until 14/15 August 1947.

The possible composition of the Boundary Commission had first been considered by the India Office in London on receipt of the revised

Mountbatten plan in late May [*PP* Vol. I, Appendix I]. For the Punjab it initially proposed a Commission of six members from both the Eastern and the Western parts of the Province, three elected by the Muslim League (Pakistan), two by the Sikhs and one by Congress (India); the relatively large number of Sikhs was evidence of thoughts then circulating as to the possibility of the creation of some kind of special Sikh State in the Punjab (a fascinating topic which we must, with some reluctance, mention only in passing). The six Commissioners would go on to choose a Chairman. If they could not agree upon a suitable candidate, a Chairman would be appointed by the Viceroy. A mechanism was suggested whereby, in the event of a disputed award by the Commission, appeal could be made either to the United Nations or the International Court of Justice at the Hague; it is interesting to see that at this very early stage of what was to evolve into the Kashmir dispute the possibility of United Nations arbitration was already latent. The India Office believed that essential to the whole process of Partition was the existence of an Arbitral Tribunal, with members to be appointed by the Governments-to-be of India and Pakistan (the India Office was at this point still contemplating the possibility of two Muslim States, Pakistan and Bengal, so it spoke of three rather than two Governments): the prime function of the Arbitral Tribunal was to resolve disputes over the division of the assets of the old British Indian Empire between the successor regimes which the Partition Council found itself unable to decide. The Partition Council was a body created on 7 June as a consequence of the revised Mountbatten plan [*PP*, Vol. I, No. 9], and representing the leaders of the major interested parties (Mountbatten in the Chair, Nehru, Patel, Jinnah and Liaquat Ali Khan), as a forum for the discussion of all questions arising from the process of the division of the old British Indian Empire into India and Pakistan. If the Boundary Commission (and behind it the Partition Council) were paralysed by internal disputes, and if the United Nations or the International Court declined to intervene, then the whole matter would be thrown in the last resort to the Arbitral Tribunal, which was seen as the ultimate umpire.

By 13 June the possibilities had been modified and refined [*PP* Vol. I, No. 16]. Now the choice put by the British to the leaders-to-be of India and Pakistan was that the Punjab Commission would consist either (a) of three members provided through the good offices of the United Nations working with six expert assessors, three each from India and Pakistan, or

(b) of an independent Chairman and four Members, two nominated by India and two by Pakistan.

Jinnah, on behalf of the Muslim League, stated [*PP*. Vol. I, No. 11] that he personally would have preferred option (a), but he would go along with Nehru in accepting option (b).

Nehru's objections to option (a), involving the United Nations, are interesting [*PP*. Vol. I, No. 14]. The United Nations might select people who were not "very suitable", that is to say not in sympathy with Congress. More importantly, the presence of the United Nations would surely introduce needless bureaucratic delays. What Nehru did not say was that, given the 15 August deadline, any option which involved the consumption of all but the absolute minimum amount of time was self-eliminating. It was essential that the Boundary Commission's work be completed by the end of the British Raj; it was, after all, British India that was being partitioned. This, of course, was why Jinnah in the end felt obliged to go along with option (b).

The India Office in London, too, was discovering that it was not so easy to organise rapidly an United Nations involvement. They had concluded, moreover, that any United Nations concern, what with the possibility of the Soviets and their friends showing an interest, might relate more to the nascent Cold War than to the best interests of peace in the Subcontinent.

The British Foreign Office soon came up with another idea [*PP*, Vol. I, No. 19]. It suggested that the two sides participating in the Boundary Commission might invite delegates from some suitable foreign power or powers, France, the United States, even Peru, to preside over the delimitation of the new Indo-Pakistani border in the Punjab. There were a number of possible variants to this theme. The President of the International Court of Justice at the Hague, for example, might be invited to appoint a bench of "neutral" judges. None found favour in London, New Delhi or Karachi.

By 20 June the Muslim League side had worked out a likely and acceptable scenario for the Boundary Commission process based upon what might be described as internal Indian institutions (and avoiding reference at any stage to such foreign bodies as the United Nations). As Liaquat Ali Khan explained to Lord Ismay, Mountbatten's chief-of-staff [*PP*, Vol. I, No. 31], the two Boundary Commissions (Punjab and Bengal), if they represented equally both sides, would certainly result in a balance of conflicting sets of recommendations. These would be handed on to

Mountbatten who could then pass them on to the Partition Council. If the Partition Council, too, failed to produce an answer, as it surely would unless Mountbatten himself were willing the exercise a casting vote and thereby assume responsibility for the consequences, then the task of making the final decision would have to be transferred to the Chairman of the Arbitral Tribunal, a body which we have already noted had been expressly devised to sort out such problems. Here, clearly, was the key position for which, it seems, the Government of India had already selected a leading British lawyer, Sir Cyril Radcliffe K.B.E., K.C., Vice-Chairman of the Bar Council in London.

On 23 June Jinnah told Mountbatten that he doubted whether the two parties, Muslim League and Congress, would ever agree on any local person as Chairman of either the Punjab or the Bengal Boundary Commissions [*PP*,Vol. I, No. 35]. He suggested, therefore, that the British might perhaps put forward the name of some distinguished member of the English Bar (an institution to which he had for many years belonged and for which he retained great admiration and respect) to act not only as an umpire whose decision would be final in the event of tied votes on the two Commissions but also as Chairman, with the same powers, of the two Commissions themselves. Mountbatten observed that just such a man, Sir Cyril Radcliffe, was already being talked about as Chairman of the Arbitral Tribunal, and it might indeed be an excellent idea to have him chair the two Boundary Commissions as well. After a few days reflection, on 27 June at a meeting of the Partition Council, Jinnah agreed. Nehru promptly concurred [*PP*, Vol. I, No. 47]. The absurdity of having Sir Cyril Radcliffe arbitrate in disputes arising from what to all intents and purposes were his own decisions soon became evident, and the Chairmanship of the Arbitral Tribunal was given to Sir Patrick Spens, the last Chief Justice of British India. While the Arbitral Tribunal did indeed meet after the Transfer of Power to consider a number of issues arising from the process of Partition, in the end it had nothing to do with the actual decisions as to what territory would go to India and what to Pakistan; and it drops out of our story. The Arbitral Tribunal formally came to an end on 31 March 1948.

His Chairmanship of the two Boundary Commissions, as was obvious from the moment of his appointment, conferred in theory enormous power to Sir Cyril Radcliffe. The award of both the Boundary Commissions was defined in the Independence of India Act 1947 in these words:

> the expression "award" means, in relation to a boundary commission, the decision of the chairman of that commission contained in the report to the Governor-General of the commission's proceedings.

Thus, to the general public it was made clear that the actual "awarding" of the boundary, in the Punjab and in Bengal, was going to be done by Sir Cyril Radcliffe; and from the outset there was an in-built assumption that he would do this on his own, his Indian and Pakistani colleagues effectively cancelling each other out. The future shape of both India and Pakistan was going, it seemed, to be determined by the opinion of an English lawyer; and, in the case of Sir Cyril Radcliffe, this was to be a man to all intents and purposes ignorant of the Subcontinent (which he had never even visited). Both India and Pakistan committed themselves to accept the Chairman's decision as binding.

To Jinnah, who showed interest in externalising the process of Partition so that it should not be dominated by established Indian (and probably pro-Congress) interests, the arrival of the apparently impartial Sir Cyril Radcliffe must have appeared to offer a real protection for Pakistan. However great his powers, they would, he evidently believed, be used to ensure fairness for Pakistan. In fact, of course, it should have been clear to any who understood the workings of the British administrative machine that an appointment of this sort was always designed to achieve the results desired by those who made the appointment, in this case Mountbatten and his backers in London. Nehru, who probably appreciated this particular aspect of the British way of life rather better than Jinnah, offered no objections to the apparent concentration of power in the person of Sir Cyril Radcliffe. He must have divined where the real power lay. Radcliffe (created Viscount in 1962) must have been peculiarly suited to such work: in later years he went on to chair, or participate in, a surprising number of British commissions and official inquiries including some dealing with highly sensitive matters of espionage and the suppression of information on grounds of national security.

The terms of reference of the Radcliffe Commission in the Punjab had virtually been set out in the revised Mountbatten plan. When asked how he wished them to be phrased, Nehru on 12 June [*PP*, Vol. I, No. 15] expressed himself entirely satisfied with the original plan wording (which, after all, had been drafted by a Congress sympathiser, V.P. Menon). This specified the criteria of Muslim and non-Muslim majority areas (the term District was carefully avoided) upon which the Boundary Commission would make its award. He did, however, modify slightly one phrase. Where in the plan [quoted above, Chapter I, Section 3] the somewhat enigmatic reference to "other factors" had been separated, by syntax if not entirely by semantics, from the act of boundary demarcation on the basis of ascertaining contiguous Muslim-majority areas, now the two were more closely linked: *"in doing so* [my italics] it will also take into account other factors". These "factors" were not identified; but there was the implication in this particular form of words that they must somehow be related to the actual process of partitioning and not to any general or wider considerations concerning the future viability of Pakistan both as a polity and an economy.

On 28 June Liaquat Ali Khan sought a slight variation in this form of words [*PP*, Vol. I, No. 56]. "In doing so" should be omitted, thus reverting to very much the form and implications of the original version in Mountbatten's draft. The final phrase should now read (as a separate sentence): "the Commission will also take into account other factors", in other words, it could concern itself with subjects totally unconnected with the Punjab boundary, and not arising directly or indirectly from the actual process of its demarcation. Mountbatten rejected Liaquat Ali Khan's proposed modification on the grounds that Jinnah had already, on 23 June, accepted the Congress wording. Liaquat Ali Khan did not pursue the matter.

Effectively, the Boundary Commissions were limited geographically to the Punjab and Bengal, and they could not explore the consequences of their work for India and Pakistan as a whole. They certainly were debarred from investigating the wider reaches of communal issues relating to the Hindus, Muslims and Sikhs and their future place in the Subcontinent. With these terms of reference, at all events, it seemed highly improbable that Sir Cyril Radcliffe was going to expand his purview to the future of the State of Jammu & Kashmir (even though it was in practice impossible to consider rationally the division of the waters of the five rivers of the Punjab, the Indus system, without taking into account who was in control of Jammu & Kashmir from whence or through which much of the Punjab water came).

It appeared to be inherent in the whole concept of the Radcliffe

Commission, though it is not spelled out in the records, that decisions would be made on "judicial" grounds and not on "political" ones. The understanding, at least on the Pakistan side, was that the only criteria to be considered were those that emerged either from strictly practical considerations such as the local operations of irrigation works and communications, or from legal issues such as those arising from land ownership and right of access to shrines (and, again, local). Major questions which affected the basic nature of Pakistan and India and their future spheres of influence beyond the confines of the border between East and West Punjab would not be considered. The Radcliffe Commission, all parties appeared to accept, was not a proper tribunal to assess in any manner, for or against, the fundamental merits of Jinnah's "two nation theory", that Muslims in the old British Indian Empire had a right to a separate political identity.

Radcliffe arrived in New Delhi on 8 July. A preliminary version of his Punjab Award was ready on 8 August, with the individual reports by the four Commissioners already completed and submitted to his office a couple of days or so earlier; and the definitive version was placed on the Viceroy's desk on 12 August. The Award was made public in both India and Pakistan on 17 August after the process of the Transfer of Power was complete. By that date Sir Cyril Radcliffe had left India, taking all his papers with him. He died in 1977 without ever throwing much light on what he had actually done in India in 1947.

There has been an enormous amount of controversy over the Radcliffe Punjab Award in that it appeared to depart from the principle of the integrity of Muslim-majority Districts by giving to India three *tehsils* (sub-districts) of the Muslim-majority Gurdaspur District, two of them (Gurdaspur and Batala) with small Muslim majorities (according, at least, to the 1941 census), thereby providing India with a practicable access to the State of Jammu & Kashmir by way of the Pathankot railhead. It has been argued that Sir Cyril Radcliffe, who was supposed to be working in total isolation from the Government of India (despite being lodged in the Comptroller's House within the compound of Viceroy's House in New Delhi), was in fact influenced by Mountbatten (or his staff) in crucial ways, not least in this Gurdaspur decision which, in the fullness of time, contributed so significantly to the language of the Kashmir dispute.

While, in the light of a large quantity of information which has surfaced in the last decade or so, one can say that there is much truth in this view, yet it must also be admitted that critics of the impartiality of the Radcliffe Award have tended to miss the real point. This we will now examine briefly.

It is clear, as we have seen, that Radcliffe was not confined to Districts. The revised Mountbatten plan had been explicit that, if need be, Districts would be rearranged in the process of Partition. "Other factors", it is to be presumed, within his terms of reference would permit him here and there to award Muslim-majority tracts to India and non-Muslim-majority tracts to Pakistan, provided that he did not depart too radically from the basic concept of contiguous areas. These considerations are often overlooked when Radcliffe has been attacked for awarding the three *tehsils* of Gurdaspur District to India. The Radcliffe Award does not set out in detail exactly why the three Gurdaspur *tehsils* were given to India, but it does indicate that any such decision was based upon the weighing of factors such as communications and irrigation works; and it would be easy enough to make out a case along these lines.

Mountbatten, long before Radcliffe set foot on Indian soil, made it plain that it was unlikely that all of Gurdaspur District would go to Pakistan: on 4 June 1947 he pointed out that it "is unlikely that the Boundary Commission will throw the whole of the [Gurdaspur] District into the Muslim majority areas". [Quoted in: L.A. Sherwani, *The Partition of India and Mountbatten*, Karachi 1986, p. 125]. In 1960 one of the two Pakistan Commissioners, Justice Mohammad Munir, announced [Chicago *Tribune*, 26 April 1960] that both he and his fellow Commissioner Justice Din Muhammad had been in no doubt from the very beginning of the Radcliffe Commission's work that the three *tehsils* of Gurdaspur District east of the Ravi were destined for India. It is interesting that in their individual reports, submitted on 5 and 6 August, the two Pakistan Commissioners, while dealing at length with Gurdaspur District (which they maintain for various reasons ought to go to Pakistan) yet do not raise the Kashmir aspect of the question; their arguments concentrate on Muslim populations and shrines, irrigation canals and like matters [*PP*, Vol. III].

For an understanding of what really happened during the course of the Radcliffe Commission in the Punjab we can only advance a number of hypotheses based on fragmentary, but weighty for all that, evidence.

The first hypothesis is that the Government of India had worked out well before Sir Cyril Radcliffe and his judges (the Indian members being

Justice Mehr Chand Mahajan and Justice Teja Singh, the latter a Sikh) had sat down, more or less what sort of Punjab boundary they wanted. The main criteria would be practical, relating to the governability of the two portions of the Punjab as administrative units. Crucial here, as has already been suggested, was the territory in which the Sikhs claimed a special interest. The act of partition between Lahore and Amritsar (almost like the separation of Siamese twins) involved a particularly tricky operation. As has also been suggested, the most logical line was from Bahawalpur State north-east along the Sutlej to near Ferozepore, and then due north across to the Ravi, running neatly between Lahore and Amritsar; the Ravi (and, for the last few miles its tributary the Ujh) would then carry the border onwards all the way to the southern limits of Jammu & Kashmir State. If District or other existing administrative borders were followed, as we have already seen, neither along the Sutlej nor the Ravi would there be a truly "river" line since boundaries tended to wander to and fro across both rivers; but such lines would probably be nearly enough "scientific" to serve, and far easier in practice to define than anything entirely new. A novice in the old Indian Political Service could have come up with this, and the available records abound with hints that this is just what someone in Mountbatten's entourage did. Sir Cyril Radcliffe's brief was to carry out an exhaustive inquiry, including public meetings and the digestion of masses of memoranda and memorials, and then, just like many a British Royal Commission, come up with the right (and expected) solution.

It is interesting to note that at the outset of Partition the Muslim League did not give much thought to the wider geopolitical consequences of cutting the Punjab in two. The approaching reality of Pakistan was an idea so new, and so overwhelming, that it drowned all else. It may well be that the Indian side, which had rather longer to ponder about the specific implications of Partition – Congress, after all, can be argued to have dreamed up the idea in its Working Committee resolution of 8 March 1947 – had speculated more intensely about what might happen if the new boundary line went a little bit this way rather than that, but there is no concrete evidence.

The old British Political Department, however, now evolving into the Indian States Department and also dealing with matters which would soon be the concern of the Indian Department of External Affairs, well appreciated the geopolitics of the Punjab and its adjacent regions. It had long understood the importance of the State of Jammu & Kashmir in the defence of Indian's Northern Frontier and the strategic significance of those key routes which gave access to that State. With the main road, the Jhelum Valley Road from Rawalpindi to Srinagar, now surely in Pakistan, India's approach to Jammu & Kashmir was perforce through Pathankot in the Gurdaspur District of the Punjab, the railhead. From here to Madhopur, and then across the Ravi by ferry to the road leading through Jammu to Srinagar over the Banihal Pass, lay India's main potential access to this key frontier region and the Central Asian tracts beyond, but only if Pathankot and the two other linking *tehsils* of Gurdaspur District on the eastern side of the Ravi went to India. This Department's opinion would almost certainly be sought in planning such a major piece of administration as the Partition of the Punjab. One may well, therefore, argue with some conviction that its advice would have been to retain within India, come what may, the three *tehsils* of Gurdaspur District on the eastern side of the Ravi (and, for the last few miles to Jammu, its tributary the Ujh). It would be prudent, whatever the eventual fate of the State of Jammu & Kashmir, to do so; and the result would be a "better" and more "natural" border.

Another hypothesis is that, during the course of the Radcliffe Commission's proceedings, challenges to this convenient line began to emerge. Both the Pakistani and the Indian sides grew increasingly aware that beyond the Partition of the Punjab lay the prospect of yet another partition or redistribution of territory of enormous significance for the future. Jinnah and Liaquat Ali Khan, who had hitherto assumed that Kashmir would become part of Pakistan, now saw that it might very well not, and the denial to India of the trans-Ravi *tehsils* of Gurdaspur began to assume a special significance. Loss of access from Jammu & Kashmir to India via Gurdaspur might force the Maharaja to look seriously towards the Government that would arise in Karachi. To leave it in Indian hands would be to offer a constant temptation to the Maharaja to try to devise some kind of association with New Delhi. The Indian side, aware of this train of thought, were increasing determined to keep trans-Ravi (or cis-Ravi in their eyes) Gurdaspur where it had originally been placed, that is to say in India.

Evidence to support this second hypothesis began to emerge around 7 August 1947. The Radcliffe Commission, Sir Cyril and his four judges, were then in Simla at the Cecil Hotel, and it would seem (admittedly from hearsay evidence, but which, none the less, probably contained more than a grain of truth) that over lunch the question of the Gurdaspur *tehsils* to the east of the Ravi (or, near the Jammu & Kashmir border, for a few miles the Ujh, a Ravi tributary) was discussed. One may well imagine that the Pakistani Commissioners repeated what they had already put in their individual reports, that two of these *tehsils* were Muslim-majority subdistricts of a District which, at least according to the 1941 figures, had a small overall Muslim majority. If the whole District were not to go to Pakistan, then ought not there be at least some compensation to Pakistan elsewhere? The proposal which then emerged, again according to hearsay evidence, seems to have been to let Pakistan have some land to the east of the Sutlej in the shape of the Ferozepore and Zira *tehsils* of Ferozepore District, both with significant Muslim majorities (55.2 and 65.2 per cent according to the 1941 census). It should be noted that the Ferozepore District had *not* (unlike Gurdaspur) been included in the Second Schedule to the Independence of India Act of 18 July 1947 which listed those Districts which could possibly form part of West Punjab, that is to say Pakistan [*TP*, XII, No. 166]; but both Justices Din Muhammad and Muhammad Munir had drawn particular attention in their reports of 5 and 6 August 1947 to the merits of bringing the Ferozepore and Zira *tehsils* of Ferozepore District into Pakistan.

This addition of the Ferozepore and Zira *tehsils* to the potential Pakistan Districts outlined in the 18 July 1947 legislation was immediately adopted officially by the Commission. On 8 August Sir Cyril Radcliffe's Secretary, Christopher Beaumont (an Indian Political Service officer whose qualifications for this task included practical experience of the administrative problems of the Gurdaspur District), prepared a note, illustrated with a map (which by some miracle has survived), on the new boundary which George Abell, Mountbatten's Private Secretary, sent to S.E. Abbott, Secretary to Sir Evan Jenkins, Governor of the Punjab [*PP*, Vol. I, No. 198, and map in Vol. IV; also *TP*, XII, No. 377]. The reason for such a communication was obvious enough. It was prudent for the Punjab Government to know its areas of responsibilities at a period when the entire region threatened to erupt in communal violence. If West Punjab after the Transfer of Power, 15 August, was now going to be responsible for the quite extensive Ferozepore and Zira *tehsils* on the east bank of the Sutlej, somebody should let its Government-to-be (under Sir Evan Jenkins) know in good time.

Sir Evan Jenkins was not the only person to learn about this proposed change. Clearly what Sir Cyril Radcliffe and his Commissioners discussed on 7 August over lunch at the Cecil Hotel in Simla had been widely reported. A.N. Khosla, Chairman, Central Waterways, Irrigation and Navigation Commission, soon heard what was afoot. He immediately wrote to Nehru in protest, because of the effect of this proposal on the Sutlej Valley Canals; and Nehru sent the letter to Mountbatten with the suggestion that he might pass it on to Sir Cyril Radcliffe [*PP*, Vol. I, No. 204; *TP*, XII, No. 395]. On 9 August Chaudhri Muhammad Ali, the Pakistan Secretary on the Partition Council, called on Ismay at Viceroy's House and found in his office an uncovered wall map which showed the new boundary with the Ferozepore and Zira *tehsils* in Pakistan [Chaudhri Muhammad Ali, *The Emergence of Pakistan*, New York 1967, p. 218]. This addition to Pakistan gave the country such a peculiar shape that even with a casual glance he could hardly fail to notice it (and, incidentally, he also spotted the presence on the Indian side of the proposed border of the three eastern *tehsils* of the Gurdaspur District). On the following day the Maharaja of Bikaner telegraphed Mountbatten that "it is strongly rumoured that the Boundary Commission is likely to award Ferozepore Tehsil to" Pakistan, and objected on the grounds of potential disruption of irrigation works vital to his State's agriculture [*TP*, XII, No. 405]. The Maharaja, it has been reported, even threatened to join Pakistan if this obstruction to his water supply were not removed.

Knowing that the Radcliffe Award was on the verge of becoming public knowledge before its official release, Liaquat Ali Khan made what must be interpreted as a last minute attempt to secure for Pakistan the three eastern *tehsils* of Gurdaspur, which Chaudhri Muhammad Ali told him (as he probably had long suspected) were destined for India. He instructed Chaudhri Muhammad Ali to call on Ismay on 11 August to protest on his behalf at the proposed Gurdaspur award which, Liaquat Ali Khan declared, he considered to be a "political" rather than a "judicial" decision, and, as such, "a grave injustice which will amount to a breach of faith on the part of the British". In a written reply, Ismay told Liaquat Ali Khan sternly and with a singular lack of sympathy that

> the Viceroy has always been, and is determined to keep clear of the whole business.... Thus I am at a loss to know what action you wish me to take on your message. In the first place, I am told that the final report of Sir Cyril

Radcliffe is not ready, and therefore I do not know what grounds you have for saying that Gurdaspur *has been* ... [original emphasis] ... allotted to the East Punjab. ... If this should be the case, you surely do not expect the Viceroy to suggest to Sir Cyril Radcliffe that he should make any alteration. Still less can I believe that you intend to imply that the Viceroy has influenced this award. I am well aware that some uninformed sections of public opinion imagine that the award will not be Sir Cyril Radcliffe's but the Viceroy's, but I never for one moment thought that you, who are completely in the know, should ever imagine that he could do such a thing. [*TP*, XII, No. 428].

Liaquat Ali Khan's sudden concern about Gurdaspur at this late date is interesting. As we shall see below, it was just about now that the Maharaja of Jammu & Kashmir was in the process of disposing of his Prime Minister, Pandit R.C. Kak, who was thought to favour, if not association with Pakistan, at least independence for the State of Jammu & Kashmir. An impending, and potentially pro-Indian, revolution in the Maharaja's Court in Srinagar, of which the Pakistani leaders were certainly aware, could not fail to concentrate attention on the future of Gurdaspur which had suddenly acquired a more acutely immediate geopolitical significance.

In the event, Pakistan did not get all of Gurdaspur. It did, however, lose the Ferozepore and Zira *tehsils*. On 10 or 11 August Sir Evan Jenkins, Governor of the Punjab, received in Lahore a telephone call by secure line from Viceroy's House in New Delhi which told him to "eliminate salient", in other words delete from his map of West Punjab these two *tehsils* which stuck out so absurdly (literally like a sore thumb) into East Punjab on the eastern (Indian) side of the Sutlej [*TP*, XII, No. 377n]. The salient duly disappeared off the face of the map.

Mountbatten and his close associates have always denied that the Viceroy had anything to do with last minute changes in Sir Cyril Radcliffe's boundary, and they imply that nothing ever took place even to suggest such a possibility. That there was indeed such an alteration by somebody the documents leave us in no doubt. Mountbatten's own part in it has been much harder to demonstrate. However, recently [*Daily Telegraph* 24 February 1992] Christopher Beaumont, Radcliffe's Private Secretary, has revealed that V.P. Menon, acting on behalf of Mountbatten, tried unsuccessfully to see Radcliffe late on 11 August, apparently to discuss boundary matters. At lunch on the following day, 12 August,

Radcliffe met Mountbatten and Ismay. Beaumont was excluded, but he is now convinced that this is when the final decision was taken about the fate of the Ferozepore and Zira *tehsils*. Beaumont kept no diary. The events he described may well have taken place on 11 August, but that they did take place is not open to serious question. His narrative combined with the documentary material now available leaves little doubt that Beaumont (who subsequently became an English Circuit Judge) was correct. The Viceroy, assisted by V.P. Menon, did indeed meddle directly with the Punjab boundary Award.

The episode of the Ferozepore and Zira *tehsils* has puzzled students for many decades. The reality, one suspects, is quite simple. Sir Cyril Radcliffe, like a good barrister, was given a brief by the Government of India, namely to defend a certain Punjab partition line which for sound geopolitical reasons had already decided upon in all its essentials. On about 7 August he allowed himself in a fit of enthusiasm to depart (perhaps on the grounds of fairness or the wish to seem fair) from his brief in the matter of the Ferozepore and Zira *tehsils*. (This possibility, which Christopher Beaumont now is inclined to doubt, was taken seriously enough by Professor Aloys Arthur Michel, a man who knew a great deal indeed about the Partition of the Punjab and its consequences [see: A.A. Michel, *The Indus Rivers. A Study of the Effects of Partition*, New Haven 1967, p.181n]). Radcliffe was brought sharply to order by Mountbatten. The final Award represented the unmodified brief, complete with an explicit declaration that the West Punjab (Pakistan) ought not on first geopolitical principles extend in any significant degree to the east of the Sutlej north of Bahawalpur State, despite the presence there of a number of Muslim-majority tracts. In other words, the whole process of consultation over which Radcliffe presided was something of a charade. Why bother with a Commission? Why did the British not simply propose the "natural" or "scientific" border which was going to emerge in any case?

One answer leaps to the mind. Mountbatten was the Great Partitioner of British India. At the same time he hoped to preserve the essential unity of the British Indian Empire by ensuring that both India and Pakistan became Dominions within the framework of the British Commonwealth. Originally he had hoped to ensure this by becoming Governor-General of both the new Dominions: he evidently believed that a joint Governor-Generalship (assisted, it may be, by a joint Supreme Command of the Armies of India and Pakistan under Field-Marshall

Auchinleck) might in time evolve into a substitute for the federal structure of the abortive 1946 Cabinet Mission plan. At the very beginning of July, however, Jinnah made it clear that he himself would be Governor-General of Pakistan, not Mountbatten. Without the joint Governor-Generalship it became far less certain that both India and Pakistan would, when the time came, opt for Commonwealth membership after all. It was, at all events, very important that Mountbatten not be seen to be responsible for some decision which would make Commonwealth membership politically difficult. He certainly could not afford to appear to favour one Dominion over the other in the matter of awarding territory. The device of the apparently impartial and totally isolated Sir Cyril Radcliffe was intended to deflect all blame for unpopular decisions (such as, for example, those relating to territory of importance to the Sikhs) from Mountbatten (and, behind him, the British Crown which presided over the Commonwealth). Sir Cyril Radcliffe was, in other words, a scapegoat of the most classic kind. It must be admitted, in passing, that the leaders of both India and Pakistan also found some advantage in this device which removed from their shoulders the onus of unpopular decisions, which in later days they could blame on the absent Sir Cyril (later Lord) Radcliffe.

Did all this have anything to do with Kashmir? In much that has been written since 1947 the Radcliffe Commission has been directly linked to the birth of the Kashmir dispute, almost as if the main function of Sir Cyril Radcliffe was to devise a Punjab boundary which ensured that the State of Jammu & Kashmir became part of the new India. This, of course, is extreme. Kashmir was fairly low on Mountbatten's list of priorities during the hectic weeks leading up to the Transfer of Power, and in no way could it be argued that the Indian acquisition of the State of Jammu & Kashmir was a major objective of the last British Viceroy. On the other hand, Mountbatten did have decided views (much influenced by his good friend Jawaharlal Nehru) about a suitable future for the State of Jammu & Kashmir, and he was not averse to promoting them if an opportunity presented itself. The last Viceroy, moreover, was fully aware of the importance in this context of the Gurdaspur District, upon which he commented on a number of occasions (for example, his remarks to the Maharaja of Indore and the Nawab of Bhopal on 4 August 1947 [*TP*, XII, No. 335]).

Suitably modified by the reincorporation into India of the Ferozepore and Zira *tehsils*, the Award of the Radcliffe Punjab Commission was complete by the evening of 12 August, when it made its way across the Viceroy's House complex to Mountbatten's desk [*TP*, XII, No. 488, Appx. I]. There is good evidence (for example, from a careful analysis of Mountbatten's Personal Report No. 17 of 16 August [*TP*, XII, No. 489]) to suggest that he either then read it or, at any rate, was fully aware of its contents. Mountbatten endeavoured to give a different impression. On 13 August, for example, he wrote to both Nehru and Jinnah to say that he was now off to Karachi and that the Radcliffe Award was still awaited: "at present, therefore, I have no idea of its contents" [*PP*, Vol. I, Nos. 216, 217]. This statement is, without a nugget of doubt, untrue.

The Radcliffe Awards for both Punjab and Bengal were formally revealed to the leaders of India and Pakistan on 16 August 1947 by Mountbatten, now Governor-General of India, in the former Viceroy's House, now Government House, New Delhi, and it was agreed to make them public the following day. Liaquat Ali Khan, the Prime Minister of Pakistan, expressed himself disgusted with the whole business; it was in his view so unfavourable to Pakistan in nearly all respects that there seemed no point in making comments in detail. Nehru, while he appeared happy enough about the overall shape of the two new boundaries, thought that the position in the Punjab might well give rise to trouble from the Sikhs (as, in due course, his daughter was to discover at the cost of her life). In the Bengal Award he was outraged by Pakistan's acquisition of the Chittagong Hill Tract, with a non-Muslim population. Neither leader at this time raised specifically the question of the future of the State of Jammu & Kashmir.

On 17 August, two days after they had become free of British rule, the people of both India and Pakistan finally were told exactly where their boundaries in Bengal and the Punjab were. In the Punjab the immediate result was a human disaster, a holocaust, with migrations and communal killings on a cataclysmic scale, a ghastly finale to the British era in the Subcontinent. Bengal, however, after the massacres of 1946, was to be spared a repetition of this horror until 1971.

It is interesting that originally Mountbatten had hoped to publish the Radcliffe Awards well before the actual moment of the Transfer of Power. On 12 August, however, when the Punjab Award had been suitably modified, he resolved to postpone publication until after the various independence celebrations had been completed. It was certainly odd to permit two new nations to begin their independent life with a most important sector of their land borders still undefined. It may be, as we shall see below, that this decision was not unconnected with the problem of the future status of the State of Jammu & Kashmir.

Professor A.A. Michel has pointed out the way in which the Radcliffe Award in the Punjab quite failed to provide an equitable division of the waters of the Indus system between India and Pakistan, a point which was to become all too apparent in April 1948 when India cut off the water supply to about eight per cent of Pakistan's agricultural land. This was as great a challenge to the survival of Pakistan as anything then happening in Kashmir, and it could easily have resulted in open war between the two new Dominions. In the event peace was patched up in May 1948, and eventually a more lasting solution to the problem of Punjabi irrigation was found in the Indus Waters Treaty of September 1960 which the World Bank helped negotiate.

There were, as Michel shows, many great problems in the division of the Indus waters into two self-contained systems, virtually none of them solved by Radcliffe. One problem, of course, totally ignored by Radcliffe, lay in the fact that a very large proportion indeed of the Indus waters either originated in the State of Jammu & Kashmir or flowed through it. If Jammu & Kashmir were to go to India, then virtually *all* the Indus waters (except those which came via the Kabul River) would be under Indian control at some stage. An equitable division of these waters, in other words, involved inevitably a division of some kind of influence over the territory of the State of Jammu & Kashmir. A division of sorts, in fact, emerged out of the Kashmir crisis which erupted in October 1947; and without the informal partition of the State of Jammu & Kashmir which resulted the Indus Waters Treaty would probably have not been a practical proposition. Without Azad Kashmir, for example, there could have been no Mangla project. Had the partition process in 1947 been handled rather differently, and with more time for its execution, it is hard to see how the question of the Indus waters would not on its own have caused the future of the State of Jammu & Kashmir to be placed on the agenda; and the manner in which it had been built up during the British period made it, of all the Indian Princely States, uniquely capable of being divided up and redistributed (given a suitable redefinition of the doctrine of Paramountcy which was not beyond the realms of possibility in 1947 had the will, understanding and time been there).

5. Jammu & Kashmir and the lapse of Paramountcy

When the revised Mountbatten plan was announced in early June 1947, no formal mechanism existed for the accession of the Princely States to either Dominion should the Rulers so wish. Indeed, even the precise terms on which accession might take place had not been worked out, though the Government of India Act, 1935, did provide some useful precedents. The whole business of the abrupt termination of the British Indian Empire seems to have taken most of the Rulers by surprise, and some were profoundly shocked by what they considered to be British perfidy, as the powerful memorandum of the Nawab of Bhopal quoted at the beginning of this Chapter makes clear enough.

On 5 July a States Department, headed by V.P. Menon, was established out of fragments of the old Indian Political Department, charged with the accession problem. In that at this moment Pakistan did not exist, it inevitably tended to concentrate its attention upon those Princely States which might reasonably be expected to accede to India. Those States which lay clearly within the Pakistani catchment area were on the whole left alone, and, in fact, Pakistan did not get around to regularising its own situation *vis à vis* the States until long after the appointed day when British sovereignty terminated.

On 8 July the new States Department informed all the Residents (representing the British Crown) in the States of the terms of accession which had now been decided by the Government of India [*TP*, XII, No. 2]. By accession the States would hand over to the appropriate Dominion (India or Pakistan) the powers of Foreign Affairs, Defence and Communications. All other powers would remain with the Ruler. The full implications of all this were discussed during the rest of July, and on 2 August V.P. Menon had ready a detailed *pro-forma* Instrument of Accession [*TP*, XII, No. 313] which the Ruler ought to sign on joining India (Menon did not strive officiously to bring States into the orbit of Pakistan-to-be). It was a document intended only for the highest class of States (those known as "fully empowered"), other States (in fact, the majority) having never hitherto enjoyed anything like full sovereignty were not going to be granted it, in theory or in practice, at this late stage. The blank form of the Instrument of Accession was duly printed and circulated to the appropriate Rulers with the request that they fill it in before the actual moment of the termination of the British Indian Empire. Nearly all did. This document will be considered again in Chapter III.

By the time of the Transfer of Power on 14/15 August 1947, only three States (other than those in the Pakistan communal catchment area which need not concern us here) had failed to accede, Hyderabad, Junagadh and Jammu & Kashmir. Hyderabad and Junagadh, the latter one of the Kathiawar States in Gujarat, both had Muslim Rulers and overwhelmingly Hindu subjects. Jammu & Kashmir had a Hindu Ruler and a Muslim-majority population. In theory the communal distinction between Ruler and subject was of no import; accession was a matter for the Ruler alone. In fact, as some in the States Department appreciated, it mattered a great deal. Sir Conrad Corfield, the last of the senior British "Politicals" with strong feelings about the rights and responsibilities of Maharajas, thought that an Indo-Pakistani exchange might be devised over Hyderabad and Jammu & Kashmir, in which Hyderabad went with India and Jammu & Kashmir with Pakistan, but he was ignored and, when he retired on the eve of the Transfer of Power, forgotten. There were also possibilities of Indo-Pakistani dealing over Junagadh.

In the event, no lasting bargains were struck. Each State met its fate very much on its own. Hyderabad and Junagadh, surrounded by Indian territory (and a stretch of coast in the case of Junagadh), were in due course swallowed up by India. Jammu & Kashmir, however, sitting as it did on the edge of both India and Pakistan, became the subject of Indo-Pakistani dispute which remains very much alive nearly fifty years on.

The Kashmir dispute has all too often been explored in the context of legal arguments which pay but token heed to the realities of politics and public opinion in the State of Jammu & Kashmir itself around the time of the Transfer of Power. To ignore internal Kashmiri political history during this crucial period is, of course, to miss an element of the greatest importance to our understanding of how the Kashmir dispute began.

It has already been noted that, unlike most Princely States, Jammu & Kashmir possessed an active and complex political life of its own. Since 1931 two major party groupings had emerged in the State, both with a common origin, the National Conference headed by Sheikh M. Abdullah, and the Muslim Conference. Both, collectively representing the Muslim majority in the State, were opposed to the absolutism of the ruling Dogra Dynasty. Their agitation (still for our present purpose treating the

Muslim and National Conferences as one) had produced a measure of constitutional development. The 1934 and 1939 State Constitutions (which the Maharaja had been obliged to grant in great measure because of their presence) had a provided for a legislature with, in the 1939 Constitution, a majority (40 out of 75) of elected members. The franchise was restricted and on a communal basis, and the powers of the legislature extremely circumscribed, but all this was much better than what was to be found in most other parts of Princely India. In the 1940s there had even been a brief period when a few elected representatives held ministerial office.

In 1946 one could, perhaps, divide public opinion in the State of Jammu & Kashmir into three categories. First: there were those who supported the Hindu Dogra Dynasty of Maharaja Sir Hari Singh. The Hindus in Jammu, where in some parts they were in a majority, and the Hindu Brahmins of the Vale, the Pandits, tended to identify with the Dogras, though there were a number of Pandit intellectuals who definitely did not. Given a choice, a majority of this element, particularly those in Jammu, might well opt for accession to India, but there were certainly to be found here some advocates of an independent Jammu & Kashmir. Second: the Muslim Conference represented the bulk of the Muslims in Jammu and the rather more conservative of the Muslims in the Vale. The Muslim Conference had some links with the Muslim League in British India, but it was very much a movement peculiar to the State of Jammu & Kashmir, and many of its members were not particularly attracted to the idea of union with Pakistan. On the other hand, it was positively opposed to union with India, and subsequently it was to become associated with accession to Pakistan. On the eve of the Transfer of Power, however, many Muslim Conference members would not have been unhappy with the idea of independence. Third: there was the National Conference, the creation of Sheikh Abdullah (which had originally – until 1939 – been called the Muslim Conference, and in opposition to which the revived Muslim Conference eventually emerged in 1941). This organisation had obtained the most publicity outside the State in the years immediately preceding the Transfer of Power, in great part because of the reputation of its leader, who not only moved in the more cosmopolitan circles in Srinagar (he was son-in-law of the European proprietor of Nedou's Hotel, the most fashionable hostelry in that holiday resort) but was deeply involved in Congress affairs in British India through his friendship with Jawaharlal Nehru.

As Sheikh Abdullah has occupied a particularly dominant position in the history of the Kashmir question, it is worth having a closer look at the man and his political platform. There is no doubt that by the middle of 1947 he was a symbol within and without the State of Jammu & Kashmir of democratic resistance to Princely rule. What precisely he stood for, and how much support, in potential electoral terms, he enjoyed, it is not so easy to determine. In 1944 he had drawn up a manifesto for a *New Kashmir*, an independent state in the Subcontinent free of the Maharaja and subject to neither Hindustan (India) nor Pakistan. Quite how secular this proposed state was intended to be is open to argument. In 1946, while the British Cabinet Mission was in India, Sheikh Abdullah launched a "Quit Kashmir" movement with the objective of the immediate ending of Dogra rule and its replacement by an independent Kashmir under the leadership of his National Conference. The Maharaja's reply was to arrest Sheikh Abdullah and put him on trial for sedition.

There can be no doubt that Nehru saw Sheikh Abdullah almost as his political twin. He tried to attend his trial, only to be arrested and effectively deported by the Maharaja from what after all was the ancestral home of the Nehru family (of Pandits), the Vale of Kashmir. From that moment Nehru identified himself so closely with the imprisoned Sheikh Abdullah that he believed that the Kashmiri leader wanted nothing better than to integrate his State into a secular Indian Union presided over by Jawaharlal Nehru. It is, perhaps, to be regretted that during these crucial weeks prior to the Transfer of Power Sheikh Abdullah remained in prison and was unable either to keep in touch with the march of events or to make his own views widely known.

In 1946, with the British Raj obviously running out of time, the question of Jammu & Kashmir's future was the subject of considerable debate in Srinagar, where the political temperature was closely monitored by the British Resident, Colonel W.F. Webb. His reports survive in the India Office Records in London, and they provide a fascinating insight into Kashmiri thoughts, hopes and intrigues during this last year or so of British India.

Early in 1946, Webb recorded, there were efforts to bring together the Muslim Conference and the National Conference; both parties sprang, after all, from the organisation which had emerged during the crisis of

1931 and in which Sheikh Abdullah was a leading spirit, and a combined party would cope far better with the challenges and opportunities presented by the impending British departure. Union, however, failed, so Colonel Webb reported, and for a variety of reasons.

For example: many Kashmiris in the Vale depended upon the tourist industry (in 1945 18,614 European – mainly British – visitors came to Srinagar), and bodies like the Kashmir Houseboat Owner's Chamber did not want, as Sheikh Abdullah was then demanding, that the British "quit" Kashmir along with the Maharaja. Who, then, would rent houseboats? Again: it was already clear that Sheikh Abdullah, unlike many other Muslims in Kashmir and Jammu, could not get along with Jinnah and his Muslim League. Sheikh Abdullah was on record that Jinnah was "not a true Moslem and ... had little knowledge of the Quoran", a view which many Kashmiri Muslims did not share. Finally: many Kashmiri leaders, including the Mir Waiz M. Yusuf Shah (of great influence among the Srinagar Sunnis), were profoundly suspicious of Sheikh Abdullah, who was seen not only to be set on his own aggrandisement but also to be of suspect theological orthodoxy (especially in the matter of the Ahmadiya community). All this complicated the National Conference-Muslim Conference discussions in March 1946, in which, apart from Sheikh Abdullah, Chaudhri Ghulam Abbas, Maulana Mahommed Sayeed Masoodi, and G.M. Sadiq (figures of great importance for the subsequent history of Jammu & Kashmir) participated, along with the Mir Waiz Yusuf Shah.

It was the "Quit Kashmir" movement, however, which brought all prospect of union to an end. As Webb described it, this phenomenon had many of the attributes of a rebellion. One aim was a popular uprising which would expel the Dogras and restore Kashmir (what was to happen in Jammu was not so clear) to native rule, which Sheikh Abdullah understood to mean a regime presided over by himself. After the State Government arrested Sheikh Abdullah in May, there were outbreaks of violence not only in Srinagar but also on Anantnag, Sopore and elsewhere (but not, interestingly enough in the context of the subject our Chapter II below, in Poonch or adjacent Baramula). The more conservative supporters of the Muslim Conference, however, were not ready for rebellion against the Maharaja. These events tended to confirm them in the view that Sheikh Abdullah was a dangerous revolutionary in politics as well, perhaps, as in religion.

The gulf between National Conference activists and Muslim Conference moderates was skilfully exploited by the Maharaja's Prime Minister, Pandit Ram Chandra Kak.

Pandit Kak was Sheikh Abdullah's most formidable adversary in the "Quit Kashmir" agitation. Kak was a scholar, a man of wide interests, no narrow Hindu bigot (his wife, Margaret, for example, was English), and he seems to have possessed a profound understanding of the people of the Vale of Kashmir, in whose language he could exert a powerfully fluent and persuasive charm and with whose traditions he was entirely at home. As the time of the British departure approached, Kak concluded that the State's best hope lay either in independence or in some form of special association with Pakistan, but, like Sheikh Abdullah, the idea of independence appealed to him above all. He was, in a very real sense, Sheikh Abdullah's direct rival, and, had there been no external pressures it is highly probable that he would have prevailed. Unlike Sheikh Abdullah, he was perfectly able to negotiate with Jinnah, and had need dictated, and opportunity arisen, would certainly have done so.

During the final year or so of the British Indian Empire, Pandit Kak acquired great influence over the less bellicose members of the Muslim Conference which at moments of crisis he was able to exploit in its arguments with the National Conference. After Sheikh Abdullah's arrest in May 1946, the National Conference announced that it would boycott all formal political functions in the State; the Muslim Conference, in part because of Kak's diplomatic skills, did not follow suit. Thus, in the January 1947 Jammu & Kashmir State elections the Muslim Conference participated (to become the largest single grouping in the *Praja Sabah*, the lower house of the legislature) while the National Conference did not. Had events turned out otherwise, the Muslim Conference could well have been an extremely effective ally for Kak's policy of a non-Indian future for the State. In April 1947, for example, Chaudhri Hamidullah Khan, Acting President of the Muslim Conference, declared in the *Praja Sabah* that if the Maharaja were to declare for independence after the British had gone, he and his party would gladly offer their lives for the cause of the Dogra Dynasty.

Unfortunately for the future peace of South Asia, Kak had powerful enemies within the Kashmiri Pandit establishment, notably Sir Kailash Haksar, who had once acted as Prime Minister of the State, his son-in-law Wattal, a contractor to the State, and B.J. Nehru, a former Financial

Adviser. This group had clashed with Kak over the awarding of certain State contracts, and they subsequently lost no opportunity to blacken the Prime Minister's reputation (as good nepotists, they constantly accused him of nepotism). One of their connections in India (if only by blood ties), Jawaharlal Nehru, believed everything they said about Kak, which only reinforced what he had already heard from his friend Sheikh Abdullah. As Colonel Webb noted in May 1946, the future Indian Prime Minister's "violently partisan attitude" was "based on untrue reports regarding Kashmir made to him by Sheikh Mohammed Abdullah's lieutenants in Delhi and Lahore who fabricate entirely false news".

Soon after Kak had Sheikh Abdullah arrested, Nehru in June 1946, accompanied by his faithful follower Dwarkanath Kachru, rushed up to the Kashmir border on the Jhelum Valley Road to try to help his friend in Srinagar. Kak had him turned back after a short detention in Uri Dak Bungalow, but Kachru was held for some three months before being what in the Subcontinent is known as "externed" (expelled from the State).

These two sets of circumstances, Kak's conflict with the Haksar-Nehru clique in Srinagar on the one hand, and, on the other, the arrest of Sheikh Abdullah coupled with the expulsion from his ancestral home of Sheikh Abdullah's Indian champion Jawaharlal Nehru, were to contribute towards Kak's overthrow a year later, with Mountbatten serving unwittingly as Nehru's ally in what was in great measure an act of personal vengeance.

Already in 1946, according to Colonel Webb (writing in July 1946), Jawaharlal Nehru had developed a definite policy for the future of the State of Jammu & Kashmir once the British had departed. Under the leadership of Sheikh Abdullah it was to be made into an anti-Pakistani (whatever shape Pakistan might eventually assume) zone to the north of the Punjab. While he might modify his ideas about the precise shape of this zone (and precision was not, in any case, Nehru's forte), the basic concept had not changed at the outset of the Mountbatten Viceroyalty in March 1947. It was to infect everything which Nehru told Mountbatten about the State of Jammu & Kashmir and Sheikh Abdullah's special position there as the voice of the Kashmiri people.

Here we have a unique set of personal connections, aspirations and prejudices all focused on a single issue. The nature of the peculiar relationship between Nehru and Lord and Lady Mountbatten during the final British Viceroyalty is beyond doubt, but we will leave it cloaked in a discreet silence here. Other relationships, such as those between Nehru and Sheikh Abdullah, and between Nehru and one of the major anti-Kak Pandit cliques in Jammu & Kashmir (there were others), have been sketched above (though some aspects of the Nehru-Sheikh Abdullah connection have yet to be explained satisfactorily – it may well have involved more than shared political opinions). Taken all together, they provide a powerful influence at the very heart of the Indian governmental establishment tending towards the proposition that the State of Jammu & Kashmir ought to end up in India rather than Pakistan.

Nehru's own involvement with Jammu & Kashmir inevitably influenced Mountbatten, whose attitudes towards that State we must now examine. There is a caveat here. It is easy to forget that, Nehru's emotions apart, there were good geopolitical reasons, well understood by the *éminences grises* of the Political Department and its successor services, to inspire powerful voices in New Delhi during the final days of the British Indian Empire to advise the Viceroy that the State of Jammu & Kashmir was by virtue of *realpolitik*, if not of right, part of India, and should so remain. One such voice was undoubtedly that of V.P. Menon, the driving force behind the Indian States Department.

The complexities of the problem of the future of Jammu & Kashmir appear first to have come to Mountbatten's notice in April 1947, while he was still pondering the initial (and abortive) version of his plan. The point at issue was what to do about the Gilgit Lease, that arrangement of 1935 by which the Government of India had acquired control for sixty years over Gilgit and its neighbourhood along the Northern Frontier [*TP*, IX, No. 254]. Should the lease remain with the successor Dominion, which in this case the Political Department evidently concluded would almost certainly have to be Pakistan, or should it be handed back to the Maharaja of Jammu & Kashmir? The Political Department view, which convinced Mountbatten, was that the lease ought to be handed back to the Maharaja before the actual Transfer of Power (still thought to be June 1948); this would give the Maharaja the opportunity to establish his authority while the British were still around to support him. When the date of the Transfer of Power was advanced to 15 August 1947, so also was the date of retrocession of Gilgit; it was now fixed for 1 August. There can be no doubt that the Political Department (after 5 July the States Department) did strive beyond the normal call of duty to ensure (without success) that Gilgit remained the Maharaja's.

It is possible that Mountbatten with his Naval background, unlike some Political Department veterans, did not fully appreciate the significance of Gilgit to the strategists of British Indian defence. It had been seen to be a key bastion against Russian expansion since the middle of the nineteenth century, and a great deal of the history of the territorial expansion of the State of Jammu & Kashmir after 1846 was inextricably involved with Gilgit and the mountainous tracts to its north. It was unlikely that the Political Department would advocate the return of Gilgit to Jammu & Kashmir unless they felt sure that State would soon be safely incorporated into some stable Subcontinental polity, which in their view tended to mean India rather than Pakistan. In that the British Resident in Kashmir was then still reporting that the odds were that the Maharaja of Jammu & Kashmir would opt for independence after the Transfer of Power [*TP*, IX, No. 37], it could well be that there was already germinating in the Political Department, soon to be V.P. Menon's States Department, some plan to frustrate the Maharaja and ensure that in the end his State was safely penned in the Indian fold.

It is also interesting that Nehru saw the Gilgit Lease rather differently. He thought that the Government of India should hang on to it for as long as possible. It was essential to have a clearer picture of Jammu & Kashmir's future before making such an important decision. As in the case of Berar (in relation to the State of Hyderabad from which the British had leased this tract at the very beginning of the twentieth century), Nehru objected on principle to handing back territory from what was going to be enlightened Indian rule to Princely autocracy. Gilgit, of course, was in Nehru's eyes a far more important matter than Berar as it involved his beloved Kashmir. It may be that at the back of his mind he saw Gilgit eventually being merged with the North-West Frontier Province, which had a Congress Ministry in power at that time, into an Indian enclave flanking that divided Punjab which was the inexorably consequence of the Congress Working Committee Resolution of 8 March. The mere existence of such a Gilgit could well force the Maharaja willy nilly into the Indian camp.

Though totally opposed in detail over Gilgit, it is interesting that the policies of both Mountbatten and Nehru relating to this remote Karakoram outpost can be interpreted to have had a common underlying objective, the eventual incorporation of the State of Jammu & Kashmir in India.

Nehru never lost an opportunity from this time onwards to expose his friend Mountbatten to arguments in favour of an Indian Jammu & Kashmir. In June, soon after the announcement of the revised Mountbatten plan, the Viceroy resolved that it would be best if all States which ought to accede to India (on terms which were then still in the process of definition) did so as soon as possible, and if at all possible before the Transfer of Power so that accession would take place under British auspices. Mountbatten, reflecting here the views of V.P. Menon, never did like the idea of a number of independent polities springing up in the wake of the departing British. Two Dominions were enough. In practice, it was evident that the big problems were Hyderabad and Jammu & Kashmir, and the Viceroy determined to visit both Rulers as soon as he could to exert the force of his personality upon them and make them come to some prompt, and proper, decision. Hyderabad is not our concern. The visit to Jammu & Kashmir began on 17 June.

Before he set out, Mountbatten had asked Nehru for a memorandum on Kashmir, a document which was just ready when he left New Delhi [*TP*, XI, No. 229]. Nehru argued most forcefully that the State of Jammu & Kashmir must join India, but not as an autocracy under Maharaja Sir Hari Singh. Accession had somehow to bring about the empowering of the imprisoned Sheikh Abdullah and his National Conference to direct the State's destiny. Sheikh Abdullah, Nehru left Mountbatten in no doubt, was the only true spokesman for the Kashmiri people, and the National Conference was the only popular Kashmiri political organisation worthy of consideration. The evidence suggests that Mountbatten was convinced.

During his time in Srinagar, the Viceroy never managed to pin the Maharaja down to a serious discussion of any kind. He found him, as had many others, both evasive and indecisive. In the end Mountbatten had to content himself with presenting to the State's Prime Minister, Pandit Kak, a summary of the main points he had hoped to discuss with the Maharaja [*TP*, XI, No. 294]. This was an interesting conversation which can be interpreted in more than one way. In the present writer's view, Mountbatten intended to let Pandit Kak know that the only hope for the survival of the Dogra Dynasty was for the Maharaja to throw in his lot with Congress and the Indian Union.

One result of the Viceregal visit to Srinagar in June was to convince Mountbatten that the real force behind the Maharaja's reluctance to join

India was provided by Pandit Kak. It was Kak who nourished thoughts of independence and, even, some special relationship with M.A. Jinnah. If Kak were got out of the way, however, Maharaja Sir Hari Singh might be convinced easily enough to do his duty and sign up with the Government in New Delhi. During the last few days of the British Indian Empire in August 1947 Mountbatten evidently tried to use the Radcliffe Commission as a weapon against Pandit Kak. The approach was extremely indirect, but it can be detected in odd phrases uttered by Mountbatten or included in his Personal Report destined for the eyes of King George VI.

What seems to have happened was this. It was hinted in a number of indirect ways that the Maharaja's sole prospect of surviving was to tie up in some manner with India. This would only be possible provided the Radcliffe Commission awarded to India the three eastern *tehsils* of Gurdaspur District, through which ran the main road from the Pathankot railhead in India to Jammu. If all of Gurdaspur went to Pakistan, of course, the Maharaja would be doomed. In order to ensure the desired allocation of Gurdaspur by Sir Cyril Radcliffe, so the whispers had it, the Maharaja had to do two things: get rid of Pandit Kak and prepare to sign an Instrument of Accession to India. Otherwise, all of Gurdaspur would go to Pakistan and Sir Hari Singh would be left to the tender mercies of M.A. Jinnah. The documentary evidence suggests that Mountbatten was perfectly aware that this covert, almost subliminal, campaign made an utter nonsense of his claim to have absolutely no control over what Sir Cyril Radcliffe might or might not decide.

The Maharaja, under this pressure, went half way. On 11 August he dismissed Pandit Kak, replacing him temporarily with a Dogra kinsman, Major-General Janak Singh, who was to act as caretaker until some more decisive figure could be found to implement whatever policy it was that the Maharaja wished to implement. On the other hand, he signed no Instrument of Accession. The best he would do was to offer to sign Standstill Agreements with both India and Pakistan in order to maintain the status quo for a while. Immediately after the Transfer of Power, Pakistan accepted the Standstill Agreement while India prevaricated.

In order to convince the Maharaja that the fate of Gurdaspur still hung in the balance, it was obviously prudent to delay the publication of the Radcliffe Award. If the Maharaja knew that Gurdaspur had gone to India, he would be under no pressure to make up his mind as to accession. As we have already seen, it is interesting in this context that Mountbatten, who originally was in favour of the publication of the Radcliffe Award as soon as it was ready, on 11 or 12 August (when the Award was indeed to hand) decided to postpone its publication until after the actual Transfer of Power on 15 August. It may well be that he hoped that right up to the last minute the prospect of all of Gurdaspur in Pakistani hands might urge the Maharaja to throw in his lot with India, a decision which was all the easier to make after the dismissal of Pandit Kak. The meeting between Mountbatten and V.P. Menon, to which Christopher Beaumont refers (on 11 August) and the lunch from which he was excluded, could well have related to this exploitation of Gurdaspur in the context of Kashmir rather than to the Ferozepore and Zira *tehsils*. V.P. Menon, while not involved in the Radcliffe process, was certainly very much concerned with anything that affected the future of the State of Jammu & Kashmir.

For a brief moment then, from about 12 August to the actual Transfer of Power in India, with Pandit Kak out of the way, Mountbatten may well have thought he really had solved the Kashmir problem with Maharaja Sir Hari Singh signing up with India in the dying minutes of the British Raj; but, if so, he woke up on 15 August to find that this had not occurred. As Governor-General of the Dominion of India Mountbatten was to be obliged in the months to come to devote a great deal more time and energy to this extraordinarily intractable matter. He had seriously underestimated Maharaja Sir Hari Singh's indecisiveness, or, as others might argue, his guile. Meanwhile, the Maharaja entered the new post-British era in the Subcontinent as, to all intents and purposes, the ruler of a sovereign and independent country, with all the challenges and responsibilities which that such a status implied. In these circumstances he would probably have fared better with Pandit Kak (now under house arrest) as Prime Minister to advise him than he did with Janak Singh or, from 15 October, Justice Mehr Chand Mahajan (a former member of the Radcliffe Commission for the Punjab and clearly dedicated to the Indian interest).

II

The Poonch Revolt, origins to 24 October 1947

The State of Jammu & Kashmir was founded in the first part of the nineteenth century by Gulab Singh, a Hindu Dogra (of Rajput descent). His ancestor Ranjit Dev had once ruled a considerable tract of hill territory between the Punjab and the Pir Panjal Range as well as several Jagirs (fiefs) in the Punjab plains; but Jammu lay at the core of his dominions. Ranjit Dev had acknowledged, from the 1760s, the invading Durrani Afghans as his overlords. When the Sikhs embarked upon their meteoric rise to power in the Punjab at the very end of the eighteenth century, Afghan influence declined in these hills. Soon anarchy reigned throughout the region.

In the circumstances, Gulab Singh (born in 1792) and his two younger brothers, Dhian Singh (1796) and Suchet Singh (1801), sons of Mian Kishore Singh, sought to re-establish Ranjit Dev's kingdom under Sikh patronage. By 1818 the three Dogra brothers had acquired a powerful influence at the court of the great Sikh ruler, Ranjit Singh. Dhian Singh soon became Ranjit Singh's most important adviser, and, after Ranjit Singh's death in 1839, remained a dominant figure in Sikh ruling circles until his assassination in 1843. Both Gulab Singh and Suchet Singh also served Ranjit Singh in various capacities. It was inevitable that all three brothers should be rewarded for their efforts by the Sikh Durbar (Court) at Lahore.

Jammu was given to Gulab Singh as a Jagir subject to Lahore in 1820; and Suchet Singh also received territories, but in parts of the Punjab which do not relate to the subsequent history of the Kashmir dispute. About the same time Dhian Singh was granted his own Jagir, which consisted of the ancient hill state of Poonch along with a number of adjacent minor hill states including Bhimber and Mirpur. Unlike Jammu, with its powerful Hindu nucleus, Dhian Singh's new possessions contained an overwhelmingly Muslim population. In its geographical shape, Dhian Singh's territory was an elongated rectangle of some 3,600 square miles of hill country on the Punjab side of the Pir Panjal Range, lying between its crest and the Jhelum River and extending southward from the Jhelum-Kishenganga confluence near Domel right down to the Chenab River where it debouches into the plains in the Gujrat District of the Punjab (and, at one time, Dhian Singh held Gujrat as well).

The collection of fiefdoms over which Dhian Singh acquired control, it is interesting to note, coincides very closely with what in late 1947 was to become Azad ("Free") Kashmir. Azad Kashmir, of course, includes Muzaffarabad on the right bank side of the Jhelum, a region which until 1846 remained under Sikh rule, and then, as part of Kashmir Province, passed to Gulab Singh. Dhian Singh also, as we have seen, possessed Gujrat in the Punjab, which at the time of the Transfer of Power became part of Pakistan and has never been connected with Azad Kashmir. None the less, it can be argued with some conviction that the core of Azad Kashmir State, often dismissed today by writers with Indian sympathies as no more than a fantasy of Pakistani chauvinism, does indeed represent a political entity in its own right of some appreciable antiquity.

Dhian Singh was too busy as a politician and statesmen in the Sikh Durbar at Lahore to play an active part in the administration of his territorial possessions; the supervision of his interests was entrusted largely to his elder brother, Gulab Singh. In the 1830s the Dogra-appointed Governor in Poonch, Shams-ud-Din, a member of the Muslim family who had ruled in pre-Sikh days, rebelled with the support of many local Muslim chieftains. This first Poonch revolt, in many ways a precedent for what was to happen in 1947, was suppressed with great determination by Gulab Singh, and, as a contemporary British observer, G.T. Vigne, noted, with extreme cruelty:

> an insurrection had taken place near Punch against the authority of Gulab Singh. He had gone in person to suppress it, and succeeded in doing so. Some of his prisoners were flayed alive under his own eye. ... He then ordered one or two of the skins to be stuffed with straw; the hands were stiffened, and tied in an attitude of supplication; the corpse was then placed erect; and the head, which had been severed from the body, was reversed as it rested on the neck. The figure was planted by the way-side, that passers by might see it; and Gulab Singh called his son's attention to it, and told him to take a lesson in the art of governing. [G.T. Vigne, *Travels in Kashmir, Ladak,*

THE POONCH REVOLT, ORIGINS TO 24 OCTOBER 1947

Iskardo, the countries adjoining the mountain-course of the Indus, and the Himalaya, north of the Punjab, 2 vols., London 1842, Vol. I, p. 241].

After Dhian Singh's death in 1843, Gulab Singh treated Poonch, Bhimber, Mirpur and the rest as if they were his own property, despite the fact that his brother had two heirs, Moti Singh (the younger of the pair), to whom had been left the Jagir of Poonch, and Jawahir Singh, who was intended to inherit the remainder. When in 1846, following his cynical neutrality during the First Anglo-Sikh War, Gulab Singh by the Treaty of Amritsar (of 16 March 1846, between the British and Gulab Singh) was permitted by the Government of India to purchase from it the former Sikh Province of the Vale of Kashmir (for 75 lakhs, or units of 100,000, of Rupees), he took the wording of this Treaty (Article I, referring to Article 12 of the Treaty of Lahore between the British and the Sikhs of 9 March 1846) to indicate that Dhian Singh's estate had come to him as well.

This view was certainly open to question; but Dhian Singh's heirs were then minors and in no position to argue very strongly. It was not until 1848 that the two boys, or their agents, were able to seek redress from the Government of India in the person of Sir Frederick Currie, Resident at Lahore. His award was interpreted by Gulab Singh (and his successors) as accepting his rights over his brother's legacy. In fact, it did nothing of the sort; indeed, its somewhat opaque language tended to confirm the *de facto* independence from Jammu & Kashmir of the two sons of Dhian Singh, including the cancellation of the obligation imposed upon them by Gulab Singh to pay the costs of a battalion of infantry in the Jammu & Kashmir State Forces. Dhian Singh's heirs, however, were still required to pay to the Jammu & Kashmir ruler an annual (essentially token) sum in lieu of customs which Gulab Singh might have collected in the territory involved, as well as a highly symbolic annual tribute to Gulab Singh, as Maharaja.

In 1852, after Moti Singh and Jawahir Singh had quarrelled, Henry Lawrence (then one of the British Commissioners administering the Punjab territory which had recently been annexed from the Sikhs) was invited to arbitrate. The question here was the determination of the precise boundaries between the two portions of Dhian Singh's estate. Lawrence reaffirmed Moti Singh's right to the Jagir (or *Ilaqa*) of Poonch, an area of some 1,600 square miles which was now defined with some care. The remainder, perhaps another 2,000 square miles or so including Bhimber, Kotli and Mirpur, was left with Jawahir Singh.

In 1858, immediately following Gulab Singh's death, Jawahir Singh was involved in a plot against Gulab Singh's son and heir, Maharaja Ranbir Singh, probably an attempt to divert the succession to the whole of the State of Jammu & Kashmir from Gulab Singh's line to that of Dhian Singh, of which Jawahir Singh was the senior representative. The British, in order to eliminate any challenge to the position of the Maharaja Ranbir Singh, who had already acquired a considerable stature in the geopolitics of the Indian Empire as a bastion of India's Northern Frontier against that Russian menace which so obsessed mid-Victorian British statesmen, deprived Jawahir Singh of all his territory; it was then was handed over formally to the Maharaja Ranbir Singh. Moti Singh, however, was yet again left in possession of Poonch, subject only to the payment of a nominal and symbolic tribute to the Maharaja.

By 1873 Poonch was to all intents and purposes just another Indian Princely State, a member of a group which the British Government of India knew as the Punjab Hill States. It ran its own administration and raised its own revenue, including customs duties. The Raja, Moti Singh, had his own army of some 1,200 men and a battery of artillery. In addition, he could call on a kind of territorial reserve of former soldiers and government pensioners, all of them Muslims and many of them having served in the British Indian Army (which recruited extensively from Poonch). In the 1890s, after the Government of India had deprived the then Maharaja of Jammu & Kashmir, Pratap Singh, of almost all his powers and was in effect directly ruling the State through the British Resident in Srinagar, the role of the Maharaja in Poonch affairs virtually disappeared. The only administrative references now made from Poonch to Srinagar were requests for the confirmation of death sentences by the British Resident. From 1906 to 1922 the Government of India provided the Raja of Poonch with an official from the Punjab who took final responsibility for the governance of the Jagir. Of the 30,000 troops from the general Kashmir region who served with British forces during World War I, no fewer than 20,000 came from Poonch; in gratitude, the Government of India awarded the Raja, Baldev Singh (who succeeded Moti Singh in 1897) the right to a personal salute of nine guns (the Maharaja of Jammu & Kashmir was a 21 gun salute Ruler).

In 1918 Baldev Singh was succeeded as Raja of Poonch by his son

Sukhdev Singh. During this reign a crisis began to develop in the relations between Poonch and the Maharaja of Jammu & Kashmir of great importance for the future.

Maharaja Gulab Singh's grandson, Maharaja Pratap Singh, died in 1925 without direct heir. He had been an extremely devout, even old fashioned, Hindu; and he looked askance at the modern ways of his younger brother, Amar Singh, who was his Chief Minister and, in this period of direct British supervision over the affairs of the State of Jammu & Kashmir, far more powerful than the Maharaja. The obvious heir was Amar Singh's son, Hari Singh, but Hari Singh, apart from sharing his father's delight in western dress and manners, had turned out to be dissolute and extravagant; the British Indian Political Department had to rescue him in London from some extremely embarrassing attempts to blackmail him. As his death approached, therefore, Maharaja Pratap Singh resolved that the succession should pass to the Dhian Singh line as represented by the younger brother and heir to the Raja of Poonch, Jagatdev Singh who, Pratap Singh declared, was the "Spiritual Heir to Kashmir".

Maharaja Pratap Singh, despite the approval of the Chamber of Princes, was overruled by the Political Department, which thought that Hari Singh, whose disreputable background might make him easier to manipulate, would prove a more amenable Maharaja. Thus Maharaja Sir Hari Singh, destined to play such a prominent part in the Kashmir crisis of 1947, came to the throne of Jammu & Kashmir State with an abiding loathing for his potential rival in Poonch, who remained in the eyes of many in both Jammu and Kashmir the true "Spiritual Heir to Kashmir"; he was determined that this threat to his authority should be suppressed as soon as a suitable opportunity presented itself.

Sukhdev Singh died in 1927. Jagatdev Singh, as the new Raja of Poonch, at once began to feel the force of the animosity of Hari Singh. The Jammu & Kashmir Government immediately produced an edict, a *Dastur-i-Amal*, in which it was specified that the Raja must from now on always appoint a Wazir (Chief Minister) selected for him in Srinagar or Jammu, and that all Poonch decisions would have to be drafted by this official. Moreover, the Raja would be subjected to severe restrictions in his right to employ any foreign (that is to say British) advisers, and it was stipulated that all Jammu & Kashmir State laws would apply in the Poonch Jagir. Finally, the Raja must agree to visit the Maharaja at least three times a year to perform some act of homage in open Durbar (Court). Although British Political Department intervention resulted in most of these provisions being removed (it considered that Poonch was "more than an ordinary Jagir", and certainly not an integral part of the State of Jammu & Kashmir), yet the final text of the *Dastur-i-Amal* of 28 January 1928 specified the performance by the Poonch Raja of two acts of homage annually to the Maharaja; and this was duly approved by the British Resident in Srinagar, E.B. Howell.

Despite the modifications to the *Dastur-i-Amal*, Hari Singh began to treat Poonch as if it were just another province in his State. In 1929 he arbitrarily dismissed Raja Jagatdev Singh's Wazir along with other Poonch officials. When Jagatdev Singh attempted to see Hari Singh, who was then staying at the Taj Mahal Hotel in Bombay, to discuss the situation, the Maharaja refused him an audience.

Two years later came what amounted to a public break in relations between the two Dogra Rulers. On 15 May 1931 a reception was held for Hari Singh at the Shalimar Gardens in Srinagar. Protocol had it that the Maharaja would arrive late, and that when his motor car reached the gateway to the Gardens, all those present would come down to the entrance to greet him. Everyone, including the Ruler of the other Jagir in the State, Chenani, followed custom except for Jagatdev Singh, who remained in the pavilion where he waited for the Maharaja to come to him just as if the two men were at least of equal status. Hari Singh was furious. For a few days the Poonch Raja was denied the right to attend any official function in the State, and then he was stripped of his entitlement to a four gun salute which had been granted him by Maharaja Hari Singh, though he retained, of course, the nine gun salute which the Government of India had awarded Baldev Singh.

In late 1936 Hari Singh launched a detailed attack on what remained of Poonch autonomy. Poonch courts were made directly subordinate to the Jammu & Kashmir High Court. The right of the Poonch Raja to raise troops from among his subjects was severely curtailed. The Poonch police were subjected to strict State supervision. All branches of Poonch administration were to be liable to inspection by the Maharaja. Finally, Poonch was denied the valuable right to levy its own customs duties. Naturally, the Raja of Poonch protested to the British Indian Political Department, and desultory discussions ensued until 1940, when Raja Jagatdev Singh died and was succeeded by his son, Ratandev Singh.

THE POONCH REVOLT, ORIGINS TO 24 OCTOBER 1947

Here was Hari Singh's chance. The new Raja was a minor. Hari Singh declared that he would not permit Ratandev Singh ever to assume any authority in the Jagir until a fresh arrangement, *patta* (charter), was devised. Meanwhile, the administration of law in Poonch would conform to the practice in the rest of the State of Jammu & Kashmir under the authority of the State Supreme Court, and all Jammu & Kashmir State taxes would apply to the Jagir. Hari Singh selected a guardian for the new Raja, Rao Bahadur Baldev Singh Pathania who had formerly been Governor of Kashmir Province. An Administrator of the Jagir was appointed, one Sheikh Abdul Qayum, a former Chief Justice. The Poonch right to collect customs duties was abrogated; in compensation, the Maharaja agreed to pay the Jagir treasury 78,000 Rupees annually.

This time the British acquiesced with scarcely a murmur; there was some talk of revision in 1943, but nothing seems to have come of it. Jammu & Kashmir State troops were helping in the War, and during that emergency the Government of India had no desire to argue about what could well be seen to be domestic matters with any of the major Princes, who were valued as bulwarks against anti-British agitation by the Indian National Congress and others.

These events played a significant part in the genesis of the Kashmir problem in ways that have to date remained rather obscure. The Poonch Rajas, despite the horrors of suppressed rebellion in the 1830s which we have noted, had developed a close and, on the whole, harmonious relationship with their predominantly Muslim subjects who came to look on them as a barrier against the imposition of far less tolerant rule from Jammu and Srinagar.

Unlike the Muslims of the Vale, who were on the whole anything but martial, and usually (and, we now know well, mistakenly) regarded as virtually inert in political matters by observers both in and without the State, the men of Poonch were by tradition soldiers. As we have seen, over 20,000 of them served in the Indian Army in World War I. In World War II the number was far higher; at its end at least 60,000 ex-servicemen returned to the Jagir. Their reaction to the political changes in Poonch was definitely negative. While the War was on, this did not in practice matter much. With the approach of the Transfer of Power, however, the Poonch problem became ever more acute. There were areas of remote countryside in what was often, along the Pir Panjal Range, extremely difficult terrain, into which the Maharaja's men did not dare to go, the

THE POONCH REVOLT, ORIGINS TO 24 OCTOBER 1947

Jammu & Kashmir equivalent of the unadministered tracts along the North-West Frontier of British India. On the eve of the British departure, in June 1947, refusal to accept the Maharaja's authority spread to more densely populated regions. Here was the beginning of the Poonch revolt.

The fiscal situation in Poonch at this moment was observed by Richard Symonds, a Quaker who was carrying out relief work in the Punjab. One of the very few outsiders with first-hand knowledge of what was going on in Poonch, he wrote in the Calcutta *Statesman* (4 February 1948) that the ex-servicemen returning to the Jagir found

> there was a tax on every hearth and every window. Every cow, buffalo and sheep was taxed and even every wife. Finally the Zaildari tax was introduced to pay for the cost of taxation, and Dogra [Hindu] troops were billeted on the [Muslim] Poonchis to enforce collection.

These taxes were not, it should be noted, imposed on Hindus or Sikhs.

The first clear sign of the Poonch revolt was the refusal by many villages and landlords dotted over the region to pay these new, and unaccustomed, taxes to the Maharaja's agents. Resistance was mainly confined, in the early stages, to the Bagh District of Poonch, the northernmost part of the Jagir. By July 1947 it was concluded in Srinagar that there was unequivocal evidence of some form of organised opposition to the recently imposed rule by the Gulab Singh branch of the Dogra Dynasty over the Poonch Jagir, a subject of extreme sensitivity which the Jammu & Kashmir Government had no wish whatsoever to discuss either with the British or with their political successors-in-waiting; the last thing they wanted was a revival of an external investigation into the status of Poonch.

By the actual days of Transfer of Power, 14 and 15 August, this essentially separatist movement had spread beyond Poonch into Mirpur and parts, even, of Jammu, and it had become inextricably involved with the question of the whole State's future, to be independent or to exist in association with either India or Pakistan. Most active opponents of Maharaja Hari Singh's rule at this moment considered that Pakistan in some way offered the best hope of salvation.

The Transfer of Power, dated to 14 August in Pakistan and 15 August in India, was accompanied in Srinagar on both those days (which just happened to coincide with a special "Kashmir Day" which had been commemorated in British India since the Srinagar crisis of 1931 when the Maharaja's men had fired into a crowd and killed a score of protestors) by the widespread display of Pakistan flags and great public excitement. The Jammu & Kashmir Government responded with the application of police force, and many casualties resulted. Repression in Srinagar was a great stimulus to thoughts about the State's political future.

Some saw the only hope for stability and peace in a rapid replacement of the Maharaja by a regime in close association with India. This was the view of many leading Hindu Pandits, including those who had supported Sheikh Abdullah's National Conference. Whether Sheikh Abdullah himself, then still in prison, thought thus is not known. Probably he still adhered to his old dream of an independent State, the "Switzerland of Asia", under the administration of the National Conference with himself at the head of affairs. Others looked to immediate opposition to the Maharaja, be it armed or political, leading to independence, or to association with Pakistan or even, in the case of Poonch, to the recovery of that autonomy which Hari Singh had abolished so brutally not so long ago.

Thus the disturbances in Poonch, up till now no more than sporadic outbreaks of unco-ordinated hostility to Jammu & Kashmir State authority, began to acquire a command structure and, in the process, turn into a true rebellion. Again, the Bagh District of Poonch seems to have provided the venue. In the last week of August a series of public meetings here, presided over by a number of local men of substance including the young landowner Sardar Abdul Qayum Khan (still, in 1993, a great figure in Azad Kashmiri politics), approved the concept of some kind of independence for the region. On 26 August (at least according to the received version on the Muslim side) a public meeting near Bagh was fired upon by the Maharaja's police. Some people at the meeting fired back, and thus battle was joined. Sardar Abdul Qayum Khan and a group of his friends withdrew to a neighbouring forest where they set up a headquarters and despatched messengers to Rawalkot and elsewhere to spread the news that open conflict had now started between the Muslims of Poonch and the Maharaja. Their influence soon spread southwards into the Mirpur region.

The various Azad Kashmiri stories of the origins of the Poonch revolt tend, naturally enough, towards the romantic, and they may well conceal events which have not been recorded and which involve unknown persons. What is undoubtedly true, however, is that in the last week of August a condition of unrest and spasmodic violence in Poonch had turned into an organised opposition to the Dogra Dynasty the like of which had not been seen since the revolt of Shams-ud-Din in the 1830s. Sir Hari Singh lacked the power, though probably he did not lack the wish, to treat the rebels as had his great-grandfather in that firm manner which, we have seen, so amazed G.T. Vigne. Thus the rebellion grew in strength as more and more ex-soldiers rallied to the cause, either bringing their weapons with them or capturing rifles from the State forces.

With all this the sources on the official Jammu & Kashmir State side do not disagree. By the second week of September the Maharaja's position in Poonch and Mirpur, at least in the countryside as the towns were still secure enough, was extremely precarious. It is recorded that by 13 September no fewer than 60,000 Hindu refugees had passed from the Poonch-Mirpur area towards Jammu and about half the total Hindu and Sikh population had fled the areas of disturbance. The Chief of Staff of the Jammu & Kashmir State Forces, Major-General Scott, advised his master the Maharaja to take serious notice of what was going on. On 22 September, in what was to be his final report before retirement, Scott made it clear to the Maharaja that on their own the Jammu & Kashmir State Forces could not hope to contain the situation.

The Poonch Revolt possessed certain features which made it particularly difficult to suppress. The region of Poonch and Mirpur lies along the Pakistan border, here marked by the course of the Jhelum River, rapid but by no means uncrossable. The inhabitants on the left bank have always enjoyed close relations with people on the other side to their west, in the Hazara District of the North-West Frontier Province and Rawalpindi and other Districts of the Punjab. There is a strong Pathan influence in Poonch, and the major martial group, the Sudhans, claims an Afghan ancestry. Elsewhere the cultural climate is essentially Punjabi. Thus, cultural and ethnic links across the Jhelum made it impossible to seal off the left (Jammu & Kashmir State, or Poonch) bank from the right (Pakistan).

The Jhelum border, of course, was of much more than local interest. The region of the Poonch revolt, essentially those lands originally acquired from the Sikhs by Dhian Singh, was a frontier zone of the Punjab to the security of which it was essential. No statesman in Pakistan who had thought about the matter could have contemplated with anything but alarm the prospect of the Jhelum river becoming the actual border with India (should Indian troops come to the Maharaja's assistance). Whatever took place on the left bank of the Jhelum could not fail to concern those responsible for the administration of the right bank. It was inevitable, therefore, that contact would be established between the Poonch rebels and the Pakistan authorities at some level, though not of necessity involving the top leadership.

Equally inevitable, however, was that at this period any such contact should tend to be made on an *ad hoc* basis and not as the expression of a carefully thought out strategy. Pakistan, in August and September 1947, was still in the process of trying to establish itself as a viable polity. Units of its Army were stranded deep in India. Its finances were parlous and much of what it considered to be its assets was locked away in Indian banks. Refugees in their millions had flooded into its territory and required resettlement and assimilation. Here was not a regime capable of detailed planning to meet a situation across the Jhelum of a kind which, prior to the Transfer of Power, had been totally unanticipated by any statesman of the Dominion-to-be. Plans made or actions taken had, perforce, initially to be the improvised work of individuals, not the formal actions of a Government.

During September and the first days of October, emerging from the logic of the situation as we have just outlined it, a number of links were established between the Poonch rebels (with representatives in the Pakistan hill station of Murree) and individuals and groups in Pakistan. Given the close connection between Poonch men and the old Indian Army, it was not surprising that a large number of informal arrangements brought men (usually old soldiers from Poonch, "Poonchies", who had served the British in the Indian Army) and some arms, mainly .303 Lee-Enfield rifles and ammunition, to the forces of what was already being known as Azad ("Free") Kashmir.

The rebels were fast establishing their own leadership structure, not, it must be admitted, without internal conflicts of such a bitterness that some of them continued, deep underground, to exert a sinister force on Azad Kashmiri politics for many years to come. A young Sudhan from Poonch, a lawyer and landowner named Sardar M. Ibrahim Khan, who was a Muslim Conference member of the Jammu & Kashmir Legislature and who had held junior office at one time as a legal officer under the Maharaja, emerged as one potential head of the Poonch liberation movement, but there were others. The great achievement of Sardar Ibrahim Khan was, during the course of September, to establish contact with a number of leading politicians and other important figures in Pakistan, including the Prime Minister, Liaquat Ali Khan, who were willing to do what they could to help in highly unofficial ways. The evidence is clear that the Governor-General, M.A. Jinnah was not personally involved.

A key meeting seems to have been held in Lahore on 12 September from which the subsequent shape of contact between certain influential individuals in Pakistan (both official and unofficial) and the Poonch rebels, whom we will from now on call Azad Kashmiris, evolved. Some 4,000 .303 rifles were offered; they were to be diverted from the Punjab Police (and, in the event, they were surreptitiously replaced by inferior Frontier-made rifles). Two commanders, Khurshid Anwar and M. Zaman Kiani, emerged as leaders of the Azad Kashmiri military. Khurshid Anwar, a former Muslim League activist, had at one time been in the Indian Army, where he attained the rank of Major. Zaman Kiani, as an INA (the pro-Japanese Indian National Army) officer, had been a divisional commander under the Japanese in their invasion of Manipur in 1944. As liaison between these men and their sympathisers in Pakistan one Colonel Akbar Khan of the Pakistan Army more or less appointed himself.

At this point the main concern of both the Azad Kashmir movement and its enthusiasts in Pakistan was to keep the Poonch revolt alive. The available sources indicate that the supply of both weapons and men from Pakistan in September was indeed slight. The Azad Kashmir army fought mainly with materiel captured from the Jammu & Kashmir State Forces, and its ranks were dominated by deserters and old soldiers from that body, augmented by friends and relatives from across the Jhelum. Some of the Pakistani supporters, notably Colonel Akbar Khan, were given to the preparation of ambitious plans. Akbar Khan was an advocate both of a pre-emptive attack towards the road from Madhopur on the Indian border to Kathua (the key to the Banihal Pass route from India to Srinagar) and of an Azad Kashmiri advance to Srinagar along the Jhelum Valley Road. A number of Akbar Khan's plans of this tendency were subsequently to be exploited by the Indians, who claimed to have captured copies of orders for what they called "Operation Gulmarg", as evidence of sinister Pakistani operational schemes for "aggression" towards Jammu & Kashmir beyond the confines of Poonch. Such proposals, however, were just then no more than ideas of an enthusiastic individual who exercised at the time no operational command.

Was there indeed, in September and early October 1947, any formal Government of Pakistan policy at all towards the State of Jammu & Kashmir? We can detect two closely related considerations which, divorced entirely from whatever might be going on in Azad Kashmir, dictated to Jinnah and Liaquat Ali Khan a basic posture towards the Government of Jammu & Kashmir.

First: at the Government of Jammu & Kashmir's request on 12 August 1947, Pakistan had on 15 August (the first possible moment after the Transfer of Power) accepted a Standstill Agreement with that State. India, incidentally, had effectively declined a similar proposal. Standstill Agreements, emerging from the practical mechanics of the Transfer of Power, provided for the continuation of essential relations, in communications, posts, trade and the like, between a Princely State yet to decided on its future status and one, or both, of the two new Dominions. The official view in Karachi was that so long as this Standstill Agreement was in existence, the Maharaja of Jammu & Kashmir would probably not join either Dominion and certainly would keep himself free from formal Indian entanglements.

Second: under the umbrella of the Standstill Agreement direct negotiations could be carried on between the Government of Pakistan and that of the Maharaja in which the shape of their future relationship could be worked out in due course. Quite what this would be was not clear. Jinnah always assumed that Kashmir, which in his mind most probably meant the Vale, would in the end enter the Pakistan sphere; after all, the K in the name Pakistan stood for Kashmir. The precise shape of future Pakistan-Kashmir relations, however, was not the subject of much debate or planning in Karachi immediately after 14 August.

In late September the Standstill Agreement started to break down. Much of the State of Jammu & Kashmir, and above all Srinagar, depended upon supplies getting through from Pakistan along the Jhelum Valley Road. Petrol, kerosene, flour, sugar, and a host of other necessities came in this way; in return was exported the timber which was so vital to the State's revenues. The free flow of traffic along the Jhelum Valley Road now began to be interrupted. The Jammu & Kashmir Government complained. Liaquat Ali Khan, apparently uncertain as to what was actually going on, answered (2 October) that he would do everything he could to get traffic moving. He did point out, however, and not unreasonably, that "drivers of lorries are for instance reluctant to carry supplies between Rawalpindi and Kohala" on the State border because of the prevailing anarchy in the aftermath of Partition. He urged the Maharaja to receive an envoy from the Government of Pakistan with whom to discuss this matter and explore ways to improve the situation.

From this moment until 20 October the Government of Pakistan worked hard at initiating direct discussions. Colonel A.S.B. Shah, a senior official in the Pakistan Ministry of Foreign Affairs, was sent up to Srinagar where he attempted to talk things over with the State Government including, after 15 October, the new Prime Minister Mehr Chand Mahajan. It was a fruitless endeavour. Mahajan claimed that Colonel Shah was trying to blackmail the Maharaja into accession to Pakistan. Colonel Shah, on the other hand, reported that he could find no person with whom he could talk realistically. The senior advisers to Hari Singh all appeared to have made up their minds that their salvation lay with India, and they showed no interest in what he had to say. In this climate of misunderstanding the Shah initiative broke down. On 18 October Mahajan told both Jinnah and Liaquat Ali Khan that if the present problems of interrupted communications, aggravated by help which the Poonch rebels were receiving from Pakistan, were not resolved at once, then his Government would be fully entitled to seek "friendly assistance", in other words turn to India for help. Jinnah made a final, abortive, attempt at peaceful negotiation on 20 October when he told Sir Hari Singh that "the proposal made by my Government for a meeting with your accredited representatives is now an urgent necessity".

Jinnah and Liaquat Ali Khan took the Maharaja's communication of 18 October to be an ultimatum. As far as they were concerned, failing any favourable response to the Pakistan Governor-General's appeal of 20 October, this was the end of negotiation.

Had there ever been a blockade? The Indian side have made a great deal out of this allegation, in which they have detected the preliminaries to Pakistan's intended "aggression" into Jammu & Kashmir. The evidence does suggest that there was indeed the development of obstacles of sorts to the passage of goods between Pakistan and the State of Jammu & Kashmir. These were not imposed by the Government of Pakistan, which was anxious in every way to strengthen the force of the Standstill Agreement. Much obstruction to traffic, however, so the British High Commission in Karachi concluded after careful investigation, was deliberately overlooked, if not actually encouraged, by subordinate officials, notably

Abdul Haq, District Commissioner for Rawalpindi, supported by his brother, Syed Ikramul Haq, a senior official in the Pakistan Ministry of Defence. Such individuals were inclined to take matters into their own hands because, regardless of the official policy in Karachi, events along the borders of Jammu & Kashmir State were following a course which those in local authority on the Pakistan side simply could not ignore. Further, in the prevailing climate of Hindu-Muslim conflict following Partition they were not disposed to go out of their way to assist any Hindu polity such as the regime of the Maharaja of Jammu & Kashmir.

There can be no doubt, moreover, that whatever the Haq brothers might have done was greatly facilitated by the prevailing anarchy in that part of the Hazara District through which ran the Rawalpindi-Srinagar road. Here, in what was really an eastward extension of the tribal belt of the North-west Frontier, powerful armed bands of tribesmen had by the beginning of October established blockades of varying duration and intensity across the major routes (so, among others, European residents being evacuated from the Vale noted), and their presence would certainly have served as a deterrent to all but the most determined lorry drivers. It is likely that without any effort at all on the part of the Haq brothers there would have been a major disruption in the flow of traffic along the Jhelum Valley Road.

The Government of Jammu & Kashmir State did not fail to react to the Poonch revolt and its extension southwards into Kotli, Mirpur, Bhimber and elsewhere. It tried to confiscate all arms and ammunition from the local Muslim population in such areas as it could control. It permitted armed bands of Hindus and Sikhs, including members of extremist organisations like the RSS (the Hindu militant Rashtriya Swayamsevak Sangh, which was to be banned in India in February 1948 following the assassination of Mahatma Gandhi) from the Indian side of the border, to execute massacres of Muslims in Jammu and in Riasi and Mirpur Districts. By the end of September Muslim refugees escaping the fury thus unleashed were flowing in ever increasing numbers both into Pakistan and into territory controlled by the Azad Kashmiri forces. There is evidence that from the outset regular troops and police in the State service joined informally and covertly, but enthusiastically, in these atrocities which, some have estimated, eventually killed at least 200,000 Muslims and drove twice as many into exile.

By the beginning of October the Jammu & Kashmir State authorities joined openly in this anti-Muslim policy by setting out to create along the State's border with Pakistan (in the region of Gujrat and Sialkot) a depopulated zone some three miles deep. Hindus here were evacuated. Muslims were either killed or driven across into Pakistan. On a number of occasions Jammu & Kashmir State Forces actually crossed over into Pakistan and destroyed villages there (well documented acts of Jammu & Kashmir State "aggression" on its territory which Pakistan has signally failed to exploit in its arguments concerning the rights and wrongs of the Kashmir situation). Early in October British observers saw in one such village on the Pakistan side of the border no fewer than 1,700 corpses of slaughtered Muslim men, women and children. Before 22 October, a crucial date in the Kashmir story, the Pakistan authorities reported that at least 100,000 Muslim refugees from Jammu were being cared for in the neighbourhood of Sialkot. The Government in Karachi might talk about negotiations, but there was a growing body of opinion in Pakistan, particularly in the Punjab, which argued forcefully for more direct action to stop the killing.

What was the reaction in India to the development of the Poonch revolt, the emergence of an Azad Kashmir and the steady erosion of the Maharaja of Jammu & Kashmir's authority? From some sources, particularly those emanating from the entourage of the Governor-General, Lord Mountbatten, one could well derive the impression that the Government in New Delhi felt, right up to the evening of 24 October 1947, that all was well in this paradise of Jammu & Kashmir. It has become clear, however, from other sources, notably the published papers of Jawaharlal Nehru and Vallabhbhai Patel, that in some circles of the Government of India the situation in Jammu & Kashmir was receiving a great deal of attention; and there were those who were determined that the State would not drift away unchecked into the Muslim sphere of influence presided over by Jinnah's Pakistan. [See, for example: Durga Das, (ed.), *Sardar Patel's Correspondence 1945–50*, vol. 1, *New Light on Kashmir*, Ahmedabad 1971; S. Gopal, (General Editor), *Selected Works of Jawaharlal Nehru*, 2nd Series, Vol. 4, New Delhi 1986].

On the eve of the Transfer of Power Jawaharlal Nehru had demonstrated what to many of his colleagues seemed to be an obsessive interest in Kashmir, his ancestral home. It was he who had tried in June 1947, and probably successfully, to persuade Mountbatten that Sheikh Abdullah and his National Conference in their alleged wish to join with India represented the true voice of the Kashmiri people. His concern with Kashmiri issues was well known at the time; and it caused no surprise. On the other hand, his Deputy as Prime Minister, and his main political rival, Vallabhbhai Patel, has often been represented as a person of far more pragmatic outlook, prepared should expediency so dictate, to let Jammu & Kashmir (or the Vale of Kashmir at least) pass quietly to Pakistan. One of the most interesting revelations of the Patel papers when they began to be published in 1971 was the extent to which this powerful Congress politician had directly involved himself in all planning directed towards an eventual Indian acquisition of the State of Jammu & Kashmir.

Nehru's interest in Kashmir was largely emotional; there he saw his personal roots in Indian civilisation. Patel had a cold geopolitical approach to the future of the whole State of Jammu & Kashmir. It was the potential Indian outlet to Central Asia. In Indian hands it would severely curtail the future freedom of international action of Pakistan. More immediately, possession of Kashmir Province would give India a direct access to the Pathan world, not only the fringes of Afghanistan but also the North-West Frontier Province of Pakistan where Congress retained a peculiar influence in an area with a virtually total Muslim population; before independence there had been a Congress Ministry here. The possibilities for the exertion of pressure upon Pakistan, directed, if need be, towards its destruction, were manifold. Patel may, as we will see in Chapter V, have seemed at times disposed towards some form of compromise with Pakistan over the Kashmir dispute; but he, far more than Nehru, also saw Kashmir's value as a lethal weapon against Pakistan.

Vallabhbhai Patel had been in close contact with a number of prominent figures in the politics of Jammu & Kashmir since at least 1946; but it is only in September 1947 that the available records begin to document his involvement with preparations for the coming Indo-Pakistani clash over the State's future.

On 13 September Patel received a request from the Jammu & Kashmir Government for a military adviser in the person of Lt.-Colonel Kashmir Singh Katoch, who was not only a serving officer in the Indian Army but also the son of the then Jammu & Kashmir Prime Minister, Major-General Janak Singh. The request was passed with approval to the Minister of Defence, Sardar Baldev Singh; and in due course Kashmir Singh Katoch was deputed to Srinagar where he undoubtedly played a significant part in the forthcoming crisis.

From this date onwards we have evidence of all sorts of Indian military aid being provided with Patel's express approbation for Jammu & Kashmir, of which the following are examples. On 28 September, at the urgent request of Maharaja Sir Hari Singh, Patel arranged for the provision of one civilian aircraft (from Dalmia Jain Airways, presumably a DC3) to run a special service between Srinagar and Delhi. By 1 October wireless equipment had been supplied to assist all-weather operations at Srinagar airport, to which supply flights could now begin to take in loads of arms and ammunition to the Jammu & Kashmir State Forces from Indian stocks (which, so soon after the end of World War II, were indeed massive). Preparations were also at this time put in hand for more effective telegraphic communications between India and Jammu and Srinagar; and the road from the Indian Punjab border near Madhopur to Jammu was now being greatly improved by the construction by Indian Army Engineers of a pontoon bridge over the Ravi leading to Kathua.

Somewhere around the second week of October the decision was taken in New Delhi to send actual troops as well as arms and equipment; some units from the Patiala State Army, at least one battalion of infantry and a battery of mountain artillery, were transported to Jammu & Kashmir. One infantry battalion was stationed in Jammu City, where it reinforced the Maharaja's major stronghold; and a mountain artillery battery reached the outskirts of Srinagar airfield. It is possible, indeed probable, that at least another battalion of Patiala infantry was sent forward along the Jhelum Valley Road to the neighbourhood of Uri where it stood in reserve behind the 4th Jammu & Kashmir Rifles guarding the two major points of access to this road from Pakistan. Some of these men travelled overland; but it may well be that some also came by air. The Patiala troop movements, the evidence indicates, were completed by 18 October. Published Patiala sources, which have surely been heavily doctored to accord with the chronology of established Indian mythology, suggest that this intervention took place at the personal request to the Maharaja, Yadavindra Singh, by Jawaharlal Nehru.

In that the Patiala State Army was at this time legally part of the Armed Forces of the Indian Union, such a despatch of units from its strength amounted in fact to direct Indian intervention in the military activities of the State of Jammu & Kashmir; but, of course, what the odd Patiala unit did was unlikely to come to the formal notice of the Indian High Command, still British dominated. The Patiala Ruler, who had been extremely active in the destruction of his State's Muslim population at the time of the Transfer of Power, was apparently only too willing to come to the aid of his fellow Maharaja; and he showed no interest in constitutional and diplomatic niceties. When India overtly intervened in Kashmir on 27 October, the Maharaja of Patiala lost no time in joining his men in the field.

There is some evidence that, by the beginning of the third week in October, Vallabhbhai Patel and his associates, including Baldev Singh at the Defence Ministry, had approved a number of other measures which involved a greater or lesser degree of direct Indian participation in the defence of the State. It is possible, for example, that Indian Army demolition experts had been provided (or promised) to prepare for the destruction of the bridges at the western end of the Jhelum Valley Road, notably that across the Kishenganga (over which ran the road from Mansehra), in the event of any incursion from the Pakistan side. Again, on 21 October (on the eve of a drastic escalation of the Kashmir crisis, as we shall see below) Patel was arranging for another Indian specialist, Shiv Saran Lal, who before the Transfer of Power had been Deputy Commissioner of Dehra Ismail Khan (in Pakistan since 15 August) and was a man well versed in matters relating to the tribes of the North-West Frontier, to go to Srinagar to advise the Maharaja on the most effective ways of dealing with those Pathans whose more active intervention in Kashmir affairs was now being anticipated, possibly by exploiting their traditional tribal animosities.

Quite as significant, perhaps, as these various practical measures was the interest shown by Patel and his colleagues (including Nehru) in the details of active politics in the State of Jammu & Kashmir. In early October, for instance, Dwarkanath Kachru (Nehru's confidential associate, as we have already seen, of whom more in Chapter III) had been in Srinagar sounding out Sheikh Abdullah's party, the National Conference, on its attitude towards the State's accession to India. Kachru warned Patel in no uncertain terms that unless something decisive were done by India, the State would drift by default into the orbit of Pakistan. Patel's principal counter to this threat, it would seem, was his advocacy of the appointment of Justice Mehr Chand Mahajan as State Prime Minister in the place of Janak Singh. Mahajan, one of the two Indian members on the Radcliffe Commission, was an undoubted supporter of accession to India. The record leaves it clear that, at least in the eyes of the Indian Cabinet, his appointment (which took formal effect on 15 October) was intended to bring that accession about; and he was believed to possess the skill and determination to do what was expected of him.

The fact that senior politicians in New Delhi had decided weeks before 15 October that such an accession was essential to Indian interests is not open to serious doubt. A letter from Nehru to Patel, dated 27 September 1947, is by itself sufficiently clear evidence for this conclusion. As Nehru then declared: winter was approaching, and the Banihal Pass, that lifeline between Jammu and Srinagar, would be snowbound; unless Maharaja Sir Hari Singh decided, or was obliged, to accede to India in the very near future, then Pakistan would take over the entire Vale of Kashmir as well as Baltistan and Ladakh. India, therefore, must act quickly, in co-operation with Sheikh Abdullah and his National Conference, to bring about the pre-emptive accession of the State of Jammu & Kashmir to the Indian Union.

During the first two weeks of October such Indian plans, either in process of execution or under contemplation, were being watched both by the Government of Pakistan in Karachi, whose sources of information were not always of the highest quality, and by those in direct command of the Poonch revolt, the Government of Azad Kashmir, whose intelligence was potentially much better because of their close contacts with Srinagar.

The history of the Azad Kashmir regime for this early period is not well documented. A Republic of Kashmir had been declared in Rawalpindi on 4 October 1947 (at a meeting held in the Paris Hotel). Its capital was to be at Muzaffarabad and its President, so press releases had it, was one Mohammed Anwar. His name was clearly a pseudonym; and debate still continues as to the true identity of M. Anwar. This Republic then passed into oblivion, for reasons as yet unclear. On 24 October another regime, this time the Government of Azad Kashmir, was proclaimed with Sardar M. Ibrahim Khan (who had also been a member of the 4 October Cabinet) as its President. What we do know for sure is that from late September there had been intense political activity in the Azad Kashmiri world by individuals representing various groups involved in Jammu & Kashmir State politics, delegates of the Muslim Conference from Srinagar, Sudhans and non-Sudhans from Poonch, and both officials and private persons in Pakistan with Kashmiri interests; and behind all these lay the organisation of the high command of the actual Azad Kashmir military, itself divided into sectors and factions. There was no formal co-ordination by the Pakistan Government, though inevitably leading Azad Kashmiri figures were in constant touch with sympathisers in Pakistan. While the 4 October Republic was abortive, yet well before its successor acquired a definitive shape on 24 October an Azad Kashmiri administration had been functioning which sufficed to provide a focus for the military elements of the Poonch revolt.

By the third week of October the Azad Kashmiri leaders had concluded that a direct Indian intervention in the State of Jammu & Kashmir in support of either the Maharaja or Sheikh Abdullah's National Conference was inevitable in the very near future. What the key warning signal was, we do not know. Perhaps the announced forthcoming assumption of office of Prime Minister by Mahajan on 15 October, perhaps news of the arrival of Patiala men to bolster the flagging efforts of the Jammu & Kashmir State Forces at some point on or before 18 October, perhaps that communication from the Jammu & Kashmir Government to the Government of Pakistan of 18 October which, we have seen, appeared to threaten the invitation of overt Indian assistance, or perhaps some event which has left no trace in the available records.

Any Indian intervention posed two major threats to the Azad Kashmir movement. First: in Poonch, Mirpur and southwards the State defenders of the main towns, like Poonch City and Mirpur, would be much encouraged; and there was a possibility of more effective sweeps by the Maharaja's men into the countryside. Second, and more crucial: a reinforced State would not only be able to use the Jhelum Valley Road to attack the Poonch rebels from their northern flank between Uri and Domel but also would bring the Indian Army to the borders of the North-West Frontier Province of Pakistan, a region where the Government in Karachi faced potential security problems of the first magnitude, as had the British before them. Here the immediate interests of the Government of Pakistan coincided directly with those of the Azad Kashmiri command.

The northern sector of Azad Kashmir, in the region of Bagh and Rawalkot, was the responsibility of Major Khurshid Anwar, a man with close family links not only with Kashmir but with the Pathan world of the North-West Frontier. By the end of September there is evidence that Khurshid Anwar was in touch with Pathan tribal leaders on the North-West Frontier, with at least the passive support of the North-West Frontier Provincial Ministry under Khan Abdul Qayum Khan (himself with Kashmiri connections), in search of weapons (which existed in abundance here). Many Pathan tribesmen were only too well aware of the communal slaughter which had accompanied Partition, and they were eager to avenge the killing of their fellow Muslims by Sikhs and Hindus (with, perhaps, the added attraction of some plunder thrown in). It was inevitable that there should arise proposals for the recruitment of Pathan tribesmen by the Azad Kashmiri forces. One great advantage of such a source of fighting men, particularly in the context of the Jhelum Valley Road, was that they could be supplied easily enough with motor vehicles. The same Pathans from among whom the tribesmen were recruited were (by some quirk of socio-economic evolution) deeply involved in the transport business in Pakistan and had easy access to lorries and buses.

In fact, of course, small parties of Pathan tribesmen had been involved in the Poonch Revolt for some time. The connection between Poonch and the North-West Frontier by way of Hazara was indeed close. Moreover, in the North-West Frontier Province tribal groups had already been organising themselves for *jihad*, holy war, since at least the latter part of September in spontaneous reaction to the communal killings in the Punjab. On 23 September, for example, a body of Gurkha and Sikh troops, who had been stranded on the North-West Frontier while the old Indian Army was being divided up, were attacked ferociously by a war party (*lashkar*) of Mahsuds, and only managed to extricate themselves after hard fighting. On that day the Governor of the North-West Frontier Province, Sir George Cunningham, noted in his diary that:

> I have had offers from practically every tribe along the Frontier to be allowed to go and kill Sikhs in Eastern Punjab, and I think I would only have to hold up my little finger to get a *lashkar* of 40,000 or 50,000. [Cunningham's Diary, India Office Records].

Thus Khurshid Anwar would have no problem recruiting tribesmen. Indeed, his main difficulty, events were to make clear, was preventing too many of them from flocking to his command.

It was perhaps in the second week in October that a decision was made to recruit a number of tribesmen, 2,000 or so, complete with transport, specifically to take part in what would be Azad Kashmir's answer to the growing Indian threat, an offensive directed from the Hazara District border of Pakistan along the Jhelum Valley Road towards Uri and, perhaps if all went well, Srinagar itself.

The plan which emerged was designed to cope with two main

problems. First: the lack of motor transport. There were no vehicles to be found among the essentially guerilla fighters in Poonch. Second: obtaining access to the Jhelum Valley Road, which was dominated by a number of guarded bridges, across the Jhelum at Kohala and Domel, and across the Kishenganga between Muzaffarabad and Mansehra.

The first problem could be solved by Pathan tribal recruitment, since, as we have already noted, those same tribesmen were traditionally connected with the bus and lorry business (as they still are today); though this particular expedient was not without its disadvantages of which Khurshid Anwar was probably well aware, arising from the undisciplined nature of such allies.

The second problem involved the elimination of the guardians of the frontier bridges, the 4th Jammu & Kashmir Rifles. The 4th Jammu & Kashmir Rifles was one of a number of mixed Dogra-Muslim units in the Jammu & Kashmir State Forces. About half the men, and a proportion of the officers, were Muslims, mainly Sudhans from Poonch. The rest were Hindu Dogras, including the Commanding Officer, Lt.-Colonel Narain Singh. The Azad Kashmiris were in touch with their fellow "Poonchies" in the State Forces; and it was not difficult to arrange for the Muslim element of the 4th Jammu & Kashmir Rifles to go along with a plan which was intended to complete the expulsion of the Dogras from Poonch, and, perhaps Kashmir Province as well.

This plan was set in motion on the night of 21/22 October, when the Muslims in the 4th Rifles rose and disposed of their sleeping Dogra colleagues, thus not only leaving unguarded the entry into the State from Pakistan but also preserving from demolition the crucial bridges across the Jhelum and Kishenganga. The Azad Kashmiri attacking forces, reinforced both by tribesmen with motor transport (some coming up from the south through Poonch and some directly from Pakistan) and by former Muslim soldiers from the 4th Jammu & Kashmir Rifles, then took control of the bridges and, also, the important provincial centre of Muzaffarabad, in passing subjecting the bazaar to a thorough looting.

The Azad Kashmiri forces, now combined under the command of Major Khurshid Anwar (but lacking promised reinforcements from Zaman Kiani's command further to the south in Azad Kashmir), on 23 October pushed on along the Jhelum Valley Road to Uri, about half way from the Pakistan border to Srinagar. Here was an important road junction, with a motorable route from Poonch City joining from the south; but there were also here a number of nullahs, or ravines, crossed by bridges which the demolition experts with the Jammu & Kashmir State Forces managed to destroy before retreating.

The State abandonment of Uri was on 24 October. The damage to the bridges, however, sufficed to delay the Azad Kashmiri advance for a day or two. As we shall see in the next Chapter, the "battle" of Uri can be taken to mark the formal opening of what might be called the Kashmiri accession crisis. Up to the occupation of Uri the Azad Kashmiri campaign was really a logical extension of the Poonch revolt, the cleaning up of the northern flank and the erection of a barrier between Pakistan and Kashmir Province. The Jammu & Kashmir State Forces at Uri (who certainly outnumbered the Azad Kashmiris) were commanded in person by their Chief of Staff, Brigadier Rajinder Singh, and were, so the available evidence suggests, reinforced with Patiala Sikh infantry. Their collapse opened up a great target of opportunity. Srinagar, the heart of Kashmir, which probably up to this point had been an objective of but the most theoretical nature, now seemed within reach. Major Khurshid Anwar had the choice of either standing at Uri and establishing a permanent barrier there, or striking on eastward in pursuit of the Maharaja's defeated men. He chose the latter. Not for the first time in history has hot pursuit been irresistibly seductive.

This was to be a fateful choice, though it is unlikely that the Azad Kashmiri commanders realised it at the time. It is probable that in due course both the Maharaja of Jammu & Kashmir and his Indian friends could have been persuaded to accept a successful defence of Azad Kashmir, even incorporating that portion of Kashmir Province containing Muzaffarabad and with a frontier at Uri. The end result could well have been the opening of talks, in which both India and Pakistan participated along with Jammu & Kashmir and Azad Kashmir, to work out the future of the region. Once they had advanced beyond Uri, however, the Azad Kashmiri forces moved away from the old and familiar framework of the Poonch revolt (involving what was essentially a marginal tract where the Maharaja's title was, as we have seen, uncertain) into the then uncharted wasteland of what was to become the great Kashmir dispute, the future of the entire State with all that this implied in geopolitical terms.

There remains one major question to answer. What part had the Government of Pakistan to play in this military venture into the State of Jammu & Kashmir? In a formal sense the Government as such took no part at all. The Governor-General, M.A. Jinnah, was kept ignorant of all details, though naturally he was aware that there was trouble of some sort brewing in Kashmir; and the Pakistan Cabinet took no minuted stance on this matter. There can be no doubt, however, that various individuals in Pakistan, both official and unofficial, did show an extremely active interest in what was afoot. We can probably divide these persons into three main categories.

First: there were those who had supported from at least 12 September the formation of the Azad Kashmir Government. Some were indeed of great seniority in Pakistan administration, including the Prime Minister, Liaquat Ali Khan. Their concern was not the day-to-day conduct of operations but rather the underlying necessity of keeping the Azad Kashmir movement afloat. In terms of organising supplies for Azad Kashmir the record suggests that these men achieved very little; their activity was largely symbolic.

Second: in the North-West Frontier Province and in the Rawalpindi District of the Punjab there were many officials both appointed and elected, from the Chief Minister of the North-West Frontier Province downwards, who were aware of the growing connection between the tribal world of the North-West Frontier and Azad Kashmir. It cannot be denied that such men did very little indeed to discourage this relationship. Some of them went out of their way to promote it.

Third: there were many individual soldiers in the Pakistan Army who appreciated the importance of the Azad Kashmir movement and felt it their duty to help it. A number of regulars took leave, or became technically "deserters", to join the fray; but in most cases this was later in the story. A few, like Colonel Akbar Khan, took it upon themselves to assume senior staff responsibilities with the Azad Kashmiri forces. Subsequently, Akbar Khan under the pseudonym "General Tariq" was to take active command in the field, but not during the events under consideration here. Some Pakistani officers merely turned a blind eye when boxes of .303 ammunition mysteriously disappeared from armouries; but again, such actions were to become more important later on. It is safe to say that there was very little regular Pakistan Army presence, direct or indirect, in Major Khurshid Anwar's column on the road to Uri between 22 and 24 October 1947.

The real Pathan tribal pressure into Kashmir Province (as opposed to Poonch) from the North-West Frontier Province seems to have started quite late in our story, around 10 October, when tribesmen in Hazara adjacent to the main road from Mansehra to Muzaffarabad (one access route to the Jhelum Valley Road), began to gather into bands and rally to the Azad Kashmiri cause with the full support of their traditional leaders. They were particularly aroused by reports of the killings of Muslims that were then going on further south along the Jammu-Punjab border. The local administrative officials did nothing to hinder them; but, even had they so wished, there was really nothing they could do with the police at their disposal.

Very soon the centre of gravity, as it were, shifted westwards to Peshawar where the Government of the North-West Frontier Province had to decide what to do about the ever increasing number of Pathan tribesmen who wanted to involve themselves in the Kashmir fighting. The instinctive reaction of many in authority, including the Chief Minister and senior Police officers, was to give the tribesmen what help they could. In practice this meant not blocking roads and, at the same time, making petrol available to vehicles bound towards the Kashmir front. The diary of Sir George Cunningham, Governor of the North-West Frontier Province and a man with vast experience in tribal matters, suggests that this began to happen on about 15 October, when Major Khurshid Anwar turned up in Peshawar on his quest for arms and, perhaps, recruits, from the North-West Frontier.

As Sir George Cunningham's diary reveals so graphically, at this stage those Pakistani leaders who understood the Kashmir situation were divided. There were some, notably in the Government of the North-West Frontier Province, who were convinced that a campaign such as might emerge from Major Khurshid Anwar's projected operation on the Jhelum Valley Road would surely bring most of Kashmir Province into Pakistan. There were, however, more sober minds who believed that, on the contrary, it would probably precipitate the whole State of Jammu & Kashmir into the arms of India and persuade the Maharaja to sign an instrument of accession to that Dominion. Of such a view was Colonel A.S.B. Shah, who had been negotiating in vain with the Jammu & Kashmir State authorities until 18 October.

The problem, once Major Khurshid Anwar's Azad Kashmiri plan was set in motion, was that it could not really be stopped. Neither the tribesmen nor the Azad Kashmiris were under Pakistan control. Indeed, any attempt to halt tribesmen on the move across Pakistan might lead to highly undesirable conflict between the Pakistan Army and the Pathan tribesmen which could well spread along the entire length of the North-West Frontier. Those Pakistan soldiers in the know, therefore, resolved to give what assistance they could and hope for the best. Aid, in fact, was effectively limited to supplying .303 ammunition, basic medical supplies and, perhaps, some motor fuel.

While senior Pakistani soldiers like Colonel Iskander Mirza (later to be to all intents and purposes the first military ruler of the new nation) were not particularly happy about the composition of the Azad Kashmiri force which was about to embark upon such a fateful venture, they could not forget that to let matters drift was probably worse. They were convinced that as soon as the road to Jammu and Srinagar from Pathankot in India was completed, which it was thought would be in January 1948, the Maharaja, confident of prompt military aid, would openly throw in his lot with India. Indian forces could then drive with ease from the Pathankot railhead over the Banihal Pass to Srinagar and the Jhelum Valley Road, whence they could approach Pakistan's vulnerable flank along the North-West Frontier. Pakistan could not stand by and just let this happen by default. The snows of winter might delay the outcome; but with spring the storm would surely break.

A real problem for the Pakistan Army was in the possible attitude of its senior British Officers. Given the existing command structure in the Subcontinent, which will be discussed again in subsequent Chapters, it was hardly likely that the British could publicly approve of initiatives by Pakistan which ran the risk, however slight, of an inter-Dominion military conflict; and it was clear that anything touching upon the State of Jammu & Kashmir fell into this category. Thus, as Iskander Mirza confessed to Sir George Cunningham on 26 October, senior British servants of Pakistan like Cunningham had, if only for their own peace of mind, been kept in the dark about what was planned for the Jhelum Valley Road on 21/22 October.

III

The Accession Crisis, 24–27 October 1947

At Uri on the morning of 24 October 1947 there occurred one of the great turning points in the history of the Kashmir dispute. As we have seen in the previous Chapter, here, about half way between the Pakistan border and Srinagar at the end of the Jhelum Valley Road, Major Khurshid Anwar's Azad Kashmiri column managed after nearly two days of fighting to break through a major road block. From the viewpoint of informed observers in Srinagar, it might well have looked as if the way to the Kashmiri summer capital was now wide open.

The Jammu & Kashmir defenders of Uri, consisting of State regulars, assorted non-combatants drafted in, and the various Sikh mercenaries or informal allies whom the Azad Kashmiri side knew collectively as "Patialas", all commanded by Brigadier Rajinder Singh (the Chief of the Military Staff of the Jammu & Kashmir State Forces in succession to Major-General Scott), were obliged to withdraw rapidly through Mahura on the road to Srinagar after having destroyed a series of bridges over nullahs (ravines) near Uri where the Jhelum Valley road was joined from the south by the key track to Poonch City over the Hajipir Pass. Major Khurshid Anwar's men took some time to devise temporary crossings; meanwhile the Jammu & Kashmir State forces had been given a brief respite. It was believed in Srinagar, however, that the Azad Kashmiri advance would probably go on. Brigadier Rajinder Singh intended to make his final stand near Baramula (close to which, on 26 October, he was to be caught in an ambush on the main Jhelum Valley Road and killed, though exactly by whom we do not know); but the morale of the Jammu & Kashmir State forces was low, and there were many desertions. State troops in the main Srinagar barracks decided to remain where they were rather than come out to meet any threat. The prognosis for a successful defence did not seem good. Sir Hari Singh's Government was convinced that something drastic had to be done, and that quickly. While some Muslim opponents of the Dogras publicly rejoiced at what was seen as coming liberation, the majority of the Hindu Pandit elite were very alarmed and on the verge of panic.

What the State Government seemed to fear most at this point was not a Pakistani annexation of great tracts of Jammu & Kashmir State territory. As the State Deputy Prime Minister, R.L. Batra, declared on the morning of 24 October (when he still thought the defences at Uri might hold), the insurgent forces were "tribesmen who are out of control of the Pakistan Government" [*Daily Express*, 25 October 1947]. This was a collapse of internal law and order rather than an act of aggression by a neighbouring state. The real danger was that the crisis would be exploited in the Vale (Kashmir Province) by opponents of Dogra rule, be they followers of the Muslim Conference (thought to favour a closer relationship with Pakistan) or of Sheikh Abdullah and his National Conference (who appeared to stand for an independent Kashmir free of the Dogras), to bring down the Dogra regime (as many believed had so nearly happened in 1931). What the Maharaja needed, therefore, was support as much against his domestic enemies as the invaders.

The Maharaja and his advisers decided, accordingly, to send the Deputy Prime Minister to New Delhi to see if he could secure (on suitable terms) any immediate assistance in men, weapons and ammunition from the Government of India. He was equipped with personal letters from both the Maharaja and the State Prime Minister, Mehr Chand Mahajan, to Jawaharlal Nehru and Vallabhbhai Patel. The Maharaja also entrusted him with what Mahajan describes as "a letter of accession to India", which was certainly no blanket unconditional Instrument of Accession but rather a statement of the terms upon which an association between the State of Jammu & Kashmir and the Indian Dominion might be negotiated in return for military assistance. The Indian side have been careful to avoid specific reference to this particular document in their descriptions of the State of Jammu & Kashmir's pleas for assistance. It is probable that it involved no more than a token diminution of the State's sovereignty. It certainly did not provide for an administration in the State of Jammu & Kashmir presided over by Sheikh Abdullah; and it rather looks as if Batra never got round to presenting it to the Indian authorities for discussion.

Deputy Prime Minister Batra arrived in New Delhi by the evening of 24 October. He spent the following day in talks with any who would listen to him; but his mission was fruitless. Alexander Symon of the British High Commission (according to his recollections preserved among the India Office Records in London), who met him on the morning of 25 October, concluded that Batra did not consider the State to be in real danger. A defensive line blocking the Jhelum Valley Road, Batra evidently believed, might yet be held. The threat, Batra reported, came from about 2,000 tribesmen from Hazara and the North-West Frontier who had entered the State by way of Domel on 22 October, transported in between 80 and 100 lorries (Indian narratives have steadily increased these figures over the years; they now stand officially at 7,000 men in 300 lorries). The repulse of such an undisciplined band ought not to be beyond the abilities of the State's Forces, particularly if bolstered by Indian supplies and reinforcements.

On the evening of 24 October, after Batra's departure from Srinagar for New Delhi, the staff of the Mahura hydroelectric power station (on the left bank of the Jhelum just to the east of Uri), which supplied Srinagar with the bulk of its electricity, abandoned their posts on hearing the approach of Brigadier Rajinder Singh's retreating troops, whom they took to be the Azad Kashmiri invaders. For a while the lights of Srinagar went out, an event which has produced its own mythology. Some Indian writers have described in obsessive detail the way in which the "tribal raiders" systematically destroyed equipment at the station. "This", one writer notes, "was the work of demolition experts and not mere tribals" [see: Rajesh Kadian, *The Kashmir Tangle. Issues and Options*, New Delhi 1992, p. 82]. In fact, nothing was blown up. Indeed, though for some weeks Mahura remained near the front line of the Kashmir conflict, the plant suffered relatively modest damage, one generator out of three put out of action, and another slightly impaired. The Mahura power stoppage, however, both demonstrated to the population of Srinagar that something serious was afoot and convinced the Maharaja that he might, in fact, be in the process of losing the whole of Kashmir Province. He seems to have then decided that it would be wise to move at once from Srinagar, now so demonstrably at risk, to the relative security of Jammu, his winter capital. Indeed, there is evidence that he was now turning over in his mind a plan to abandon Kashmir Province entirely (and, perhaps, permanently) to whoever might be able to control it, and content himself with the secure possession of Jammu, the old Dogra heartland whence

Gulab Singh over a century ago had expanded to build up his little empire on the fringes of Central Asia.

Batra's arrival in New Delhi on 24 October brought to the Government of India first-hand news that something was happening in Kashmir; but what he had to say had certainly been reinforced by intelligence already to hand from the military and elsewhere of a far more alarming nature. Mountbatten, it has been said, first heard of the "crisis" that evening while at a buffet dinner given for the Siamese (Thai) Foreign Minister. This seems extremely unlikely. Reports from Kashmir had been pouring into New Delhi all day. British press correspondents, for example, or their stringers in Srinagar, had been busy filing stories about the situation in Kashmir. Some echo of all this must have penetrated the Governor-General's circle. However the news reached him, it sufficed to convince Mountbatten of the urgent need to convene the Defence Committee of the Government of India, over which he presided; and this was done for the following morning. The Defence Committee at this time consisted, apart from Mountbatten in the Chair, of Jawaharlal Nehru as Prime Minister, Vallabhbhai Patel as Deputy Prime Minister, Baldev Singh as Minister of Defence, as well as the Minister of Finance and Sir Gopalaswami Ayyengar as a Minister Without Portfolio, and the three Commanders-in-Chief, Lockhart (Army), Elmhirst (Air Force) and Hall (Navy).

Thus it was that on the morning of Saturday 25 October the Kashmir crisis was considered by the Indian Defence Committee headed by Mountbatten as Governor-General, rather than by the Indian Cabinet to which it was subordinate but where Mountbatten had no place and Jawaharlal Nehru would have occupied the Chair; and from henceforth Mountbatten was to assume a prominent (and, some observers thought, increasingly partisan) role in the evolution of Indian attitudes towards the growing crisis.

The situation in Kashmir was presented to the Committee in such a manner as to accentuate its gravity. The threat to the Maharaja which was developing along the Jhelum Valley Road was now represented as a systematic invasion by tribesmen from the North-West Frontier, sponsored by Pakistan and directed towards the occupation of the entire State of Jammu & Kashmir, rather than as part of a local rebellion with its origins deep within the internal history of that State. If the tribesmen continued their advance, it was argued that sooner or later they must reach the borders of the Indian Punjab and, perhaps, even threaten Delhi (more or less in the footsteps of the great eighteenth century invader of India, Ahmad Shah Durrani). The problems of the old North-West Frontier of British days would thus have made an eastward quantum leap.

From henceforth the Indian side, and its British sympathisers like Mountbatten, publicly ignored all that had to do with the Poonch revolt. Although they were quite well aware, as the published papers of Jawaharlal Nehru make clear, of the true nature of the events in Poonch and Mirpur, they now decided to keep this information discreetly concealed. The enemy in the State of Jammu & Kashmir were described as "raiders", not "insurgents" or "rebels". They were well armed, existed in large numbers, and were directly sponsored by the authorities in Pakistan. Their sole motive it was decided, beyond obeying their Pakistani masters, was plunder and the mindless killing of Hindus and Sikhs. As Nehru, immediately following the Defence Committee meeting of 25 October, put it in a telegram to Attlee, the British Prime Minister:

> a grave situation has developed in the State of Kashmir. Large numbers of Afridis and other tribesmen from the Frontier have invaded State territory, occupied several towns and massacred large numbers of non-Muslims. According to our information, tribesmen have been equipped with motor transport and also with automatic weapons and have passed through Pakistan territory. Latest news is that the invaders are proceeding up the Jhelum valley road towards the valley of Kashmir. [1948 *White Paper*, Pt. IV, No. 1].

To meet this threat, the Defence Committee decided to supply the Maharaja with arms and ammunition; and arrangements were made to provide air transport (largely by switching B.O.A.C. aircraft, which had originally been chartered for transporting refugees, probably, indeed, European residents from Kashmir, with those of Indian civil airlines, such as Dalmia Jain and the closely related Indian National, so that the B.O.A.C. aircraft could keep the civilian services going while the Indian planes moved troops) for this purpose.

The question of the necessity for Kashmir to accede to India as an essential element in an offer of any direct Indian assistance was next discussed by the Defence Committee. It would seem that Mountbatten then raised these two key points. First: accession had to come before intervention. Second: such accession would require subsequent ratification by the people of the State of Jammu & Kashmir, pending which it could only be considered as provisional. Accession, however, provisional or not, would give India a reasonably legitimate, and publicly defensible, position in the State while at the same time deny such a position to anyone else, that is to say Pakistan and its friends and allies. Subsequent popular ratification would, if Mountbatten's assessment of the will of the Kashmiri people were correct (influenced as it surely was by Nehru's high regard for Sheikh Abdullah and his National Conference), confirm the Indian position without exposure to the charge by the international community against India of aggression or expansionism.

The concept of the plebiscite, of course, was already well enshrined in the whole process of independence in the Subcontinent. Plebiscites had been held in the North-West Frontier Province and Sylhet on the eve of the Transfer of Power. At the very moment when the Kashmir crisis was developing, the Indians were still proposing that the problem of Junagadh (where, it will be recalled, a Muslim ruler with an overwhelmingly Hindu population had opted for Pakistan) should be solved by a plebiscite. The Indians, incidentally, were also simultaneously solving the Junagadh issue by the creation, backed by the threat of Indian force, of a puppet Hindu regime in the shape of a Provisional Government headed by Samaldas Gandhi, the Mahatma's nephew; and within hours, as the Defence Committee in New Delhi still pondered on what to do in Jammu & Kashmir, this menace persuaded the Nawab of Junagadh to abandon his State for Pakistan (just when Sir Hari Singh was fleeing from Srinagar to Jammu to escape the forces of the Government of Azad Kashmir).

Jawaharlal Nehru was far from happy about plebiscites and provisional accessions in the Kashmir context. He saw in the whole Kashmir affair a plot masterminded in Pakistan (of which he claimed he had private evidence); and he suspected that excessive concern for constitutional niceties could well give rise to delays and, thus, play into the hands of Jinnah and his fellow conspirators. What was called for, he felt, was not so much the formalities of accession as some pragmatic arrangement whereby the Maharaja's Government might be obliged to collaborate politically with Sheikh Abdullah and his National Conference, bolstered in power by Indian arms. Only thus could the Pakistani plot be foiled. The first priority was immediate military assistance (always provided the position of Sheikh Abdullah as the real political force in the State were established); and, as V.P. Menon pointed out, it would technically be quite proper for India to send its forces to the State of Jammu & Kashmir without its prior accession to India, be it definitive or provisional. Such an intervention, however, could well look to the world at large suspiciously like an Indian *coup d'état* to dispose of the Maharaja and to entrust the affairs of all of the State of Jammu & Kashmir to Nehru's good friend Sheikh Abdullah, a consideration which may have disturbed Mountbatten and some other members of the Defence Committee even if it did not then trouble unduly Jawaharlal Nehru (who, however, came very rapidly to appreciate the strategic and tactical value of accession in any form whatsoever).

The final decision on the accession question was postponed for a few hours. It was agreed in principle that India should undertake some form of military intervention in Kashmir and that preparations should be started forthwith. Meanwhile, V.P. Menon was instructed to go up to Srinagar at once to investigate the situation on the spot. On his return, either that evening or early the following day, firm plans could be made on the basis of much better information. Menon was to be accompanied by a small party of senior Indian Army and Air Force officers to explore the practical aspects of intervention; they would, no doubt, also take this opportunity to confer with India's military representative in Srinagar, Lt.-Colonel Kashmir Singh Katoch.

This Defence Committee of 25 October was motivated by a sense of urgency. Catastrophe, it seemed, would strike the State of Jammu & Kashmir at any moment. Interestingly enough, right up to 26 October this was not the impression which the general public in India would have derived from the available information.

Three examples should suffice to illustrate this point. First: Batra, in his public statement in Srinagar of 24 October, had indicated the existence of no immediate crisis. Second: the *Times* correspondent in Srinagar, writing on 26 October, treated the events along the western end of the Jhelum Valley Road as more comic than grave. He reported that

> eye-witness accounts of the fighting around the township of Uri ... reveal a somewhat farcical state of affairs with the Kashmir army and the rebel Muslim peasantry aided by Muslim deserters and tribesmen from the Hazara District of the North-West Frontier Province blazing away indiscriminately at one another, with mortars and machine guns for hours on end without inflicting any casualties. It would appear that neither party really knows how to conduct guerilla warfare in the mountainous countryside. [*Times*, 27 October 1947].

Third: in New Delhi on 26 October a spokesman for the States Department was still declaring that the Government of India had no interest in whatever conflict might be in progress in the State of Jammu & Kashmir; and, moreover, should that State decide to join Pakistan, this would be accepted with good grace by the Indian side.

Yet here, at the meeting of the Indian Defence Committee of 25 October, the leadership of India was acting in a manner verging at times on panic. There can be no doubt that Mountbatten was convinced that a disaster was looming in the State of Jammu & Kashmir. Clearly intelligence reaching him indicated that what was happening along the Jhelum Valley Road was by no means farcical. It promised to bring about the collapse of the regime of Sir Hari Singh with extremely unfortunate consequences. A large tract of territory which Mountbatten evidently considered in all justice ought to go, if it went anywhere, to India, was about to fall into the hands of Pakistan, a triumph to M.A. Jinnah, no friend of the Governor-General of India, and a blow to the prestige of Jawaharlal Nehru with whom the Governor-General had by this time identified himself far beyond the bounds of objectivity (for reasons about which we will not speculate here). Mountbatten undoubtedly agreed with the assessment of the situation which Nehru presented to Attlee on 25 October, perhaps drafted immediately after the Defence Committee meeting, that matters were "grave" indeed.

According to the Nehru telegram to Clement Attlee of 25 October (part of which has already been quoted above), gravity here also had geopolitical implications in that

> Kashmir's northern frontiers ... run in common with those of three countries, Afghanistan, the U.S.S.R. and China. Security of Kashmir, which must depend upon its internal tranquillity and existence of stable government, is vital to security of India.

Perhaps this rationale impressed Mountbatten no more than it did Clement Attlee. There is no evidence that during his time in India Mountbatten was particularly worried about the possible expansion of Soviet influence into the Subcontinent or that he was agitated by any of the other phobias of the great age of Imperial rivalries now passed (at least for the British), though, of course, he may well have believed that there were those in London who still held these anxieties to such a degree that they might view more sympathetically what India was about to do if it were presented in this particular kind of light. There were, moreover, a number of officials in the service of the new Government of India who had served their apprenticeship in the old British Political Department and who still had the instincts of players of the Great Game; thus such warnings continued to surface for a while longer, though by the beginning of 1948 they no longer accorded with the *zeitgeist* of non-aligned India.

Mountbatten may not have been unduly worried about the advance of Soviet influence. There was, however, another factor which did concern him very much indeed. There were at that time many British subjects resident in the Vale of Kashmir (certainly more than 200 and perhaps, it was reported at the time, as many as 450) whose safety, it appeared to him, would be threatened if the conflict moved eastward along the Jhelum Valley Road to Srinagar (as Mountbatten evidently thought probable). If they were now at risk, there would certainly be a great deal of concern in Britain; and if harm came to them, the consequent publicity would in no way enhance the Mountbatten image. This was a point of some particular importance since in just over three weeks the Mountbatten (Battenberg) family would celebrate their triumphal union with the House of Saxe-Coburg-Gotha-Windsor (the marriage of Mountbatten's nephew with Princess Elizabeth, heir to the British Crown). Mountbatten, one can well imagine, would have been unhappy to attend the Royal Wedding knowing that he was being blamed for the deaths of British men and women.

What could he do about it? He was reluctant even to contemplate the use of the remaining British troops in India in the rescue of these people from the Vale. Auchinleck had wanted to send some of these men on a rescue mission to the Vale at once; but Mountbatten had refused on the grounds that the British should not interfere in internal matters in India or Pakistan. In any case, such an option was quite academic since the British forces in the country had now so run down that but a single effective infantry battalion remained, the Royal Scots Fusiliers, inadequate for anything but rounding up the odd British resident in the remoter hill stations of Kumaon and Garhwal. It must have seemed to Mountbatten that only the Army of independent India could guarantee the safety of these British residents. Here was one reason why he should have been so enthusiastic about direct Indian intervention in the Kashmir imbroglio.

In the early afternoon of 25 October V.P. Menon flew to Srinagar in a chartered aircraft. He was accompanied not only by the senior Indian Army and Air Force officers but also by Dwarkanath Kachru, Secretary and confidential agent of Jawaharlal Nehru, who had for some time been a link between the Indian Prime Minister and the Jammu & Kashmir National Conference (and probably carried on this occasion some communication for Sheikh Abdullah, and, it may be, for D.P. Dhar, a young Kashmiri Pandit who in the days ahead would play a crucial part in liaison between the Indians and various State institutions). Dwarkanath Kachru, as has already been noted, as Secretary of the All India States' People's Conference, had in June 1946 been arrested, together with Nehru, on the Kashmir border by the Maharaja's men when Nehru had been trying to attend Sheikh Abdullah's trial in Srinagar; at this time Sheikh Abdullah was Vice-President of the States' Peoples' Conference, so he and Sheikh Abdullah were old political associates. Dwarkanath Kachru stayed on in Srinagar after Menon's return to Delhi. Shortly after Menon's arrival at Srinagar, Sheikh Abdullah left that place by air for the Indian capital (possibly in Menon's aircraft); and in New Delhi he was lodged in Nehru's residence. It seems likely that this journey was expedited, if not inspired, by what Dwarkanath Kachru had to say.

Srinagar, Menon was to report, was to all intents and purposes defenceless. There were somewhat improbable reports put about in India that at this time Sheikh Abdullah had organised an effective force of armed volunteers to keep order in Srinagar and, if need be, defend it; but all Menon could see were a few National Conference ruffians on some street corners, armed with *lathis* (sticks). The regular police had totally disappeared. It was widely believed, at least by the wealthier Hindus, that ferocious Islamic hordes were rushing along the Jhelum Valley Road and would at any moment enter Srinagar unopposed.

The Maharaja was in the process of abandoning the place and removing his Government to Jammu in the comparative safety of the other side of the Banihal Pass (which would soon be snowbound). Menon said that it was he who persuaded him of the wisdom of going; but the evidence is overwhelming that Sir Hari Singh had decided that discretion was the better part of valour long before Menon came on the scene. He departed in a spectacular motor cavalcade (depriving his summer capital of virtually all the more respectable, comfortable or roadworthy cars) at dawn on 26 October; and he could hardly be expected to reach Jammu before late that evening. The Maharaja declared, so Menon was to relate, that he would do anything the Government of India might ask in order to secure prompt assistance; but he discussed no specifics with the Indian official at that time and certainly signed no papers. A little later V.P. Menon, after a night with scarcely any sleep, took off for Delhi accompanied by M.C. Mahajan, the State's Prime Minister. Also on the aircraft were the Indian Army and Air Force officers, having completed their military appreciations and contacted whomsoever they needed to contact.

In New Delhi on Sunday 26 October several distinct sets of negotiations or discussions concerning the Kashmir situation took place, involving Sheikh Abdullah, M.C. Mahajan, and V.P. Menon with various Indian politicians and officials including Mountbatten, Nehru and Baldev Singh; and not all who participated in any one were of necessity aware of what was going on elsewhere.

The earliest of these meetings was that between Sheikh Abdullah and Jawaharlal Nehru and some of his Cabinet colleagues at Nehru's New Delhi residence. Talks may even had started late the night before. The major points were: how Sheikh Abdullah would react to the planned Indian military intervention; whether he would consider working (even if temporarily) in harness with Sir Hari Singh, from whose prison he had been released a bare month before, and with the Maharaja's Prime Minister, Mahajan; and, finally, what would be his view of the future relationship to be established between the State of Jammu & Kashmir and the Indian Union. No record of these discussions has ever been published beyond a broad hint that Sheikh Abdullah took this opportunity to request formally Indian military aid. It is probable, however, that in his own mind he saw his Kashmir as being in the future a far more autonomous polity than was anticipated in New Delhi and more along the lines set out in his *New Kashmir* manifesto of 1944 (but, if so, it would seem that on this occasion he prudently kept his real thoughts to himself).

Once they had landed at Safdarjung airport, at about 8.00 a.m., Menon and Mahajan went their separate ways in New Delhi, Menon eventually to the Defence Committee and Mahajan immediately to call on Jawaharlal Nehru.

This was Mehr Chand Mahajan's day, which produced its own set of discussions.

When he arrived at Nehru's residence, in York Road, Mahajan found not only the Prime Minister but also Sardar Baldev Singh, the Minister of Defence, and Sheikh Abdullah (who made his appearance late in the talks, but was secretly listening in an adjoining room from the outset). Mahajan requested unconditional Indian military help to save Srinagar from the "raiders". Nehru said that this would not be so easy. It took time to get troops together, he pointed out, let alone transport them. It was clear that India sought conditions, in particular that the Maharaja must sign some form of instrument of accession to India and that he would agree to place the conduct of his government in the hands of Sheikh Abdullah. Unaware that he was offering just what Nehru wanted, Mahajan, so he related in his memoirs, proposed in despair that in return for the required military aid he would recommend to the Maharaja both accession to India and the granting of political power to "the popular party" of Sheikh Abdullah. It was essential, he said, that the Indian Army fly men to Srinagar at once. Without immediate help, he concluded, he would have no option but to go to Lahore and see what terms he could negotiated with Mr. Jinnah. The mention of Lahore nearly brought discussions to a halt; but then Sheikh Abdullah made his belated appearance and confirmed what Mahajan had just said about the gravity of the situation. Indian military assistance on these two conditions, some kind of accession (undefined in detail) and a Sheikh Abdullah government, was agreed. The terms were subject, of course, to the Maharaja's approval. He had certainly not authorised Mahajan to go so far as this, particularly with respect to Sheikh Abdullah, and it was by no means improbable that, even at the very last moment, he would refuse to ratify such an unpalatable formula.

Nehru then went off to the Defence Committee meeting at about 10.00 a.m. He returned to his residence in the late afternoon or early evening to inform Mahajan (who had spent the middle of the day resting at Baldev Singh's house) that the Indian Cabinet, following the advice of the Defence Committee (which had met once more in the late afternoon), had resolved to give the Maharaja military assistance including troops. Nehru asked Mahajan to set out at once by air for Jammu, along with V.P. Menon, to tell the Maharaja what had been decided and to obtain his signature for what Mahajan rather mysteriously calls "certain supplementary documents about the accession". Mahajan, however, refused to leave New Delhi until his aerodrome officer at Srinagar reported by radio that the Indian forces had in fact landed, that is to say not before about 9.00 a.m. on 27 October. Nehru agreed: "you can fly to Jammu next morning", he said. [Mehr Chand Mahajan, *Looking Back*, London 1963, pp. 151–153].

Mahajan does not elaborate in his memoirs; but it seems reasonable to suppose that he was not prepared to recommend to his Master the

THE ACCESSION CRISIS, 24–27 OCTOBER 1947

Maharaja drastic constitutional measures, such as Nehru had indicated were now called for, until he was absolutely sure that the Indians would actually turn up in Srinagar. If for some reason the Indian intervention aborted, by remaining formally uncommitted the Maharaja still preserved the option of at least trying to arrange a deal of some kind with Pakistan, whose forces had much easier access to this critical area by way of the Jhelum Valley Road.

Mahajan's movements for 26 October 1947 are quite simply worked out on the basis of his own published narrative, which is corroborated by other evidence, not least that provided by Jawaharlal Nehru himself (and now published in his *Selected Works*, Second Series, Vol. IV). Menon's movements (and the third set of discussions with which they were involved), on the other hand, present a number of difficulties. In his own account he maintains that he went up by air to Jammu and back to New Delhi in the afternoon of that day, 26 October, accompanied by Mahajan; and he describes certain features of that trip and its consequences in great circumstantial detail. [See: V.P. Menon, *The Story of the Integration of the Indian States*, London 1956, pp. 399–400]. In that this account is clearly false – there can be no doubt now that he did *not* go to Jammu on 26 October, or even leave the Delhi region, with or without Mahajan – it is perhaps easier to describe what Menon really did during the course of 26 October 1947 on the basis of other evidence.

At about 10 a.m. on that fateful day, 26 October, V.P. Menon delivered his report to the Defence Committee, where Mountbatten again took the Chair. His story was grim. The Jammu & Kashmir State Forces were in disarray, Muslim troops (roughly one third of the total) having deserted to the invaders, taking their weapons with them. The invading force, he reported, was now only some 35 miles from Srinagar in the region of Baramula (which was doubtful, since the first Azad Kashmiri men only began approaching the outskirts of that town in small numbers that night of 26 October). While the National Conference, Sheikh Abdullah's organisation, might resist the "raiders", Menon thought, the Muslim League (or Muslim Conference, the distinction is not clear in the sources) in Srinagar was at that very moment arming its members in preparation to assist the invading force; thus adding civil war to the external threat which Kashmir now faced. The Maharaja's nerve had gone. In his mind he had written off Kashmir Province as lost. He would settle for safety in Jammu.

Menon's report clearly indicated that if India were ever to occupy Kashmir Province it would have to act quickly. Military problems were then considered by the Defence Committee. While risky, military involvement was possible (on the basis of some preliminary planning). The 1st Battalion of the Sikh Regiment could be deployed. Aircraft were available – not the hundred or so about which V.P. Menon and others have written (these were to come later), but, in fact, four planes of the Royal Indian Air Force (as it then still was) and six chartered machines from Indian civil airlines. Ten aircraft, however, would suffice to take the bulk of a single battalion and its equipment into Srinagar in relays during the course of a day. It all depended, really, on whether the "raiders" were holding the airfield when the planes first arrived.

Mountbatten declared in his formal report to King George VI that while he took full responsibility for the despatch of the Indian forces to Srinagar at this juncture, he was only prepared to do so subject to the formal accession of the State of Jammu & Kashmir to India. "The accession", he said, "would fully regularise the position and reduce the risk of an armed clash with Pakistan forces to a minimum". He believed that without accession and with the State of Jammu & Kashmir retaining its theoretical independence, the Pakistan forces could in fact intervene with the same justification as those of India if not, at least in the Indian Governor-General's eyes, with the same moral force. The result could well be an open, and escalating, inter-Dominion war in which, especially at this juncture in the history of the rise of the House of Battenberg, Mountbatten definitely did not wish to participate. With accession, of course, the entire weight of the Commonwealth could be made to press down on Pakistan to prevent its attacking what was now, even if provisionally, part of India, another Commonwealth nation. Pakistan, Mountbatten believed (and at this moment correctly), would be extremely reluctant to initiate such a conflict.

While Mountbatten thought accession expedient in the short term, in the longer term he felt it essential that the decision of a single man, the Maharaja, which was what accession was when all was said and done, must be confirmed or rejected by the voice of the people. There would have to be a plebiscite in which the inhabitants of the State of Jammu & Kashmir could decide to join either India or Pakistan, or even to stay independent. Before such a plebiscite were held, he advised that India and Pakistan should get together, perhaps at the next meeting (due shortly) of the Joint Defence Council (a body devised around the time of the Transfer of Power to solve problems arising from the partitioning of the old British Indian defence establishment between the two new Dominions) to consider the future defence of the State of Jammu & Kashmir whatever way the vote might go. Nehru, to all this, observed that he had no objection to an independent Jammu & Kashmir provided it remained within the Indian sphere of influence.

An interesting feature of this meeting was that all present, including Mountbatten, seem to have been convinced that the Government of Pakistan (including the Governor-General, M.A. Jinnah) were directly responsible for the events along the Jhelum Valley Road, even though there was as yet no clear account available as to exactly what was happening. The Defence Committee suggested that Nehru should send a telegram to his opposite number in Karachi, Liaquat Ali Khan, asking him to take steps to prevent further infiltration into the State of Jammu & Kashmir from Pakistan; but this was to be worded with great care so as not to appear to be an invitation for Pakistan to intervene further in the State on the pretence of restoring order. Inter-Dominion communication, however, did not seem to the Defence Committee to be a matter of particular urgency; and there was no suggestion that, before Indian troops themselves intervened directly in the conflict, the Indian side should make any attempt to arrange an Indo-Pakistani meeting at the highest level to try to sort out the situation. In the event, no high level Indian contact with Pakistan was attempted until well after intervention was an accomplished fact and the State of Jammu & Kashmir's alleged accession to India had been made public.

The Defence Committee concluded its meeting by considering what formal paperwork should arise out of the accession issue. It was clear, given the various conditions that had been injected into it by Mountbatten, with his desire for ratification by plebiscite, and Nehru, with his insistence upon a Sheikh Abdullah administration, that no extant *pro forma* Instrument would do. Some special formal document would have to be drafted. There could well be a letter from the Governor-General to the Maharaja setting out the conditions for accession. It might also be prudent to have in hand the text of a letter, written in the name of the Maharaja, to the Governor-General, accepting terms and adding clarifications. Suitable documents should be prepared at once (which implied some quick drafting) to be taken by V.P. Menon to Jammu for the Maharaja's signature where appropriate.

It is at this point that the hitherto established narrative diverges dramatically from the facts. Menon related that he did indeed go up to Jammu that afternoon (26 October), accompanied by Mahajan, and that he persuaded to Maharaja to sign what was needed. We have already seen that Mahajan has denied that part of this story in which it is claimed that he went to Jammu with Menon that day. It is now clear beyond a shadow of a doubt, on the basis of a wide range of sources including Nehru's own correspondence and the records of the British High Commission in New Delhi, that Menon, too, did not go to Jammu on 26 October.

What is true is that at about 3.45 p.m. V.P. Menon drove out to Willingdon Airport with the declared intention of going to Jammu. However, he found there that it was considered too late for a flight to an airfield with no night landing facilities (as Menon, an official with a mastery of detail, must have known); and by 5.00 p.m. Menon was back in New Delhi where he was visited in his private residence by Alexander Symon of the U.K. High Commission (who had already gone out to meet him at Willingdon Airport a little earlier). Menon told Symon he would now be going to Jammu the following morning.

It is curious that at this evening meeting on 26 October Menon gave Symon absolutely no hint as to quite what a massive crisis was brewing. Yet it looks as if he saw Symon immediately after an extremely brief meeting of the Defence Committee at which it was confirmed that overt Indian intervention in Kashmir should go ahead the following morning. The published accounts, such as that given by Hodson [H.V. Hodson, *The Great Divide*, 2nd Edition, Karachi 1985, p. 455], report that this decision was only reached after the Instrument of Accession, duly signed by the Maharaja, was to hand. In fact, there was at this point no signed Instrument. All that was available was Mahajan's agreement to put the Indian terms to the Maharaja with a recommendation that they be accepted; but no guarantee that they would be.

This absence of a completed Instrument of Accession that evening of 26 October was pointed to by Mountbatten himself when Ian Stephens of the Calcutta *The Statesman* newspaper came to dine with the Governor-General and Lady Mountbatten. Stephens recorded the main points which were raised by his host about the storm then brewing in Kashmir [see: Ian Stephens, *Pakistan*, London 1963, p. 203]. Mountbatten said that

THE ACCESSION CRISIS, 24–27 OCTOBER 1947

"the Maharajah's formal accession to India was *being* [my italics] finalised", in other words that it was still an incomplete process. The Indian troops, however, were going in to Kashmir come what may. Mountbatten then delivered what to Stephens seemed an extraordinary anti-Pakistan diatribe. The real enemies in Kashmir were the Muslim League and its leader, M.A. Jinnah. They had planned the whole invasion, aided and abetted by certain British officials; and at this very moment, 26 October, Jinnah was waiting in Abbottabad ready to ride in triumph to Srinagar. Where Pakistan had plotted without scruple, India had acted with impeccable openness and honesty. Stephens was shocked at the way in which Mountbatten had become, it then seemed to him, more Hindu than the Hindus (others were to note this phenomenon over the next few days). Mountbatten appeared to have accepted without question every rumour hostile to Pakistan. The story of Jinnah at Abbottabad, which was completely without foundation (he was then in Lahore), was a good example; and subsequently it has entered the mythology of the Kashmir dispute. It is clear from this account that Mountbatten had reached a state of mind where such niceties as the actual completion of the accession process had ceased to matter. What had to be done was to get the gallant Indian troops into Srinagar without delay to frustrate Jinnah's vile conspiracy.

At about 9.00 a.m. on 27 October 1947, carried by ten Dakota aircraft, the 1st Sikhs started landing at Srinagar under the command of Lt-Colonel Dewan Ranjit Rai; and what happened there will be considered elsewhere. On the same morning, so the London *Times* reported:

> Mr. Mehr Chand Mahajan, the Prime Minister of Kashmir, and Mr. V.P. Menon, the Secretary of the States Department, left for Jammu, the capital, where the Kashmir court is now in residence, to obtain, it is learnt, formal confirmation of accession by the Maharaja. [*Times*, 28 October 1947].

Rumours that some kind of Instrument of Accession by the Maharaja of Jammu & Kashmir to India had been signed started to circulate in New Delhi around 1.00 p.m.; and they were confirmed over the telephone to the UK High Commission by Sir Gopalaswami Ayyengar at 4.15 p.m.

One conclusion would seem to emerge from this very well documented narrative. In contrast to what Mountbatten had originally advised, the actual Indian intervention in Srinagar took place *before* the Maharaja had signed anything indicating his intention to accede to India. At 9.00 a.m. on Monday 27 October 1947 the State of Jammu & Kashmir existed in the same constitutional limbo of insecure independence that it had enjoyed since 15 August following the lapse of British Paramountcy. Mountbatten was certainly aware of this state of affairs. Perhaps he thought that in the circumstances the Maharaja's signature to an Instrument of Accession was but a mere formality.

But was it a mere formality? The fact is that it would have been much better, on the kind of arguments which Mountbatten was himself applying, had the Maharaja been fully signed up before a single Indian soldier ever set foot on Kashmiri soil. What actually happened undoubtedly laid India open to the charge of jumping the gun. Moreover, it could always be argued, and with a significant degree of conviction, that the Maharaja had only signed *because* the Indians had occupied his summer capital, in other words, that he had signed under duress. It should cause no surprise, therefore, to find that in a number of official accounts (from the Indian side) which emerged not long after 27 October 1947, it was stated that the Maharaja *had* indeed signed an Instrument of Accession before the Indian intervention. Two examples must suffice.

First: just before 1 November 1947 the three British Commanders-in-Chief of the Indian Forces, Lockhart (Army), Elmhirst (Air) and Hall (Navy), were persuaded to issue a joint declaration to the effect that they had taken part in no advance planning for the Kashmir operation prior to 25 October 1947. The final paragraph of this unusual document read:

> at first light on the morning of 27th October, *with Kashmir's Instrument of Accession signed* [my italics], the movement by air of Indian forces to Kashmir began. [Quoted in: J. Korbel, *Danger in Kashmir*, revised ed., Princeton 1966, p. 87].

Though often quoted, the reason why this particular declaration was produced at all has been hard to discover. In fact, it seems that it was concocted for Mountbatten to show to Jinnah, Liaquat Ali Khan and other Pakistan leaders when he visited Lahore on 1 November (as we shall see below) in his abortive venture to settle the Kashmir crisis on a Governor-General to Governor-General basis. It was clearly important to demonstrate to the Pakistanis that there had been no history of British conspiracy behind the Indian intervention at Srinagar airfield on 27 October. Had Mountbatten not supported this particular chronology with all his authority, the Pakistani leadership might have investigated with greater care the story of the Maharaja of Jammu & Kashmir's accession on 26 October. As it is, they have generally to date accepted (in public at least) this tale, to their considerable diplomatic disadvantage over the years.

Second: the Government of India *White Paper on Jammu & Kashmir*, which was laid before the Indian Constituent Assembly in early March 1948, and which represents the Government of India's first full official explanation of its position *vis à vis* Kashmir, contains in the Introduction the following:

> on the 25th [of October] the Government of India directed the preparation of plans for sending troops to Kashmir by air and road. Indian troops were sent to Kashmir by air on the 27th, *following the signing of the Instrument of Accession the previous night* [my italics].

By early 1948 the place of the 26 October Instrument of Accession in the armoury of Indian advocacy had been well established, so the function of this particular sentence requires no exegesis. There can be no doubt, however, that its presence in a *White Paper* has confused many students in subsequent years.

The reasons for this increasing emphasis upon the desired chronology, that intervention indeed followed the completion of accession, are not hard to detect. The accession argument was a major consideration in keeping Pakistan out of direct involvement at the very beginning of the conflict, when M.A. Jinnah wanted to send in the Pakistan Army and was dissuaded by the threat, repeated to him personally by Auchinleck (who flew up to Lahore on 28 October to reinforce the acting Pakistan Commander-in-Chief, Gracey, on this point) of withdrawal of all British Officers mainly on the grounds that they could not be involved in an inter-Dominion war. As Auchinleck put it to Jinnah, "there would be incalculable consequences of military violation of the territory of Indian Union in consequence of Kashmir's sudden accession". The same factor continued to operate in this manner for many months before Pakistan was able to come out openly and formally in support of the Azad Kashmiri forces; though, it must be admitted, before 1947 was over senior British Officers, including Messervy, the Commander-in-Chief of the Pakistan Army, were not adverse in private to giving those actively involved in Kashmir operations the benefit of their advice and experience, just as was happening on the Indian side (albeit rather more openly).

The ritual of accession, moreover, proved extremely convenient to

Indian diplomats to justify all sorts of actions in the State of Jammu & Kashmir which at first sight might conflict with the commitment to a plebiscite, and it enabled India to reject any Pakistani proposals for simultaneous withdrawals on both sides. As Sir G. S. Bajpai, India's top diplomatist, put it to the British High Commissioner in India, Sir Terence Shone, on 18 November, the legal point was that the Indian forces were in Kashmir because they had been invited to go there by a State which had acceded to the Indian Union. This put India in quite a different situation from Pakistan which was meddling in territory where it had no right to be; if there were any withdrawing to be done, Pakistan would have to do it first. Over the years the accession argument has grown ever stronger in Indian official thought, and today it probably represents the most powerful public justification for the Indian decision to retain at all costs those parts of the State of Jammu & Kashmir which it now holds; Kashmir is an "internal" Indian matter. Successive Indian Prime Ministers, dutifully echoed by their diplomats, have so declared; and the majority of Indian citizens doubtless so believe to this day.

The fact that accession must have actually followed intervention presented the Indian bureaucracy at the time with some problems. Whatever documents resulted from the accession process, and something had to be produced almost at once, would have to show the desired sequence of events. Thus there was made public on 28 October the text of a pair of letters, one from the Maharaja to Mountbatten, bearing the date 26 October, and the other from Mountbatten to the Maharaja, with the date 27 October. Both were almost certainly drafted by V.P. Menon; and we have no direct evidence as to when the Maharaja's letter was actually signed (if, indeed, it ever was), but we can be sure that it was not on 26 October.

The Maharaja's letter as published lays out the classic Indian case for intervention. The mass infiltration of tribesmen from the Frontier, transported on motor vehicles assisted by the Pakistan authorities in their transit of Pakistan territory, is described in detail. The consequence was this:

> with the conditions obtaining at present in my State and the great emergency of the situation as it exists, I have no option but to ask for help from the Indian Dominion. Naturally they cannot send help asked by me without my State acceding to the Dominion of India. I have accordingly decided to do so and I attach the Instrument of Accession for acceptance by your Govern-

ment. The other alternative is to leave my State and my people to free-booters. On this basis no civilized Government can exist or can be maintained. This alternative I will never allow to happen as long as I am Ruler of the State and I have life to defend my country. [Quoted, for example, in: P.L. Lakhanpal, *Essential Documents and Notes on Kashmir Dispute*, 2nd edition, Delhi 1966, pp. 55–57].

Stirring stuff; but it would have possessed more force had it actually been written by the Maharaja on the stated day when, in fact, Sir Hari Singh was in the process of abandoning Kashmir Province for the relative safety of Jammu and showed no signs of wishing to defend anything. It did, however, for those who drafted it, get round the awkward problem of the date of the Instrument of Accession, which was firmly put into 26 October.

Having promised to fight to the death to remain Ruler of his Sate, in the next paragraph of this document Sir Hari Singh virtually abdicated. "It is my intention", the letter stated, "at once to set up an Interim Government and ask Sheikh Abdullah to carry out the responsibilities in this emergency with my Prime Minister". Thus Nehru's principal fee for Indian aid to the Maharaja's State was paid (and thus began, also, the problem of Sheikh Abdullah which was to complicate India's handling of that portion of the Jammu & Kashmir under its control for decades to come).

The question of the plebiscite, on which the Maharaja was given nothing to say in this letter, was dealt with in Mountbatten's formal reply in these words:

> consistently with their policy that in the case of any State where the issue of accession has been the subject of dispute, the question of accession should be decided in accordance with the wishes of the people of the State, it is my Government's wish that as soon as law and order have been restored in Kashmir and her soil cleared of the invader the question of the State's accession should be settled by a reference to the people.

But what of the Instrument of Accession itself, that key document, the formal title deed and act of conveyance as it were? The Maharaja's letter to Mountbatten, with the date 26 October 1947, has, as we have seen, a reference to an Instrument of Accession: "I attach the Instrument of Accession for acceptance by your Government". But, in that this letter was surely drafted in New Delhi by V.P. Menon or his colleagues long before the Maharaja set eyes on it (if he ever did), it does not prove that such an Instrument was ever signed, merely that it could possibly have been discussed with the Maharaja when Mahajan and Menon caught up with him in Jammu on 27 October. He may have signed then; on the other hand, he may have put off signing but permitted a reference to the Instrument to remain in the letter. It is quite possible, of course, given his state of mind at the time, what with his flight from Srinagar and his fear of the Pathan invaders, that he may never have looked at the letter at all or even have been made aware of its precise contents. Be that as it may, the Maharaja's letter dated 26 October 1947 gives us absolutely no clue as to what the "Instrument of Accession" actually looked like.

The Indian 1948 *White Paper* reproduces a sample text of an Instrument of Accession such as was devised by the States Department on the eve of the Transfer of Power (as had already been noted in Chapter I above). This was a document which derived from the Indian Independence Act, 1947, and the Government of India Act, 1935. It was, in fact, a printed form with spaces left for the name of State, the signature of the Ruler, and the day of the month of August 1947. There was also space for the Governor-General's acceptance, again with a blank for the day of the month of August 1947. It was a singularly unsuitable document for the rather special circumstances in the State of Jammu & Kashmir in October 1947. It related specifically to the British Indian Empire prior to the Transfer of Power on 15 August 1947 and not to the transfer of sovereignty by what was now an independent polity. It contained no provision either for a plebiscite or for the delegation of powers such as was now being proposed in the case of Sheikh Abdullah. It is interesting that in the document reproduced as Pt. I, No. 29 in the Indian 1948 *White Paper* all the spaces are left blank. This is not a representation of *the* document signed by the Maharaja, merely an example of the kind of document he *might* have signed (particularly had he opted for India prior to the Transfer of Power). One may well wonder why the Government of India, had it indeed been in possession of a properly signed Instrument, did not publish it as such in the 1948 *White Paper*; it would certainly have been the documentary jewel in India's Kashmiri crown.

A version of this *pro forma* (complete with the printed date August 1947, with the printed August duly crossed out and October written in) with the signatures of the Maharaja and Mountbatten was eventually produced by 1971 to serve as the frontispiece of the collected correspondence of Sardar Vallabhbhai Patel [Durga Das, ed., *Sardar Patel's Correspondence 1945–50*.

Volume I. New Light on Kashmir, Ahmedabad 1971]; and this text continues to be exhibited or quoted by Indian officialdom. The best that can be said about this item is that it raises grave doubts as to its authenticity. Despite much search, there is good reason to believe that the original Maharaja's copy of this, or any other, form of Instrument of Accession has failed to turn up in the Jammu & Kashmir State Archives. There are well informed people who deny that any such document ever existed.

The point is this. Having got the Indians committed to his defence, and having secured the despatch of Indian troops to Srinagar without signing anything, there were sound reasons (above all for one of Sir Hari Singh's devious and indecisive cast of mind) why the Maharaja should continue to withhold his signature from any documents which so limited his freedom of action, potential or actual. The Indians would have to go on defending him, come what may. Eventually, perhaps, he might rid himself of Jawaharlal Nehru and Sheikh Abdullah, both of whom he detested. The Indians, of course, could never admit that the Maharaja had not signed the Instrument of Accession once they had so publicly announced that he had. There the matter must rest until fresh documents surface to justify a firmer verdict one way or another.

IV

The War in Kashmir, October to December 1947

It is not our purpose here to describe in detail the conduct of the First Indo-Pakistani War over Kashmir. There are, however, a number of aspects of its initial stages, helpful in the understanding of its origins and fundamental nature, which have not received the comment they deserve. We lack good impartial military histories of this conflict. There are numerous Indian accounts, none entirely satisfactory; and military historians from Pakistan have shed very little light indeed on these opening stages of the first Indo-Pakistani Kashmir war. The subject, even today, is too political for the vast majority of Indian or Pakistani writers; they cannot resist the urge to garnish their narrative with patriotic polemic.

Moreover, the initial stages of the fighting were surrounded in deliberate mystery by the two sides. Both India and Pakistan were involved at various levels in clandestine policy concerning the State of Jammu & Kashmir long before the key dates of 22 and 27 October. Neither has been particularly anxious to explore its own activities (even though anything but reluctant to comment on those of the other party). The result has not been conducive to the delineation of a sharp picture of what actually was happening.

Another feature of this particular war which certainly served to confuse the historiography of the Kashmir question is that at the highest level the armies of the two major protagonists were both commanded by British officers. The Indian Commander-in-Chief, Sir R. Lockhart, took a keen interest in Kashmir operations from the outset, as indeed did the Indian Head of State, the Governor-General Lord Mountbatten. Operational command of the Indian forces on 27 October and the days that immediately followed was exercised from New Delhi by Lt.-Gen. Sir Dudley Russell. The Pakistan armed forces were also under a British Commander-in-Chief, on 27 October Gen. Sir Douglas Gracey in the absence on leave of Sir Frank Messervy; but on this side, shortly after news of the overt Indian intervention was received, and M.A. Jinnah proposed sending in his own men in riposte, by a deliberate act of policy British commanders debarred themselves and all their British subordinates from any personal involvement in Kashmir. This self-denying ordinance was imposed on the express orders of the Supreme Commander, Field-Marshal Sir Claude Auchinleck, who was, to make a peculiar situation even odder, notionally in charge of the forces on *both* sides (until 30 November 1947, when this inherently unsatisfactory arrangement was brought to an end, with Auchinleck leaving India on the following day).

The British factor influenced the recording of the Kashmir crisis in a number of ways, some crude and some subtle.

For instance: there has been a tendency on the part of many British observers (Lord Birdwood is a good example) to assume, if only out of politeness, that certain British dignitaries were telling the truth even when probability suggested that they were not. The phenomenon which has helped keep alive the myth of the chronology of accession preceding Indian intervention (which we have discussed in the previous Chapter), has also preserved all sorts of other fables which are today not so easy to detect, let alone expose for what they are. Many official British observers of what went on in Kashmir Province during those first days of crisis felt, or were instructed, that it was their duty not to make their experiences public. It is a fact that quite a number of British officers in the armed forces of both India and Pakistan unofficially involved themselves in early Kashmir operations to a degree that went far beyond the bounds of benevolent neutrality; we will examine one example, the affair of Major W. Brown and the Gilgit Agency, a little further on in this Chapter. With a very few exceptions, they kept silent (something at which the British military seem, when they so wish, to be quite as good as the Silent Service) in after years.

British silence, however, broken on the whole by none but semi-official spokesmen like Alan Campbell-Johnson (whose mission it was to praise Mountbatten not to bury him, even in the pages of his diary), has completely failed to remove suspicions. Most Pakistanis today believe that Mountbatten, as the last Viceroy of British India and the first Governor-General of independent India, systematically stacked the cards against them during both Partition and the genesis of the Kashmir dispute. This is, to some extent at least, almost certainly so. It is surprising, therefore, to find that many Indian writers are quite prepared to assume that Mountbatten, following some obscure policy of neo-imperialism generated in Whitehall, was busy bringing Pakistan into existence and then keeping it alive for reasons of British self-interest, and perhaps, also the interest of its American ally (and master).

Such suspicions, evident among the uninformed of a later age, were also present in 1947 and influenced the decisions of some of the major parties in the opening days of the crisis. M.A. Jinnah had no trust whatsoever in the integrity of Mountbatten. Jawaharlal Nehru was soon to lose faith in the British Commander-in-Chief of his army, Sir R. Lockhart, whom he suspected of carrying on a clandestine correspondence with his British cronies in Pakistan, and failing to inform the Indian Cabinet about all he knew. This element of suspicion of the British, sometimes justified and sometimes not, certainly hampered British attempts at mediation immediately following 27 October 1947. The historian cannot ignore it; it has contaminated much Indian and Pakistani writing on the genesis of the Kashmir problem with an element of what can only be described as paranoia.

The very presence of the senior British officers, even without the flowering of such suspicions, and even if in the Indian case many of the officers concerned were exceptionally co-operative, had another profound effect on the nature of the record. A great deal of Kashmir military planning, both in India and in Pakistan, had perforce to be made by Indian and Pakistani soldiers in such a way that it at least appeared that the British officers (BOs) had no inkling as to what was afoot. Thus an element of charade has entered into many of the documents, be they records kept by the Governor-General of India or those compiled by humbler British military officers and civilian officials. Such play-acting has all too often been taken by subsequent researchers to represent reality.

We must return, now, to the progress of the war in Kashmir.

The threat to which the Indians responded with their overt intervention on the morning of 27 October 1947 involved far more than a band of Pathan tribesmen roaring along the Jhelum Valley Road in a convoy of dilapidated buses. There were, in fact, at least three operations in progress on what we shall continue for convenience to call the Azad Kashmiri side, (1) the Poonch sector, (2) the southern or Mirpur sector, and (3) the northern sector along the Jhelum Valley Road.

First: in the Poonch Jagir the Azad Kashmiris had by 27 October secured control of virtually all the countryside up to the main crests of the Pir Panjal Range. The geography here was important. While this tract was separated from West Pakistan by no more than the Jhelum River, which could be crossed easily enough in many places, from the Vale of Kashmir it was walled in by the Pir Panjal mountains which presented great difficulties even to experienced local travellers let alone military formations. Access from the rest of Azad Kashmir to Poonch City was, for example, simple enough from the south-west. From the Vale that City was by no means easy to reach; perhaps the best route was by way of Uri to its north on the Jhelum Valley Road, to which it was linked by a motorable track of indifferent quality which crossed the Hajipir Pass. Other passes were far more formidable; and at this stage in the conflict were certainly beyond the capabilities of most, if not all, motor transport.

In this area, the heartland of the original Poonch revolt, the Jammu & Kashmir State on 27 October still retained Poonch City, where its garrison along with the remaining Hindu and Sikh inhabitants put up a strong defence, soon to be assisted by Indian air power; and in the end (in the summer of 1948) the Indians were able to join up with this outpost, despite the blocking of the Uri road, and retain it in their part of the State. To do so, however, involved considerable feats of military engineering of a kind which could not be applied to many a population centre of lesser psychological importance. Thus elsewhere, towns like Bagh and Rawalakot were soon snatched from their State garrisons by the Azad Kashmiris.

Second: south of Poonch Jagir the main front lay along the borders of Mirpur Province with Riasi and Jammu. Here the Indians were able from the outset to apply considerable pressure because they had a good logistic connection with India from the Pathankot railhead through Madhopur and across the Ravi by pontoon bridge (constructed by Indian Army engineers on the eve of the Indian intervention) to Kathua and Jammu. This route not only provided access to the south of Azad Kashmir, but was in addition the first leg of the main road across the Banihal Pass to Srinagar, the key alternative to air transport for operations in the Vale.

It was, of course, also the means of approach to a sector of border between Jammu and West Pakistan in the plains where geography favoured the more conventional forms of warfare including the use of armour. There was always a possibility that, should the conflict escalate, the Pakistan side might launch an attack here, along the axis Sialkot-Jammu or Sialkot-Akhnur, in an attempt to sever the Banihal Pass lifeline (and, indeed, such attempts, which some leaders on the Azad Kashmiri side had advocated in 1947, were made in the Indo-Pakistani Wars of 1965 and 1971). It followed, therefore, that a significant proportion of Indian strength in this quarter would have to be withheld from Mirpur operations to provide a reserve against the possibility of a direct intervention by Pakistan. It is probable that the bulk of the Indian forces from the outset were concentrated here, where they also acted as a counterthreat aimed at Pakistan in the Punjab.

On 27 October 1947 the situation on this southern sector seemed to be that most of the major towns (like Mirpur and Kotli) were held by the Jammu & Kashmir State Forces, possibly with some assistance from the Patiala infantry which had been sent to Jammu some days prior to the formal Indian intervention; but the countryside was controlled, if not always permanently occupied, by the Azad Kashmiris. In other words, it was a classic guerilla war situation for which many recent parallels can be drawn. The Azad Kashmiris, even though pressing towards Akhnur on the Chenab, a place which in the strategic thinking of the day pointed like a dagger at the main Jammu-Srinagar road across the Banihal Pass, were as yet unable to do more than threaten; they were not equipped for assaults against fixed positions defended with any skill at all. This situation would change during the course of November, as the Azad Kashmiris acquired experience, more skilled leadership and better weapons (many of them captured from the Jammu & Kashmir State Forces).

This was, moreover, a sector where communal relations had been shattered by the Maharaja's policy of precautionary elimination of Muslim threats (what today in another context would be called "ethnic cleansing") from September onwards. Here was the scene of great, though virtually unrecorded, massacres of Muslims by Sikhs and Dogras which reached a climax on the very eve of the overt Indian intervention in Kashmir, and continued in Jammu territory controlled by the Maharaja through November and December 1947. In regions so affected, survivors showed no love whatsoever for the old order; the Azad Kashmiris here did not lack for support among the remaining Muslim population.

Following their open intervention, of course, the Indian strength on this sector increased vastly; but never to such an extent as to threaten to overwhelm the Azad Kashmiri defenders. During the course of 1948 a stalemate was reached which has persisted more or less to the present day. A front line was stabilised which ran south from the Indian controlled

Poonch salient, passed just west of Naoshera (which remained in Indian hands), and reached the old Punjab border (now that of Pakistan) a few miles to the west of the Chenab River. The Jammu & Kashmir State town garrisons to the west of this line were unable to hold out against Azad Kashmiri siege, many falling during the course of November 1947. The extreme south of this sector was really an extension of the Punjab plains; and here fighting could take place on a surprisingly large scale, so that in successive Indo-Pakistani Wars this was to be the scene of great clashes of armour and the use of tactical air power, at times of a magnitude which would have aroused notice in World War II.

In the final week of October 1947 the Azad Kashmiri military command in these two sectors, Poonch and the southern front including Mirpur, was, it would seem, largely entrusted to a small group of former Indian National Army (INA) officers with Kashmiri affiliations, of whom the most important was M. Zaman Kiani, who had during World War II fought on the Japanese side as a divisional commander at Imphal (a battle in which General Douglas Gracey had been actively involved on the opposing side). Liaison between the Poonch and Mirpur commands and that of Major Khurshid Anwar (on the third, and northernmost, sector to be described below) appears to have been somewhat defective at this early stage of the conflict. Thus Khurshid Anwar's operations from Domel all the way to the approaches to Srinagar took place in virtual isolation from what was happening in Poonch and Mirpur, even though some of its major objectives were of the greatest strategic importance to the commanders of these two sectors.

Third: there was the northern sector through which ran the Jhelum Valley Road. This was a corner where Kashmir Province touched upon the Hazara District of the North-West Frontier Province, where, in fact, the State of Jammu & Kashmir marched with the Pathan tribal world. Through it ran the only good land communication between Pakistan and Srinagar, the Jhelum Valley Road, which was approached on the Pakistan side by two routes meeting at Domel beside the Jhelum-Kishenganga confluence. One, by way of Muzaffarabad from Mansehra (which involved bridges over both the Jhelum and its Kishenganga tributary), led across the Indus from Peshawar, the capital of the North-West Frontier Province. The other, across the Jhelum from Pakistan at Kohala, and then along the left bank of the Jhelum to Domel, was the road from Rawalpindi and Lahore by way of the Murree hill station. Both these access routes to the Vale of Kashmir were connected with the nearest railhead in Pakistan, Havelian, a few miles south of the cantonment town of Abbottabad. In order to secure their positions in Poonch and Mirpur from any northern threat, and at the same time to retain communication with northern and eastern Poonch, notably the towns of Rawalkot and Bagh, it was essential for the Azad Kashmiri forces to occupy this part of Kashmir Province, certainly as far eastward along the Jhelum Valley Road as Uri. As a secondary, though extremely tempting, objective, this same tract promised to be the key to the capture of Srinagar itself and the union of all Kashmir Province, the Vale, with Poonch and Mirpur, to form a greater Kashmir free of Dogra rule.

It is this particular (northern) sector which occupied the centre stage in the opening scenes of the first Kashmir war; and many accounts of that conflict treat it as if it were the only front. In fact, as we have already suggested, within the context of a viable Azad Kashmir any operation along the Jhelum Valley Road beyond Uri towards Srinagar was a tactical sideshow, though it might hold out glittering prospects of strategic gain in the longer term. Indian commentators, and their sympathisers, have been disposed to emphasise one element, the defeat of the "raid" on Srinagar, to the virtual exclusion of all others. We must now examine such evidence as is available as to what exactly that "raid" was.

At Uri on 24 October the column commanded by Major Khurshid Anwar, some 2,000 strong (consisting of men from the old Poonch revolt, former members of the 4th Jammu & Kashmir Rifles, and a number of Pathan tribesmen from various North-West Frontier groups), having pushed back the Jammu & Kashmir State Forces and their allies but confronted with destroyed bridges, was not able to resume its advance until the following day. On the evening of 26 October a few small detachments approached the outskirts of Baramula, a substantial town of some 15,000 inhabitants on the Jhelum some 35 miles to the north-west of Srinagar; but the town was not to be taken over by the Azad Kashmiris and their allies until the course of the following day – according to Brigadier Hiralal Atal, in a telegram to General Roy Bucher, at 1500 hours on 27 October [see: Hiralal Atal, *Nehru's Emissary to Kashmir*, New Delhi 1972, p. 44]. Indeed, there is excellent evidence that at the moment that the first Indian Sikhs arrived at Srinagar airfield Baramula was still unoccupied.

For the story of the war as seen from the Azad Kashmiri side over the next few days we have the narratives of Khurshid Anwar and other participants; these, needless to say, do not agree in all respects with the many Indian accounts, of which in some ways that of Lt.-General L.P. Sen is the most interesting (though not all Indian soldiers would accept it as gospel). The story which follows in this Chapter is the distillation of a large number of narratives and reports related or written from many points of view.

By 27 October Khurshid Anwar's force had been much depleted, men having perforce been left behind to secure the extended line of communications; and the situation grew worse with every day. Only three or four hundred men advanced to Patan, some 15 miles north-west of Srinagar, on or shortly before 31 October. Here they encountered an Indian blocking force in positions along the Srinagar road; and there followed, it appears, a series of clashes for control of the place. Meanwhile, Khurshid Anwar took about two hundred men in an attempt to approach Srinagar from the south by a flanking march. Only 20 or so men, however, actually came into direct contact with Indian forces guarding Srinagar airfield, on 3 November. Khurshid Anwar was then obliged to pause. Further attempts to advance having failed despite some reinforcements, on 7 November his column began to withdraw towards Uri, giving up Baramula and abandoning the prospect (for the foreseeable future, it was to transpire) of entering Srinagar. For a week after their arrival on 27 October the Indian regulars had been left virtually unmolested to build up their strength both through Srinagar airfield and, increasingly, by land convoys from Pathankot via Jammu over the Banihal Pass.

Major Khurshid Anwar was perhaps not the greatest of soldiers, though undoubtedly brave and energetic; and a few days after the withdrawal from Baramula he was to be seriously wounded in action and obliged to retire from the fray. His deputy, Major Aslam Khan, an officer of Kashmiri origin who described himself to the British journalist Sydney Smith (of the *Daily Express*) as a "deserter" from the Pakistan Army (he had, in fact, recently served in the Pakistan Army after a career in the Jammu & Kashmir State Forces, where his father had once held high rank), was a competent professional who was to show some ability in operations in Baltistan a little later on. The conduct of the final stages of this campaign strongly suggest that the main objective was the Kohala, Domel, Muzaffarabad region, flanked by Uri; beyond that lay targets of opportunity which were attacked with strictly limited forces.

This is what the Azad Kashmiri sources suggest. Indian accounts differ in a number of respects. The magnitude of the danger is amplified. Organised military action is detected in every incident when some isolated tribesman opened fire upon Indian troops. It is made quite clear that Srinagar was saved from a frightful fate at the very last moment. Had the intervention been postponed by a few hours, so Indian accounts have it, the result would have been catastrophe. Behind this hyperbole, so characteristic of military bulletins from virtually all nations, a story of sorts can be discovered which is capable of collation with what we now know from the other side.

When the men of the 1st Sikhs began to disembark from their Dakota aircraft at Srinagar airfield on the morning of 27 October, their commander, Lt.-Colonel Dewan Ranjit Rai, clearly did not believe that the landing ground was in any direct danger. As soon as his force was present in company strength, he secured (not without difficulty because of the large number of vehicles commandeered by the Maharaja for his departure to Jammu the previous day) transport from the local State authorities and took himself off with his men towards Baramula, more or less abandoning his base. Quite what he had in mind is not clear. Perhaps he hoped to meet the remnants of the State forces and their Patiala Sikh allies. More probably, he had been instructed in New Delhi to make his way along the Jhelum Valley Road as far as he conveniently could to the west of Srinagar in order to establish a symbolic road block. This might stop no tribal hordes, but it would certainly make an approaching patrol of Pakistan Army armoured cars think twice before initiating an overt inter-Dominion shooting war (which might then spread to the Indo-Pakistani borders both West and East). During the morning of 27 October, before the Pakistan authorities had been warned off by Gracey and Auchinleck from sending in their own regulars, the arrival of such forces could well have seemed to the Indian high command to be the greatest danger to their Kashmiri ambitions. In the event Lt.-Colonel Ranjit Rai was ambushed and killed; and many of his men ended up, for no obvious immediate good purpose, in positions near Patan astride the Baramula-Srinagar road (and about 15 miles from the vital airfield). The defence of the Srinagar airfield was soon to become the responsibility of other units who arrived as the airlift from India proceeded.

By reading between the lines of several Indian accounts of what was happening in Baramula and its surrounding country at this moment it

THE WAR IN KASHMIR, OCTOBER TO DECEMBER 1947

becomes obvious that this was no countryside through which small groups of Indian troops should wander. In Baramula itself, as the Azad Kashmiri forces entered the town in strength during the course of 27 October, the Muslim population took to the streets to welcome them as liberators from Dogra rule. It would seem that at the same time there developed a significant amount of guerilla activity in the countryside, either the action of men who had made their way over the mountains from Poonch through the Gulmarg district to the neighbourhood of Baramula and Patan, or of members of a local Kashmiri resistance to the Dogras. No doubt some of the latter had acquired weapons from State sources, be they defeated troops or captured armouries. It may well be that both Brigadier Rajinder Singh, the Jammu & Kashmir Chief of Staff who had been ambushed the pervious day, and Lt.-Colonel Rai, who died in a similar manner on 27 October, were victims of such people rather than organised Azad Kashmiri opposition.

The Azad Kashmiri force under Khurshid Anwar and Aslam Khan, which advanced from Baramula through Patan in their flanking movement southward of Srinagar contained the bulk of what might be called the professionals, mainly Poonch men (the majority Sudhans), either old soldiers who had served in British Indian Army or former 4th Jammu & Kashmir riflemen. Left behind in Baramula were assorted groups of tribesmen from the North-West Frontier Province and, even, it is possible, Afghanistan. Discipline was not the strongest characteristic of such men; and their officers experienced serious difficulty in keeping them under control, particularly when stories began to circulate of the arrival of the Sikhs (who had been generally accepted by the tribesmen as the greatest scourge of the Muslims in the communal massacres which accompanied Partition, and the legitimate foe in any *jihad*, holy war) at Srinagar airfield. The inevitable killing of Sikhs and Hindus in Baramula, particularly merchants who had remained to guard their stock, now began to be accompanied by indiscriminate looting and a considerable amount of rape, applied as much to unfortunate Kashmiri Muslims as to the infidel.

Usually these outrages did not lead to massacre; but in a few cases, where leaders completely lost control over their men, an orgy of killing was the result. This was certainly the case at St. Joseph's Convent, the site of what was to become one of the most publicised incidents of the entire Kashmir conflict. Here nuns, priests and congregation, including patients in the hospital, were slaughtered; and at the same time a small number of

Europeans, notably Lt.-Colonel D.O. Dykes and his wife, met their deaths at tribal hands.

This horrible affair, it would seem, took place on 28 October. At about the same time, one of the key eye-witnesses to what happened in Baramula, Sydney Smith of the London *Daily Express*, was captured by some Pathan tribesmen. Smith had driven out that morning from Srinagar to see what was afoot, and had managed to pass through what Indian sources imply was a battlefield (but clearly, if so, was only so in spots) only to blunder into a tribal band which, instead of murdering him, took him prisoner. He was soon rescued by a Pakistan Army convoy which had turned up on the scene in an attempt to seek out and evacuate any Europeans still in the Baramula-Gulmarg region; and a few days later he was brought back to Abbottabad where he re-established contact with the *Daily Express* to produce a highly dramatic account of the events in Baramula [*Daily Express* 10 November 1947]. Despite the sensationalism, Smith's account makes it clear that what happened was something which has occurred with almost all armies at one time or another; some troops had, under the stress of circumstances, run amok. Order was eventually restored. Smith speaks particularly highly of one Afridi leader, Suarat Hyat he called him, whose courage undoubtedly saved many lives that day, including Smith's.

Smith's conversation with his captors throws a certain light on the Pathan tribal state of mind at this time. He was told that the main tribal aim was the overthrow of Dogra rule in Kashmir; next, and a very close second, came the extermination of Patiala State followed by the capture of Amritsar, which was seen as the Sikh capital. Clearly the Sikhs were the main enemy, and the Patiala Sikhs, whom these men believed they had already encountered in their advance along the Jhelum Valley Road, seemed to be the worst Sikhs of all. In this frame of mind some of the tribesmen evidently responded rather emotionally to the news that yet more Sikhs were now descending from the air a few miles down the road in the direction of Srinagar.

The Indians side has maintained, largely on the evidence of European and American press reports which date to several days after the Indian reoccupation of Baramula on 8 November, that many thousands of people were killed there by the tribesmen (notably the reports in the *New York Times* by Robert Trumbull). The town was by this time virtually deserted, the Muslim population having fled, initially to avoid the attentions of tearaway tribesmen and then in fear of the advancing Indian Army, which was seen to represent the return of the Dogras and the vengeful wrath of Sir Hari Singh. The unfortunate Baramula residents may also, to judge from photographs published by the Indians, have suffered severe bombardment by Indian mortars and, perhaps, artillery; and this may have reinforced their reluctance to remain in this unhappy place. By subtracting the number of those who remained in Baramula when the Indians arrived, or who turned up shortly after, from the pre-crisis population of some 14,000 or so, casualty figures of up to 13,000 have been calculated. These, of course, are nonsense. What happened in Baramula was nasty; but it was certainly no nastier than what had happened to Muslims at Sikh and Hindu hands in many a town in the Punjab and Jammu a month or two earlier, and which was to contribute towards making this period of Asian history such a blemish on the record of the liquidation of the British Empire. It is probable that the total Baramula casualties were not more than 500, perhaps less.

The Baramula affair has become central to the Indian mythology about Kashmir. The intervention of 27 October 1947, be it legal or not, with or without the Instrument of Accession, has been justified by the fact that this horror was in progress; and only through Indian action could it have been prevented from spreading to Srinagar itself. To this claim one can offer two points in reply. First: as we have already suggested, it may well be that the very fact of the Indian intervention on 27 October actually guaranteed in reaction that some kind of cataclysm should take place on the part of the extremely unsophisticated tribesmen. There seems to be little doubt that the Baramula affair followed the Indian arrival at Srinagar airfield. Second: whatever happened in Baramula that day is nothing when compared to what has happened to Kashmiri men, women and children at Indian hands since 1989. Those massacres which it is argued did not take place on 27 October and the days which immediately followed were not prevented; they were merely postponed for two generations.

It has become axiomatic, and not only on the Indian side, that the Baramula massacres lost the Azad Kashmiri forces a great deal of support and good will among the Muslim inhabitants of the Vale of Kashmir including the large population of Srinagar. Here is one perceived base for Sheikh Abdullah's popularity, which most observers at this time, including some Pakistani leaders, believed was overwhelming among the people of the Vale; he was seen to have been the instrument of salvation from tribal massacre and rapine. It is interesting to find, therefore, (so circumstantial reports reaching the British High Commission in New Delhi indicated) that in fact on 30 October, a day or two after the events in Baramula (and the day after the formation of a Sheikh Abdullah Emergency Government), well attended anti-Sheikh Abdullah meetings were being held in Srinagar where it was announced that the present National Conference control over the city would soon disappear. The Afridis, it was said, were coming to rescue the Srinagar Muslims; and they would instal a true Islamic regime. Those police loyal to Sheikh Abdullah (all other police had disappeared by this time), were pelted with mud and stones when they tried to break up these assemblies. On at least one occasion they opened fire, killing a number of Kashmiri demonstrators.

A feature of the advance to Baramula by the Azad Kashmiris and their Pathan followers was the way in which tribal groups, never in themselves very large, came and went. Most of the original tribesmen who entered Baramula by 28 October were gone a day or so later. Some uncontrolled parties then spread out into the countryside, where they extended, independently, the area of plunder and rape to many villages before making their way back to the Jhelum Valley Road and transport home. Others mounted lorries and buses in Baramula and withdrew directly through Pakistan to the Frontier. Their place was taken by fresh groups, some of whom represented private ventures totally outside the command structure of Azad Kashmir.

The fact of the matter was that, once the Indian arrival at Srinagar was known, the authorities in Pakistan were for the moment quite unable, and in some cases so angry as to be unwilling even to try, to police the road from the North-West Frontier to the Kashmir front. The way was open to any who wished to use it.

Thus the considerable body of tribesmen whom the Indian forces ambushed at Shalateng, about five miles west of Srinagar on the Srinagar-Baramula road, on 7 November, does not appear to have been in any way part of the formal Azad Kashmir military organisation; rather it looks very much like a gathering of a number of freebooting parties which had driven along the Jhelum Valley Road to a point well beyond the Azad Kashmiri advance outposts. This body displayed a total lack of military prudence; and the result, according to some Indian sources, was the killing by Indian forces of over 600 men and the capture of more than a hundred vehicles. It was a massacre which had little military significance. Major Khurshid Anwar's men were already withdrawing to the west of Baramula.

Until 7 November the road from Pakistan to Baramula was used by others who were neither malevolent nor directly involved in the conflict. Sir George Cunningham, for example, the Governor of the North-West Frontier Province, on two occasions during this first week of November sent small convoys of lorries to Baramula from Peshawar with the mission of trying to find out what was happening and, if possible, rescuing any stranded British residents. The Pakistan Army, too, despatched patrols along this route with the same objective (but with great care not to get involved in any conflict with the Indians). A surprising number of individuals, including Sydney Smith of the *Daily Express*, as we have already seen, were picked up by such Pakistani parties and evacuated by way of Kohala and Abbottabad. Some unpublished contemporary British accounts show clearly that between 28 October and 7 or 8 November the situation both along the Jhelum Valley Road and in the adjacent tracts of Pakistan in the Hazara and Rawalpindi Districts was chaotic (even more so than it had been since the end of September), what with the temporary local collapse of law and order, the movement of refugees and the coming and going of opportunistic tribal groups. Not all these marauders came from the North-West Frontier. There is, for example, a report of a party of some 200 Muslims from the United Provinces which had somehow made its way at this time across from India to join in the *jihad* (and the loot); the Indians too, it would seem, experienced problems in policing their roads.

By 14 November, when the Indians had moved westward along the Jhelum Valley Road to reoccupy Uri, the situation stabilised. Khurshid Anwar, wounded, had withdrawn; and his place (until February 1948) was taken by Colonel Akbar Khan (also known by the pseudonym General "Tariq"). Akbar Khan, an experienced soldier (he had won the DSO during World War II), was able to establish some measure of discipline over the tribesmen who remained with him, and to inject into the Azad Kashmiris a degree of tactical and strategic professionalism which had often been lacking hitherto. A front between the Indian Army and Azad Kashmir was soon consolidated just to the west of Uri. Both in the portion of Kashmir Province (with Muzaffarabad as its capital) which remained in Azad Kashmir, and in the adjacent tracts of Pakistan on the right bank of the Jhelum River, political order was restored. Soon after this, heavy falls of snow brought all military activity here to a halt for the rest of 1947.

Meanwhile, a fourth sector had opened to the north of the Jhelum Valley Road, involving what, in the subsequent language of the Kashmir question, was often referred to as the Northern Areas (including Gilgit, Hunza and Nagar, and Baltistan). This, too, can to some degree be described as a reaction on the Muslim side to the arrival of 1st Sikhs at Srinagar airfield on 27 October.

In 1935 the Maharaja of Kashmir, Sir Hari Singh, had leased that part of the Gilgit Wazarat on the right bank of the Indus (in which lies Gilgit town), plus most of the Gilgit Agency and a number of dependent minor hill states including Hunza, Nagar, Yasin and Ishkuman, to the Government of India. For a period of sixty years the whole leased region would be treated as if it were an integral part of British India, administered by a Political Agent at Gilgit who was responsible to New Delhi, initially through the British Resident in Kashmir but, by 1947, through the British Political Agent at Peshawar. The Maharaja's rights in the leased territory were nominal. He no longer kept any troops there. Security was maintained by the Gilgit Scouts, a locally recruited Corps with British Officers in command and financed by the Government of India.

In April 1947, as we have already seen, with the prospect of the imminent British departure from the Subcontinent and the lapsing of British Paramountcy over the many Indian Princely States, the Government of India resolved to return all the Gilgit leased areas to the Maharaja of Jammu & Kashmir. Formally, this transfer appears to have taken place on 1 August 1947. The day before, 31 July, the Maharaja's Wazir, or Governor, Brigadier Ghansara Singh, had arrived in Gilgit. The populations of this region, solidly Muslim (mainly Shia) with the exception of a number of Hindu and Sikh merchants and shop-keepers in Gilgit town, were not consulted in any way about their return to Hindu Dogra rule after a dozen years under the British; and they expressed no enthusiasm whatsoever for what Ghansara Singh had to offer.

The real power in this remote corner of what was really Central Asia, the Gilgit Scouts, certainly did not welcome their reassignment to the service of the Maharaja. Their Commandant, Major W, Brown, and his Adjutant, Captain Mathieson, were in considerable doubt as to what they ought to do. Their service contracts had now, over their heads, been transferred from the Government of India to the Government of Jammu

& Kashmir State. They knew that their men were unlikely in any crisis to remain loyal to a Hindu Ruler. At the same time, they were reluctant to take any action which could be construed as open mutiny. In the event, they managed to hold the ring until the end of October 1947, despite the great traumas that accompanied Partition in the Punjab, without major catastrophe. They kept the Gilgit Scouts in check. The new Wazir, Ghansara Singh, occupied his official residence in the grandeur of impotence. The Gilgit Scouts were the *de facto* rulers, but Ghansara Singh's *de jure* position was not explicitly challenged.

On 27 October 1947, the day of the overt Indian intervention in the Vale of Kashmir, the nearest outposts of effective Jammu & Kashmir State power were two points on the Indus, Bunji and Skardu. Bunji, on the left bank of the Indus a few miles downstream from where it is joined by the Gilgit River, was home to the 6th Jammu & Kashmir Rifles, like the 4th Jammu & Kashmir Rifles a mixed Hindu-Muslim unit. Further upstream was Skardu, the capital of Baltistan, part of the vast Ladakh District of the old Jammu & Kashmir State, where there was a small garrison of troops who remained loyal to the Maharaja. Skardu at this moment was very much a sideshow, but Bunji, controlling the direct road from the Vale of Kashmir to Gilgit, was not. Here, apparently as yet another positive reaction to the arrival of the Indian 1st Sikhs at Srinagar airfield, the Muslims in the 6th Jammu & Kashmir Rifles mutinied, just as had earlier their brethren from the 4th Jammu & Kashmir Rifles in the Domel region. The Hindu elements were suppressed. Several Muslim officers from Bunji then made their way to Gilgit to contact the Gilgit Scouts and put to them various proposals for the future conduct of administration in the region, including the declaration of some kind of independent state, or group of states, in these mountains.

At the same time, Muslim tribesmen from all over the Gilgit Agency and its dependencies started to gather in Gilgit town. They clearly had two objectives. In the short term they wished to work out their anger against India by killing any Hindus and Sikhs they could find, which in practice meant the shopkeepers in Gilgit bazaar. In the longer term, they wanted to join with the political malcontents in Gilgit and the adjacent mountain states in the destruction of the established structure of authority. Faced with the prospect both of political chaos and massive bloodshed, Major Brown had to make some hard decisions very rapidly.

Brown at this time was just 26 years old. His only British colleague,

Captain Mathieson, equally youthful, was then several days march away in Chilas. As his superiors came to appreciate, Brown faced no easy task. The first step, in which Brown probably followed events rather than directed them, was the confining of Ghansara Singh and his associates under house arrest by the men of the Gilgit Scouts, many of whom wished to go further and slaughter the Maharaja's representative along with every other Hindu and Sikh in the Gilgit region. Brown managed to restrain his men, but in the end he felt that the situation demanded external political aid, which could only in the circumstances come from Pakistan. Having secured the offer of accession to Pakistan of the Rulers of both Hunza and Nagar (which, incidentally, Pakistan did not officially accept until March 1948, and only then after the two Rulers had aroused Liaquat Ali Khan, the Pakistan Prime Minister, by telling him that unless they received some formal acknowledgement of their earlier offer, they would seriously consider joining the Soviet Union), Brown formally told his men on 3 November that the Gilgit Scouts now served the Government in Karachi. On the morning of 4 November the Pakistan flag was raised over his headquarters.

The most interesting feature of this course of events, what Brown himself described as a *coup d'état* and its sequel, was that it took place entirely without any planning on the part of either the Pakistan civil or military authorities. Two weeks passed before the Government of Pakistan was able supply an administrator to take over civil power in the region, during which it was effectively exercised by Brown on his own. Brown was certainly not acting as a party to a British conspiracy, though it must be admitted that neither his immediate superior in Peshawar, Colonel Bacon, nor indeed Colonel Iskander Mirza, Defence Secretary to the Pakistan Government, were particularly unhappy when they heard about what was going on. Questions were asked in London about what junior British Officers were doing on the edges of the roof of the world; the age of Kipling and of men who would be king was over. It was resolved that Brown would be removed at the earliest opportunity, which turned out to be in January 1948, when he handed over to Aslam Khan (once Major Khurshid Anwar's deputy and now a Colonel and back in the official service of Pakistan).

All the same, both Brown and his British "masters" have been attacked by many Indian writers. This was, they have said, all part of an Anglo-American plot to maintain, using Pakistan as a surrogate, a Cold War foothold on the fringes of Soviet Central Asia. Curiously, a number of Pakistani commentators have attempted to deny that Brown had anything at all to do with the events in Gilgit. For example: the official Pakistani military history of the Frontier Corps, which appeared in 1967, states that the man who led the Gilgit "revolution" was one Subadar Major M. Babar Khan, and that Major Brown was in fact arrested by the Gilgit Scouts along with Brigadier Ghansara Singh, which is nonsense. No doubt there are elements of chauvinism, not to mention jealousy, at work in all this. Brown received no decoration from the Government of Pakistan, though the British eventually gave him a by no means munificent MBE. (In August 1993 Pakistan awarded Major Brown a posthumous SP – Star of Pakistan).

There can be no doubt that the events in Gilgit, following on the arrival of the Indians at Srinagar airfield on 27 October, were to transform the nature of the Kashmir conflict. The front, which would soon be established from a point just to the west of Uri southward, would now be extended to the north so that, running more or less east along the right side of the Jhelum Valley, it stretched to the upper Indus and then ended inconclusively in the glaciers of the Karakoram where today (1993) its terminus is still, in the Siachen glacier, a subject of Indo-Pakistani armed contest. Pakistan would retain a direct territorial contact with China, to be of immense geopolitical significance in years to come. India would not acquire a direct territorial contact either with Afghanistan or with the North-West Frontier Province, and thus miss obtaining the consequent opportunities for intrigues with Pathans both in and outside Pakistan to the detriment of that country's integrity. It was a failure which would without doubt contribute towards the survival of West Pakistan in future years.

Had Major Brown not acted as he did, all might have turned out quite differently. The men of the Gilgit Scouts knew nothing of Pakistan. Their outlook was provincial in the extreme. Left to themselves they would have disintegrated into violently squabbling factions advocating a variety of improbable goals: a federation of Karakoram states; independence for all including such micro-states as Gupis; even some re-establishment of the old relationship between Hunza and China (which the British had formally terminated only in 1936). Pakistan would not have intervened; the region was too remote and the leaders of the new Dominion were thinking about more pressing matters than the future geopolitics of

Central Asia. Sooner or later, once India had established itself firmly in the Vale of Kashmir, a column would have made its way from Srinagar to Bunji and then on to Gilgit. The whole political shape of South Asia would have been changed.

In due course the Gilgit Scouts sought to extend their area of influence eastward into Baltistan and Ladakh. In Ladakh they failed by a whisker to capture Leh, but Skardu in Baltistan eventually fell to them after a dramatic siege. All this, however, was in the future. Shortly after Major Brown had brought Gilgit into the Pakistan fold, winter set in and operations ceased until 1948. The nature of the Kashmir war, however, had been changed fundamentally. Up to the Gilgit *coup d'état* it could be argued that the conflict was between Azad Kashmir on the one hand and the Maharaja assisted by his Indian allies or masters (depending on how one regarded the reality and significance of accession) on the other. Now a third player was introduced, the Gilgit Scouts, who were not subordinate in fact, and indeed never so regarded themselves, to the Azad Kashmir regime which in due course was established in Muzaffarabad. The Gilgit Scouts owed their loyalties to Pakistan. In their area of operations, what came to be known as the Northern Areas, there were polities like Hunza and Nagar which had acceded to Pakistan. Despite Indian arguments of great complexity, it was impossible now to deny with any conviction that Pakistan had a legitimate interest in the Kashmir conflict which directly involved sectors of its sovereign territory.

One further byproduct of the overt Indian intervention of 27 October must be mentioned in passing. The State of Chitral, the major Princely State at the northern end of the Pakistan-Afghanistan border along what in British days had been known as the Durand Line, had in the nineteenth century accepted a tributary relationship to the Maharaja of Jammu & Kashmir, and this had been confirmed, under British supervision, in 1914. The relationship was essentially similar to that which, it has been argued, obtained between Hunza and Nagar and the Maharaja. On 6 October the Ruler of Chitral, the Mehtar, formally repudiated all ties with Jammu & Kashmir State. On 2 November, stimulated by the mounting crisis in the Vale of Kashmir following the arrival of the 1st Sikhs at Srinagar airfield, and its repercussions in Gilgit, the Mehtar acceded formally to Pakistan. Up to this point, it seems, he had been flirting with the idea of some kind of independence, possibly in association with Afghanistan.

THE WAR IN KASHMIR, OCTOBER TO DECEMBER 1947

In early November 1947, with the overt Indian intervention in the Vale of Kashmir a few days old, leading Indian politicians such as Jawaharlal Nehru, Vallabhbhai Patel, and Sardar Baldev Singh, and senior officials like V.P. Menon, started to visit Srinagar and what they clearly considered to be "liberated areas". The Indian Army, as one would expect in such a situation, put on a good show, aided by D.P. Dhar, an extremely articulate Kashmiri Pandit official acting as liaison between Sheikh Abdullah's regime and the Indians (he was destined later for great things). One result of these visits was to reinforce the politicians' belief in the rightness of their cause. The provisional accession under consideration by the Indian Cabinet on 26 October was rapidly evolving in Indian political orthodoxy into the mandate for a permanent Indian occupation justified by the worthiest humanitarian criteria.

There was, it must be admitted, a certain irony here. As the Indian politicians became increasingly committed to war, so some of the Indian professional soldiers began to appreciate that the campaign was probably only capable of the most limited objectives. Far better a negotiated settlement with Pakistan than the continued, and needless, shedding of blood. Moderate military voices, however, were drowned in the clamour of Indian moral rectitude. India, the politicians intoned, had a duty which could not be shirked; they must save the people of Kashmir from the tribal menace.

What was the tribal menace? How many tribesmen from the North-West Frontier and Afghanistan actually took part in these first weeks of the Kashmir conflict? Jawaharlal Nehru and other Indian leaders spoke at times as if the entire Azad Kashmir side consisted of nothing but Pathan tribesmen, the "raiders". As far as they were concerned, at least in public, there was no Poonch revolt (a view made abundantly clear by default in the Indian 1948 *White Paper*). By March 1948 Indian officials were saying that there were at least 124,000 "raiders" marauding in Jammu & Kashmir State.

The precise facts are not easy to ascertain. Sir George Cunningham, Governor of the North-West Frontier Province, kept in his diary (now among the India Office Records in London) a careful account of those tribal movements to and from the Kashmir front which came to his notice, and he was undoubtedly better informed than most. On 7 November 1947 he worked out that there must be about 7,000 Pathans involved in the Kashmir fighting in one way or another and on all fronts, of which

2,000 were Mahsuds, 1,500 Afridis and 1,200 Mohmands. The remainder were made up of a wide range of people including some from across the border in Afghanistan (not to mention the Muslims from the United Provinces in India). About 2,000 tribesmen were, it would seem, active along the Jhelum Valley Road. The rest were scattered over the Poonch and Mirpur regions of Azad Kashmir. No tribesmen remained long at the Kashmir front; groups were constantly going home to be replaced by fresh recruits. By March 1948 the Azad Kashmir command had decided that it would like to maintain a maximum level of some 2,000 Pathans, preferably Mahsuds, on the Uri sector (nearest by road to the North-West Frontier Province); elsewhere it felt it could probably manage well enough without any tribesmen at all, though it was, of course, willing to recruit a selected few such men for what had by now become its regular units. On no account did it want any more Afghans.

If tribesmen really wished to go to Kashmir, it would be hard for the Pakistan authorities to stop them without actually fighting them. A conclusion, evident already before the events of 22 October at Domel, was that to stand up against the tribes in this respect would result in a revival of trouble on the extremely difficult North-West Frontier where it was hoped that the Islamic Pakistan would do far better in keeping the peace, and much more cheaply, than had the British. Moreover, any forceful opposition of this kind would most probably have failed. As Sir George Cunningham reflected in his diary on the urge of some tribesmen to go to Kashmir: "at any rate there is no question at present of resisting the movement from this side, any more than a Turk in France in the twelfth century could have resisted the Crusade". In the event, after the first heady days of October and early November 1947, tribal enthusiasm for Kashmiri adventure dwindled considerably.

As 1947 drew to a close, it was already possible to detect a pattern in the Kashmir conflict. The combination of the Azad Kashmiris and the Gilgit Scouts, with varying degrees of assistance both moral and material from Pakistan, had produced the beginnings of a stalemate, and this the cleverer soldiers on both sides appreciated. There would, of course, be much fighting in the future. 1948 saw both the epic struggle for Poonch and, later in the year, the Indian victories at the Zoji La and Kargil which achieved control over the Leh-Srinagar road and not only gave India possession of the Ladakhi capital but also access to the desolate Tibetan borderlands without which the Sino-Indian conflict of the late 1950s would certainly have assumed a rather different form. By the beginning of 1948, however, astute observers could well have concluded that some kind of partition of Jammu & Kashmir State, between India on one hand and entities well disposed to Pakistan on the other, had been brought about in practice. It could follow that the preferable solution to the Kashmir problem lay in formalising this state of affairs and accepting the existence of legitimate Indian and Pakistani spheres in the disputed region. Already during the course of November 1947, it is certain, the British Commonwealth Relations Office was thinking along these lines in their quest for a mediated solution to the Kashmir crisis, as we shall see in the next Chapter.

V

To the United Nations, October 1947 to 1 January 1948

After 15 August 1947 Lord Mountbatten, once Viceroy presiding over all of British India and (as Crown Representative) those Princely States which acknowledged British Paramountcy, became Governor-General of an independent India with ultimate responsibility to an Indian Cabinet in New Delhi headed by Jawaharlal Nehru. Those bits of the old British Raj which were now Pakistan had, in effect, become foreign, and his constitutional attitude towards them was, perforce, that of an Indian looking out beyond the frontier. It took a while for all the implications of this fact to sink in, but by October 1947 it was clear to many of those concerned with the affairs of the Subcontinent that Mountbatten was no longer (some said he had never been) a neutral and impartial figure.

The main bridge now between India and Pakistan was not the Indian Governor-General (as it might just possibly have been had he become Governor-General of Pakistan as well) but the British Commonwealth Relations Office (which had absorbed the old India Office). It represented the Commonwealth, a body to which the two new Dominions had been persuaded (not without difficulties) to belong and which, through periodic conferences of Prime Ministers provided a potentially most valuable venue on neutral ground for meetings between the Indian and Pakistani leadership. The Commonwealth Relations Office also maintained High Commissioners in both New Delhi and Karachi, and thus provided a direct, and rapid, link between the two capitals.

The importance of the British at this juncture is easy to understand. Until August 1947 the whole Subcontinent had been under British dominion. Its civil service had been established by the British and its laws framed or approved by them. English was the language of the elite of all groups and cultures by which they communicated on political matters, and it was the key to higher education. The Army was organised on the

British model, had fought in two great World Wars under British Generals in fields of battle sometimes far removed from India, and even after independence a significant proportion of the officer corps in the two new Dominions was still British. Following the Transfer of Power British models for government and administration were retained. When in trouble, in these early days of independent life the leaders of both India and Pakistan turned instinctively to their British friends.

Thus it is not surprising that to the outside world the Indian Subcontinent immediately after the Transfer of Power still looked very much like a British preserve (what in other times might have been called a sphere of interest or influence), and squabbles between the successors to the British Indian Empire were still interpreted as if they were really British domestic quarrels. Even in the United States, where there was great interest in the idea of democracy and self government in place of British imperialism, the initial reaction to a crisis in Indo-Pakistani relations was to leave it to the British to sort out. All this, of course, would change. By the end of 1947 the United States was doing a considerable amount of thinking on its own about the details of South Asian politics and international relations (though still relying greatly on the British Foreign Office, rather less well disposed as it happened towards Pakistan than was the Commonwealth Relations Office, for information on the state of play in Kashmir). Other states, too, within the Commonwealth and without, would soon begin to work out their own policies. Nothing, indeed, helped accelerate this process as much as the involvement of the United Nations in the Kashmir question right at the start of 1948. This not only symbolised the British inability to cope with the problems of their former subjects, but also made South Asia a matter of great interest to countries whose diplomats hitherto possessed but the slightest knowledge of the geography, history and politics of the region.

In the weeks that immediately followed the outbreak of the Kashmir crisis in October 1947, however, it still seemed quite natural for the main burden of attempted pacification between the two successor Dominions to the British Raj to fall on the British High Commissioner in India, Sir Terence Shone, and his opposite number in Karachi, Sir Laurence Grafftey-Smith, both directly responsible to the Secretary of State for Commonwealth Relations in London, Philip Noel-Baker, a man of peace if there ever was one.

The first British High Commissioners to India and Pakistan are an interesting pair. Shone, the son of a General, had been in military intelligence during World War I, after which he had joined the diplomatic service. His last two posts had been Minister in Cairo and Minister in Syria and the Lebanon. He was, in other words, part of the British Foreign Office Arabist establishment with no previous experience of the Hindu world and its unique attitudes towards truth and reality. Grafftey-Smith was equally removed from the old Indian establishment. His diplomatic career had begun in the old Levant Consular service, and he been posted to Arabia, Iraq, Albania and Egypt (where he coincided with Shone). For a brief while during World War II he was sent outside the Arab world to Madagascar, but in 1945 he became Minister to Saudi Arabia before, in 1947, arriving in Karachi. Here was another of the Foreign Office Arabists, like Shone with no Indian predilections.

Where many of the old British India hands looked upon Pakistan as, at best, something extremely unwelcome, a sort of Oriental Eire, the consequence of a presumptuous splitting in two of the great British achievement in political unification of the Subcontinent, Shone and Grafftey-Smith fully appreciated that the idea of an Islamic society, and its inherent dislike of subjection to non-Muslims, was reasonable enough. It is possible that their attitude, while it did not resolve the Kashmir dispute in these initial stages (and nobody else at that time did any better), helped prevent it escalating into an all out Indo-Pakistani war in which the Muslim side might have been swamped (as, there can be no doubt, some British observers either anticipated or hoped). Attempts at mediation by these two remarkable men, under the highly moral pacifist supervision of Philip Noel-Baker, were indeed genuine. Their efforts were appreciated as such by the Pakistan side and often regarded with profound suspicion both by Mountbatten and by his Indian colleagues like Jawaharlal Nehru and Vallabhbhai Patel.

For nearly two months before Kashmir erupted in late October 1947, both Shone and Grafftey-Smith had gone to considerable trouble to find out what was actually happening in and around this "Switzerland of Asia" and what was in the minds of its indecisive Maharaja, Sir Hari Singh, and his subjects. By 22 October it had become clear to the two High Commissioners that, if given a free choice, the people of the State of Jammu & Kashmir, or at least those living outside parts of Jammu and Ladakh, would probably opt for a future in some kind of association with Pakistan. They clearly did not believe the doctrine that Nehru was continually expounding to Mountbatten, namely that Sheikh Abdullah was the sole legitimate voice of the Kashmiri people and that his influence inclined them strongly towards membership of an Indian secular state. Even after lurid reports of the Baramula massacres had marred the image of Pakistan in some Kashmiri quarters, both Shone and Grafftey-Smith appear to have remained convinced that Kashmir (Jammu and Ladakh were something else) *ought* (following the logic of Partition, if for no other reason) to go to the Muslim side of the Subcontinental great communal divide.

There was abundant evidence reaching the two High Commissions, particularly during the first half of October, that any attempt to bring about the Maharaja's accession to India would produce violent reactions elsewhere in South Asia. Not only would Pakistan resent it (though, perhaps, it could eventually be soothed through diplomacy) but others, less amenable, would take extreme umbrage. Shone sent one of his staff, Major W.P. Cranston, to Srinagar from 10 to 14 October to survey the scene. Cranston's report emphasised a number of points which the Indian side have tended ever since to suppress or ignore. There was indeed a civil war raging in Poonch. In Jammu at that very moment the Maharaja was engaged in a series of massacres of Muslims which some observers have considered to have been the nastiest of all in that wave of atrocities which followed immediately upon the Transfer of Power: conservative estimates suggest over 200,000 deaths here between August and December 1947. These events, naturally enough, set hordes of refugees on the move into Pakistan. Even if the Pakistan authorities might be persuaded to condone, however reluctantly, the accession of the State of Jammu & Kashmir to India, Cranston made it clear that there were people outside direct Pakistani control along the tribal belt of the North-West Frontier, some of them on the Afghan side of the Durand Line, who could well, aroused by reports of the killing of their fellow Muslims, take matters into their own hands and swarm across Pakistan into the State. Both the Mehtar of Chitral and the Nawab of Dir, powerful Rulers from the Frontier world, had warned the Maharaja most vigorously of this political reality.

All such reports reaching Shone were transmitted to Grafftey-Smith, and vice versa, and all reached the Commonwealth Relations Office in London. Thus the British diplomatic representatives in South Asia were not entirely taken by surprise by the events of 22 to 26 October. Trouble was clearly brewing in and around the State of Jammu & Kashmir. What did surprise them somewhat was the Indian response, seconded with such fervour by Mountbatten.

The first formal notification of the crisis which the British Government in London received from India was Nehru's telegram to Attlee of 25 October, which has already been noted in Chapter III. Explaining the Indian thinking about the possibility of helping the Maharaja of Jammu and Kashmir to resist the tribal "raiders", Nehru declared that:

> I should like to make it clear that [the] question of aiding Kashmir in this emergency is not designed in any way to influence the State to accede to India. Our view, which we have repeatedly made public is that [the] question of accession in any disputed territory or State must be decided in accordance with the wishes of the people and we adhere to this view. [1948 *White Paper*, Part IV, No. 1].

Shone promptly arranged for the text of this communication to be made available to the Pakistan authorities in Karachi (to whom Nehru managed to postpone sending a version of the text until two days later, 27 October, when it had already been overtaken by events).

The implication of the 25 October telegram seemed clear enough. The Indians were going to go slow on the Jammu & Kashmir accession question, thus leaving the settlement of the final sovereignty of all of the State, or its constituent parts, as a matter for inter-Dominion negotiation, and, indeed, prior to the opening of such negotiation they might also refrain from military intervention. So, at least, the British Government in London hoped.

Thus Attlee replied to Nehru on 26 October in these terms:

> I am clear ... that the use of armed force is not the right way to resolve these difficulties. I cannot conceive that, at best this could result in anything but the most grave aggravation of communal discord not only in Kashmir but elsewhere. Further, it seems unlikely that the Pakistan Government, or indeed any Government, could resist the temptation to intervene also with its own forces if you intervene with yours. This could lead to open military conflict between the forces of the two Dominions resulting in an incalculable tragedy.

Attlee urged Nehru to persevere in this apparent policy of restraint. Meanwhile:

> I also suggest for your consideration, as I am suggesting to Prime Minister of Pakistan, that it might be most useful step towards settlement of difficult

question of Kashmir's future if it could be discussed by you, Mr Liaquat Ali Khan and Maharaja of Kashmir as soon as possible at some suitable place.

The British evidently believed that it was just possible that Nehru might follow this advice, and even in Pakistan it was thought that the crisis was more likely to result in negotiations than in either overt Indian intervention or the Maharaja's formal accession to India. On the morning of 27 October, as (unknown to him) Indian troops were actually landing at Srinagar airfield, Grafftey-Smith reported to London a conversation with a very senior Pakistani official who expressed the view that

> the one thing most likely to stop the trouble in Kashmir would be a declaration by the Government of India that they would not accept the accession of Kashmir (even if the Maharaja proposed it) except after a plebiscite in the State. Such a view, if it was to have any value, should obviously not be accompanied by infiltration of Indian troops ... into Kashmir.

While Grafftey-Smith doubted whether Nehru would make such an explicit declaration, he certainly considered it worth a try to ask the Indians to do so; it might at least reinforce the merits of moderation. Particularly interesting here is the contrast between Grafftey-Smith's hopes and what Mountbatten was actually up to. While the British Government in London, and its representatives in the Subcontinent, hoped for inter-Dominion negotiations without either Indian intervention or Jammu & Kashmir's accession to India, Mountbatten was deeply committed to a policy of Indian military activity, coupled with accession, which would make such negotiations quite impossible.

When it became known during the course of 27 October that India had actively intervened in the State of Jammu & Kashmir and, moreover, had declared that the Maharaja had acceded to that Dominion, the British Government was dismayed. On the following day in a telegram to Nehru, Attlee could only repeat despairingly his earlier proposal for a tripartite conference involving India, Pakistan and the Maharaja of Jammu & Kashmir. There can be no doubt that in the immediate aftermath of the reported accession of Jammu & Kashmir to India, Philip Noel-Baker at the Commonwealth Relations Office, at this time also representing the views of Attlee, found extremely disturbing the way in which the Indians had apparently gone about inducing the Maharaja to join up with them.

The South Asia experts at the Commonwealth Relations Office were at this moment convinced that major errors had been committed by the Government of India in the conduct of its Kashmir policy.

First:

> in accepting, even provisionally, the accession of Kashmir to India. Military help could have been sent without accepting the accession of the State.

(It is an interesting, but hitherto unexplained, fact that the Commonwealth Relations Office officials never commented upon the questionable chronology of accession, for which all the evidence they needed was available in their own files by the middle of November 1947: perhaps they never noticed or, perhaps, they just not did want to know, it may be naturally reluctant to challenge the veracity of a personage as royal as Mountbatten).

Second:

> in sending troops without any attempt to secure prior high level consultation with the Pakistan Government, or even informing them in advance ... that this action was not intended to prejudice Kashmir's future but simply to prevent slaughter within the State, with wide and dangerous consequences to the communal situation outside it.

A final error was "in selecting Sikh troops for despatch to Srinagar". The Commonwealth Relations Office concluded that "all this suggests that one objective of the Government of India was to secure Kashmir's accession to India". It added charitably that "this may not have been Mr Nehru's intention," but "the Pakistan Government could hardly be expected to put any other interpretation on the action of the Indian Government".

The Commonwealth Relations Office indeed had a point. It is striking how little effort India actually made during these crucial days from 25 to 28 October to establish any contact with Pakistan. It was as if, having decided to resolve the Kashmir question by force, Nehru and his colleagues were determined to avoid any risk of other solutions being proposed at the last minute of which they would morally be obliged to take some notice.

The first direct high-level Indian communication with Pakistan over Kashmir seems to have been on 27 October (and after the Indian troops had started landing at Srinagar airfield), when Nehru sent Liaquat Ali Khan a version of his telegram to Attlee of 25 October, of which, as we have seen, the British had already supplied a text to Karachi.

The next contact between the two Dominions took place through the British military net. When M.A. Jinnah, Governor-General of Pakistan, had had time to reflect upon the implications of the reported Indian intervention at Srinagar airfield and the Maharaja's accession to India, which was late in the evening of 27 October, he felt profoundly betrayed by the Indian side; what was happening seemed to be a direct violation of the promises implicit in Nehru's telegram to Attlee of 25 October, to which reference has been made above. In a state of considerable rage and disgust he rang up the acting Commander-in-Chief of his Army, Sir Douglas Gracey, to order that Pakistan troops be sent in along the Jhelum Valley Road to challenge the Indians. Had this happened, of course, the Pakistan men would have encountered Lt-Colonel Rai's 1st Sikhs (less their dead CO) outside Baramula (armoured cars could have got there quite easily from Rawalpindi along the Jhelum Valley Road by noon on 28 October), and, no doubt, if inter-Dominion war had not erupted, which was in fact unlikely, at least serious inter-Dominion discussions would have started. Instead, Gracey ignored Jinnah's orders and sought instructions by telephone from his superior, Field Marshal Sir Claude Auchinleck, in New Delhi (who was still Commander-in-Chief of the armies of both India and Pakistan).

Auchinleck backed up Gracey's attitude, and said that he would come to Lahore early the next day, 28 October, to explain in person the facts of the situation to Jinnah. If Jinnah insisted on throwing the Pakistan Army into the Kashmir fray, Auchinleck told him, the British Government would have no option but to order the withdrawal of all British officers (BOs) from the Pakistan Armed Forces. Jinnah, following Gracey's opinion as to the current weakness of the Pakistan Army, reluctantly accepted that he could not get far at this time without the British officers. He gave in and withdrew his orders to Gracey.

In retrospect this was probably a great lost opportunity. Had Jinnah persisted it may well be that, in the end, the British officers would not have been withdrawn: it was, after all, an act which implicitly involved the withdrawal of British officers from India as well (unless the Attlee administration was prepared to find itself fighting alongside India against Pakistan, which seems improbable whatever some pro-Indian British officials might have argued), and would have been a severe blow to the British position in the whole of South Asia. Instead, the British might have been driven to impose some realistic Indo-Pakistani negotiations (perhaps using the same sanction on India as well as Pakistan, the withdrawal of British officers) at that crucial moment when the issue was still in the balance and neither side was too deeply committed. Jinnah, however, gave in to his military advisers, and that was that.

There are already a number of questions to be answered. Can it be true that Gracey had no suspicion as to what was afoot on the Indian side, in that senior British officers in the Indian Army played such a part in planning the Kashmir operation from at least 25 October? It seems unlikely, unless Gracey's access to any old boy network was extremely defective; and while not everybody liked Gracey, he had a circle of firm friends within the old Indian Army. Further, what did Auchinleck, notionally in supreme command of both Indian and Pakistani forces, know? He surely must have had more than an inkling of Indian thinking, experienced as he was in the Indian Army and its ways. If so, then had he discussed the matter with Mountbatten, and had any decision been taken as to what policy he ought to pursue? Finally, had the implications of the chronology of the Maharaja's alleged accession to India been explained to him?

If Auchinleck had received (and believed) the version of the accession story which was then already being put about by Indian politicians and officials, that India was only defending what was rightfully its own (accession having preceded intervention), then he would have found it hard indeed to condone the kind of action which Jinnah wished Gracey to initiate, however much his personal sympathies might have lain with Pakistan and all it stood for. A commander in his supreme position simply could not agree to authorise the troops of one member of the British Commonwealth, Pakistan, to attack what was now (after accession) the sovereign territory (even if provisionally) of another, India. Here was the first dividend from the manipulation of the chronology of the accession narrative already being paid out to the Indian side; it was destined in the longer run to continue to be a highly profitable Indian investment.

Jinnah was very suspicious about what Auchinleck had to say, though he does not seem to have blamed the messenger for the message. Auchinleck reported that

TO THE UNITED NATIONS, OCTOBER 1947 TO 1 JANUARY 1948

Jinnah withdrew orders ... [for Pakistan troops to enter Kashmir] ... but is very angry and disturbed by what he considers to be sharp practice by India in securing Kashmir's accession.

Quite what that sharp practice was, of course, Jinnah found it hard to specify; and his successors have been under the same difficulty ever since. They knew there was something funny about accession, but they were unable to put their fingers on the precise irregularities. They certainly did not appreciate all the chronological problems which have been examined here in Chapter III. They knew that what India actually did, overtly intervening on 27 October, conflicted with the implied assurances of Nehru's telegram to Attlee of 25 October. But all this was rather vague. The Pakistan side then, and subsequently, was unable to come up with specific charges adequately substantiated. In his telegram to Attlee of 29 October, Liaquat Ali Khan did indeed hint that the timing of accession was dubious, but he could supply no detailed evidence to support Jinnah's broadcast declaration that "the Government of Pakistan cannot recognise accession of Kashmir to Indian Union, achieved as it has been by fraud and violence". It is interesting that Pakistan has done no better since. For example: the *White Paper* produced by the Bhutto administration in 1977 quite failed to exploit those implications for the accession question set out in M.C. Mahajan's autobiography which had been available to Pakistani diplomats since 1963.

The Indian side, as insurance against too much international credence being placed on the "fraud" issue, by 29 October was bolstering up its own case with all sorts of fresh, or freshly expanded, arguments. Thus V.P. Menon then explained to Alexander Symon, the British Deputy High Commissioner in New Delhi, that it was still worth keeping in mind the geopolitical issue touched upon in Nehru's telegram to Attlee of 25 October. He told Symon that

> on a long-term view there was a very real danger of Russian penetration through Gilgit, in fact there were already portents of this in the unusually large numbers of foreign 'traders' who had recently been reported to have been seen there with plenty of gold in their possession. In this connection it was important to bear in mind that the Muslim inhabitants of Kashmir Province with its long international frontier were "have nots" to a man and would thus be easy and immediate prey to communist propaganda if orderly government were replaced by tribal rule. The next step would be India itself,

which faced many difficulties and ... might be fertile ground for communist propaganda.

This was good traditional "Great Game" stuff, but quite out of tune with Nehru's own non-alignment and sympathies with the socialist world. India soon dropped all anti-communist arguments; these were in the language of that Anglo-American imperialism which was shortly to be pointed to as one of the supports for the Pakistani conspiracy against India's rightful interests in the State of Jammu & Kashmir. "Great Game" or no "Great Game", however, India has continued to develop the underlying theme, that India, as the senior and most responsible power in the Subcontinent, has a duty to defend the whole region by such steps as the restoration of order in the State of Jammu & Kashmir.

One achievement of Auchinleck's visit to Lahore on 28 October was to secure a proposal from Jinnah (who made it clear that he would not accept the Maharaja's accession to India as legitimate) to the Indian leadership for the holding of a plebiscite to decide the future of the State of Jammu & Kashmir. Jinnah's plan was that full powers in the State should be granted to the Indian and Pakistani Army Commanders-in-Chief, Sir Rob Lockhart and Sir Frank Messervy, both British, to serve as Joint Commissioners with the task of restoring order and determining the popular will. The idea of consulting the people, already touched upon in Nehru's telegram to Attlee of 25 October, had been stressed in Mountbatten's letter to Maharaja Sir Hari Singh dated 27 October (and published the following day). It is not clear whether Jinnah had seen the text at this point, but it seems probable that Auchinleck brought a copy with him. At all events, Jinnah was the first to propose detailed arrangements for the holding of a plebiscite to which Mountbatten had only referred in the most general terms. In order to discuss a plebiscite and other related matters, notably the prompt termination of the actual fighting, Jinnah suggested that a Special Conference on the Kashmir situation be held in Lahore on the following day, 29 October. As communicated to Nehru by way of Lord Ismay, still acting as Mountbatten's right arm, the Conference was immediately accepted by India.

However, various Indian politicians and officials soon began to have second thoughts. V.P. Menon told Mountbatten that for Nehru to go to see Jinnah in Lahore now would be a bit like Chamberlain going to visit Hitler in Munich. He also declared that it was extremely undesirable to permit the creation of a any forum which might legitimise a Pakistani interest, let alone military presence, in any portion of the State of Jammu & Kashmir. Pakistan, he argued, had absolutely no business in the State and, therefore, no grounds for calling a Special Conference on this subject. Moreover, the very fact of the Special Conference could well cast doubt on the validity, albeit conditional, of the Maharaja's claimed accession to Indian which gave that Dominion a unique legal posture in the State, in that it might imply that the status of the State of Jammu & Kashmir was still in doubt. Such a risk more than counterbalanced any benefits which could possibly derive from a Special Conference. Vallabhbhai Patel, too, left no one in doubt that he opposed the idea of Indians going "crawling" to Jinnah on any terms whatsoever.

Mountbatten, who at this point really did want to get some sort of talks going, reluctantly agreed to drop the Lahore Special Conference idea for 29 October. Instead, he suggested that the Joint Defence Council meeting, which had been scheduled for New Delhi on 1 November, might be transferred, as a gesture of good will to Jinnah, to Lahore; and there, in passing as it were, the Kashmir crisis might be talked about in intervals between other business. This compromise was accepted by Nehru and, very reluctantly, by Vallabhbhai Patel. Mountbatten then rushed off to telephone Jinnah before anyone could change their minds. Jinnah, although suspecting that behind this postponement lurked some subtle Mountbatten-Nehru plot, agreed to the new arrangements.

Doubts on the Indian side, however, persisted. R.K.S. Chetty, the Finance Minister, objected to anyone from India, including Mountbatten, going to Lahore or anywhere else in Pakistan at any time and on any terms to talk about Kashmir. Gopalaswami Ayyengar declared that while Mountbatten might go, great political harm would be done if he insisted on Nehru's coming with him. Above all, it was evident with every passing hour that Nehru came to cherish less and less the prospect of meeting face to face the formidable, and extremely angry, M.A. Jinnah. Fortunately for Nehru, at the eleventh hour, on 31 October, the Pakistan Government published statements about what it maintained was the fraudulent nature of Indian (that is to say Nehru's) policy in Kashmir, repeating the words used by Jinnah in his recent broadcast. On reading this, Nehru said it was more than he could "take". The Pakistan leadership had insulted him; and he could not possibly be expected to go to Lahore. Mountbatten, supported by Ismay, agreed that because of "such a deliberate slap in the face" by Pakistan, "it was now out of the question to expect Pandit Nehru to go to Lahore". When he was told of this conclusion, Mountbatten recorded, "Pandit Nehru was apparently so delighted that he skipped off quickly to the next room and started telephoning his Cabinet colleagues to tell them that I had let him off". It was decided to plead in Nehru's case a diplomatic illness to justify his absence from the Lahore encounter.

The preliminaries to the Lahore meeting (as outlined here) have been described in great detail in a special report by Mountbatten, dated 11 November 1947, which is preserved in the India Office Records in London. This fascinating document is also a prime source for what actually happened at Lahore on 1 November, one of the crucial moments in the evolution of the Kashmir dispute.

Mountbatten, accompanied by Lord Ismay, arrived in Lahore on the morning of 1 November. He passed about 45 minutes with the Pakistani Prime Minister, Liaquat Ali Khan, who really was ill (unlike Nehru) and in bed at his private residence. After lunch he spent three and a half hours with the Governor-General, M.A. Jinnah, and then went back to talk briefly with Liaquat Ali Khan before returning to New Delhi.

Mountbatten opened his discussions with Jinnah by explaining the Indian plebiscite proposal which was now on the table, essentially the holding of the vote following the withdrawal of the Azad Kashmiri forces and their allies and with both the Indian Army and Sheikh Abdullah still in place. Jinnah objected to this particular scheme for a number of reasons. He felt that the State of Jammu & Kashmir, with its massive Muslim majority, belonged to Pakistan as of right as an essential element in an uncompleted Partition process. He feared that India was not sincere about free plebiscites but was merely trying to create precedents for some future electoral ploy in Hyderabad (where the desire of a Muslim ruler to govern his non-Muslim majority population in independence was already promising to become the next great trouble spot in the Subcontinent after Kashmir). Above all, he believed that any plebiscite held in the State of Jammu & Kashmir, under the protection of the Indian Army and with Sheikh Abdullah being permitted a free rein, would surely be manipulated so as to result in a victory for the Indian interest.

Jinnah then turned to the question of how the whole Kashmir situation had been brought about by Indian intrigue; but his language here was somewhat lacking in precision. It is evident that the Governor-General of Pakistan, though convinced that something was highly suspect about what was alleged to have taken place, had not yet seen through the various accession charades, and perhaps he never did. The possibility that he might stumble on something approaching the truth, however, clearly worried Mountbatten. He had already gone to the trouble, for example, to equip himself with that strange document, the denial by Lockhart, Elmhirst and Hall, the Army, Air and Naval Commanders-in-Chief in India, that they had anything to do with Kashmir planning before 25 October, and this version of history he now presented to the Governor-General of Pakistan. Here, in passing but firmly for all that, it was stated that the Maharaja's accession to India had taken place before "first light on the morning of 27 October" when the first Indian regular troops started their flight to Srinagar airfield. It may well be that Jinnah did not have total faith in the Indian Governor-General's veracity, but he was certainly too polite to challenge it to his face. Thus, obliquely and by default, a Pakistani seal of approval of sorts was accorded to the 26 October accession date which only grew stronger with the passage of time.

On the assumption that attack was the best defence, Mountbatten emphasised that the fundamental blame for the Kashmir crisis lay with Jinnah and his colleagues in Pakistan. The real problem, Mountbatten argued, was to be found in Jinnah's inability, or reluctance, to control his Pathan tribes. Not so, Jinnah replied. The problem, he maintained, arose entirely from India sending troops to Srinagar airfield. With the discussion fast approaching an impasse, Ismay now suggested that "the main thing was to stop the fighting"; and he asked Jinnah if he had any definite proposals to make.

Jinnah then outline the following plan. Both sides, that is to say the Pathan tribesmen and the Indian troops, must withdraw at once and simultaneously. Jinnah and Mountbatten would then assume full powers to take control in the State of Jammu & Kashmir and sort out all matters including the organising of a meaningful (and fair) plebiscite. Jinnah told Mountbatten that if he were ready to fly with him at once to Srinagar, he could guarantee that in twenty-four hours the business would be settled once and for all by the two of them on their own. Mountbatten replied that this might be all very well for Jinnah, who was evidently complete master in his own house; Mountbatten, however, was a constitutional Governor-General with no executive powers and responsible to the Indian Cabinet. He would naturally report back to his Indian masters what the Governor-General of Pakistan had to say, but he could not commit his political superiors in New Delhi to any line of policy or any specific action.

All this suggested strongly to Jinnah that the Indian side was merely playing for time. If real power rested not with Mountbatten but with Nehru, why had the Indian Prime Minister not come to Lahore? Jinnah doubted the truth of Mountbatten's assurances that Nehru really was sick in bed; and his suspicions were soon confirmed by reports (probably correct) from New Delhi that during 1 November Nehru had been out and about as normal. As far as Jinnah was concerned, the main achievement of the Lahore talks was to convince him, if he indeed needed convincing, that Mountbatten had been so absorbed into the Indian establishment as to be trusted about as much as Jawaharlal Nehru or Vallabhbhai Patel. The Lahore encounter did not, as the British Commonwealth Relations Office had hoped, do anything to bring the fighting in Kashmir to a halt.

Following the Lahore meeting of 1 November, efforts by the British to broker some kind of Indo-Pakistani settlement of the Kashmir issue went on, and, until the formal reference (by the Indian side) to the United Nations on 1 January 1948, the British were the only active mediators in this unhappy situation. They explored no fewer than seven possibilities, each of which, alone or in combination with others, might help bring about a solution: (1) tripartite discussions involving India, Pakistan and the Maharaja of Jammu & Kashmir as to the future of the State; (2) bipartite Indo-Pakistani talks on the same subject; (3) a plebiscite or referendum in the State; (4) mediation between India and Pakistan by some external entity, be it a leading British politician or lawyer, a representative of another country, or an International body other than the Security Council or General Assembly of the United Nations; (5) the granting to the State of Jammu & Kashmir of independence or autonomy, perhaps under joint Indo-Pakistani supervision of some kind; (6) partition of the State between India and Pakistan; (7) some kind of direct general supervisory involvement in the State of Jammu & Kashmir by the Security Council or General Assembly of the United Nations following a formal reference to that body.

The idea of tripartite talks involving the Maharaja Sir Hari Singh was dead by the time of the Lahore meeting on 1 November 1947. The Indian side, however, continued to experiment with the concept of some kind of Kashmiri participation by seeking to bring in the Head of the Maharaja's

Emergency Government, Sheikh Abdullah, as a legitimate party, which, of course, was anathema to the Pakistan side. Neither India nor Pakistan then showed much interest in what the future held for the Maharaja of Jammu & Kashmir.

Bipartite Indo-Pakistani discussions, by correspondence or meetings at various levels, started shortly after the Indian intervention on 27 October, and they have continued, with gaps due to exceptionally strained relations (including wars), until the present; but it must be admitted that for more than forty years these means (despite a handful of what can possibly be interpreted as near misses, notably in 1953 and, perhaps, 1962-3) have quite failed to produce a formula for settlement.

The British tried initially to reinforce the concept of a bipartisan approach by repeating to each side their communications with the other, and, where possible, addressing both sides in much the same language. Within a few days this device began to annoy the Indians who detected in it a British condonation of Pakistani wickedness, and, indeed, of a powerful bias towards Karachi which could not be tolerated. By 31 October, Lord Ismay (on behalf of Nehru by way of Mountbatten) was asking Sir Terence Shone to make sure that London included from time to time in its messages to the Indian leadership some passage explicitly critical of Pakistan. As V.P. Menon put it to Alexander Symon, the Deputy UK High Commissioner in New Delhi, the tone of Attlee's telegrams to Nehru to date had failed to show a real "appreciation of the difficult position in which the Government of India had been placed".

The idea of some kind of an independent or autonomous State of Jammu & Kashmir briefly surfaced in the very early days of the dispute. On 29 October, for example, V.P. Menon told Alexander Symon that

> one possible solution was for the establishment of Kashmir as an independent state subject to (a) joint Dominion control over her external affairs and defence which was necessitated because of her international frontier and (b) a standstill agreement with each Dominion on communications.

V.P. Menon, however, thought that while in theory there was much to recommend such a scheme, in practice it was unlikely to yield results. Nehru also, about this time, looked at the independence option; and he said he had no objection provided that the whole State of Jammu & Kashmir remained within the Indian sphere of influence and had nothing to do with Pakistan, which was not particularly helpful. It is interesting that of late (at least since 1990) the independence or autonomy of Jammu & Kashmir, or parts of it, subject to Indo-Pakistani joint supervision of some kind, has again been discussed by a number of those who seek an end to the ghastly violations of human rights which are now such a feature of the Kashmiri landscape. All joint supervision projects, however, suffer from the basic fault of the 1947 proposal. Given the massive ill will already present in 1947, and today (1993) enormously magnified, any Indo-Pakistani joint supervision of anything would lead but to protracted, and in all probability ultimately fruitless, argument. Pakistan, of course, would hardly welcome any plan which accepted the independence of the State of Jammu & Kashmir, but still within India's exclusive sphere of influence. India, on the other hand, continues to declare that it will never let the whole of the State of Jammu & Kashmir fall into the exclusive sphere of influence of Pakistan.

While it is clear that the Indian leadership was in no way predisposed towards the idea of an independent State of Jammu & Kashmir (even if prepared from time to time to give academic consideration to the possibility), it is fascinating to find that in these early days of the dispute India's nominee for the headship of a Jammu & Kashmir administration within the Indian fold, Sheikh Abdullah, was indeed profoundly attracted to such a prospect. He had advocated Kashmiri independence in 1946. He was still advocating this on 28 January 1948, when as a member of the Indian delegation to the United Nations he called on the U.S. Representative, Ambassador Warren Austin, to discuss the Kashmir situation. Austin concluded that

> it is possible that principle purpose of Abdullah's visit was to make clear to the US that there is a third alternative, namely, independence. He seemed overly anxious to get this point across, and made quite a long and impassioned statement on subject. He said in effect that whether Kashmir went to Pakistan or India the other dominion would always be against solution. Kashmir would thus be a bone of contention. It is a rich country. He did not want the people torn by dissension between Pakistan and India. It would be much better if Kashmir were independent and could seek American and British aid for development of country. [*Foreign Relations of the United Sates (FRUS) 1948*, Vol. V, Pt. 1, Washington 1975, p. 292, Austin's memorandum, 28 January 1948].

Ambassador Austin, of course, made it clear to Sheikh Abdullah that independence was not an option on offer. The only question before the

Security Council was whether Kashmir should go to India or to Pakistan. It is not difficult to see why in 1953 India found it expedient to remove Sheikh Abdullah from his post as Prime Minister of the Kashmir Interim Government.

The idea of the partition of the State of Jammu & Kashmir aroused much British interest at this time, and until at least the end of February 1948 it remained the favoured Commonwealth Relations Office solution to the problem (and Sir Alexander Cadogan of the Foreign Office was still considering a partition scheme in October 1948: see *FRUS 1948, V, 1, p. 424*), perhaps achieved (as Sir Owen Dixon on behalf of the United Nations was to propose in 1950) by means of a series of regional plebiscites. After all, it could well be argued that the whole Kashmir dispute was really the result of the incomplete nature of Partition in the Punjab on the eve of the Transfer of Power. Once Partition was completed by dividing up the State of Jammu & Kashmir (as an extension to the northern end of Radcliffe's boundary), the problem might go away and the two Subcontinental Dominions get down to the real business of learning to live with each other.

V.P. Menon had raised, rather negatively, the idea of partition in a conversation with Sir Terence Shone on 13 October, more than a week before the great Kashmir crisis erupted. Menon observed that

> the Maharaja [of Jammu & Kashmir] was finding it extremely difficult to come to a decision on accession. One suggestion that Kashmir Province might become part of Pakistan with the Maharaja remaining as ruler of Jammu only and acceding to the Indian Union only in that attenuated capacity did not ... appeal to the Maharaja.

Indeed, Menon thought that rather than face such a partition, the Maharaja would prefer to come to some arrangement with Pakistan. Whether Menon was telling the truth as then perceived in New Delhi, or not, we cannot say. It is interesting, all the same, that this partition option was very much on the table in Srinagar at this stage, as Major Cranston discovered when he was there from 10 to 14 October 1947. He reported to Sir Terence Shone that there was then much talk among local State worthies about the possibility of Jammu joining India, and the Vale, including Srinagar, joining Pakistan, perhaps with the Maharaja remaining nominally sovereign over both parts of the State. It seems likely that the Maharaja himself had speculated with some interest along these lines (contrary to what Menon had told Symon), and had discussed the possibility, directly or indirectly, with Nehru, who greatly disliked the idea of the dismemberment of his ancestral State. There is evidence, however, that the idea of such a partition still held some appeal for the Maharaja on 26 October as he withdrew with his cavalcade from Srinagar to Jammu across the Banihal Pass, abandoning the Vale of Kashmir – something was better than nothing.

The obvious merits of partition struck a number of British observers as the crisis developed. As Auchinleck put it on 3 November 1947, in a despatch to the Ministry of Defence in London:

> I suggest that there is only one practical solution which is for the parties to agree now to the partition of the State giving the Muslim portions, namely Kashmir, Mirpur, Poonch, to Pakistan and the Hindu parts such as Jammu to India. I see no prospect of settled peace in this area for years to come. A partition on these lines might improve the general relationship between the two Governments. The Maharaja would suffer but he merits little consideration. ... He might retain the title of Maharaja of Jammu.

The British High Commission in New Delhi agreed that there was a great deal of truth in Auchinleck's argument, but insisted that it was not up to the British to put such proposals either to India or to Pakistan.

A number of British officials in the service of Pakistan were likewise much attracted by the prospect of partition of the State of Jammu & Kashmir as a solution to the crisis which threatened to destroy what remained of the British achievement during three centuries in the Subcontinent. Thus Sir George Cunningham, Governor of the North-West Frontier Province, wrote to M.A. Jinnah on 1 December 1947 that

> the general feeling seems to me to be that Poonch and Mirpur must at all costs come into Pakistan, while Jammu, or a part of it, might go to India, and that for the rest a plebiscite, under impartial control, would be reasonable. [Cunningham Papers, India Office Records].

Cunningham, if by "general feeling" he included Jinnah, Liaquat Ali Khan, and other senior Pakistanis, was probably in error. Chaudhri Muhammad Ali, for example, who at this time reflected fairly accurately the views of the Pakistani leadership, "reacted most violently" when Ismay touched on the partition idea on 8 November.

Pakistan, indeed, from the outset showed great distaste for partition plans, an attitude which can still be detected today. There was one slightly paradoxical reason (among others) for this. The Indians always used the Kashmir case as an argument for the legitimacy of the secular state, which it was claimed India was. Implied was a challenge to the legitimacy of Pakistan as a state at all in that it was an arbitrary, and wilful, withdrawal of an Islamic rump from the rest of the former British Indian Empire. Treating the State of Jammu & Kashmir as a single entity which might as a whole vote for Pakistan, in some strange way reinforced Pakistan's validity, the equal to India, as a non-communal state among the community of nations. Partition, inevitably on the basis of Muslim or non-Muslim populations of the various regions involved, could only emphasise the communal nature of Pakistan to which Indians pointed with such disdain. This is not entirely rational, but it has exercised great psychological influence.

More rational was the Pakistan appreciation that any talk of partition could easily drift from communal criteria to a decision to divide the State of Jammu & Kashmir on the basis of who held what territory at the time. In that from the outset (27 October) India held Srinagar, the result would be Pakistan's permanent loss of the capital of Muslim Kashmir and a city of great symbolic and economic importance. Partition, in other words, could all too easily mean no more than accepting as the legitimate international border a *de facto* cease-fire line. Such a view of partition in the State of Jammu & Kashmir was indeed tacitly or explicitly to be adopted by the Indian side from time to time from the mid-1950s onwards. It usually aroused an extremely hostile reception in Pakistan.

By February 1948 the British had discovered that the prospects for a negotiated partition of the State of Jammu & Kashmir between India and Pakistan along the lines indicated by Auchinleck in the passage quoted above were virtually nil. They then concentrated on the plebiscite, a concept to which, after all, Mountbatten had given his endorsement in the published exchange of letters between the Maharaja of Jammu & Kashmir and the Governor-General of India relating to accession.

There was nothing very new about the idea of the plebiscite as a means of solving Subcontinental problems. As we have seen, it surfaced during the actual process of partition prior to the Transfer of Power in August. In September it had been actively considered in the context of Junagadh, a State with a Hindu majority population whose Muslim Ruler had at the very last moment of the British Raj decided to accede to Pakistan. As a solution to the Junagadh issue, Jawaharlal Nehru had made the following proposal to the Defence Committee of the Indian Cabinet on 30 September:

> we are entirely opposed to war and wish to avoid it. We want an amicable settlement of this [Junagadh] issue and we propose therefore, that wherever there is a dispute in regard to any territory, the matter should be decided by a referendum or plebiscite of the people concerned. We shall accept the result of this referendum whatever it may be as it is our desire that a decision should be made in accordance with the wishes of the people concerned. We invite the Pakistan Government, therefore, to submit the Junagadh issue to a referendum of the people of Junagadh under impartial auspices.

As in Junagadh so quite logically in the mirror image situation of the State of Jammu & Kashmir, an argument of which it is certain both Mountbatten and Nehru were aware. The Pakistan side, too, saw the point. It hoped that, handled with caution and skill, Junagadh might somehow be exploited as a precedent for Jammu & Kashmir.

The great problem about the plebiscite was not so much the idea as such, but how it would be implemented. Jinnah, on 28 October, accepted that a truly impartial plebiscite was probably the best answer to the Kashmir problem. As we have already seen, what he then urged was that the two Commanders-in-Chief, Lockhart in India and Messervy in Pakistan, should be appointed Joint Commissioners for the conduct of a plebiscite, during which time they should be authorised to use in concert such troops as might be required to keep order and ensure fairness. Jinnah, however, refused to consider any electoral process which could be conducted under the sole umbrella of the Indian Army and subject to the unchallenged influence of Sheikh Abdullah. Basically, with or without Sheikh Abdullah, this has remained Pakistan's objection ever since to plebiscite proposals floated or supported by the Indian side.

The Indians, on the other hand, have maintained from the outset a posture where a plebiscite can only be accepted if Pakistan has withdrawn all its "raiders" from every part of the State of Jammu & Kashmir, throughout which it is argued they have no right whatsoever to be. When Nehru first thought seriously about the implications of a plebiscite in the State of Jammu & Kashmir, just after the accession crisis, he explored the idea of substituting for it, by a political magician's sleight of hand, an electoral victory of Sheikh Abdullah and his party in some kind of local Jammu & Kashmir State process on a franchise and under conditions which, it must be admitted, were easy enough to manipulate, even in the presence of a limited number of observers from a body such as the United Nations. It may be that this was at the back of his mind in his much quoted broadcast over All India Radio on 2 November 1947 when he said that:

> we have declared that the fate of Kashmir is ultimately to be decided by the people. That pledge we have given ... not only to the people of Kashmir but to the world. We will not, and cannot back out of it. We are prepared, when peace and law and order have been established to have a referendum held under the auspices of the United Nations. We want it to be a fair and just reference to the people, and we shall accept their verdict. I can imagine no fairer and juster offer. [*1948 White Paper*, Pt. IV, No. 8].

In later years India from time to time claimed that such a "reference to the people" had indeed been made through various elections (all to some degree rigged) held in that part of the State of Jammu & Kashmir which it controlled. This has done nothing to increase Pakistan's confidence in the impartiality of any plebiscite which might be held in regions where Indian power reigned.

During the first days of the Kashmir dispute, in late October and November 1947, the idea of the plebiscite was actively explored by British officials both in London and in New Delhi. On 30 October, only three days after the overt Indian intervention in Kashmir, Attlee put a detailed plebiscite plan to Nehru. There would be an appeal to the tribesmen, mainly from the Pakistan side and exploiting the vast personal influence in the Pathan world of Sir George Cunningham, Governor of the North-West Frontier Province, to withdraw along the Jhelum Valley Road to Pakistan. The Indians would agree to withdraw *all* their troops once the tribesmen had left. At the same time, all Jammu & Kashmir State troops would pull out from Poonch (and, presumably, Mirpur) where the sole civil and military power would now be that of Azad Kashmir. There would then follow a plebiscite, if possible supervised by neutral (probably British) observers. At the same time, India would reaffirm that the "provisional accession" of the Maharaja of Jammu & Kashmir to India would in no way prejudice the final outcome of the plebiscite. If the vote went for Pakistan, then accession would be null and void.

Other plebiscitary projects continued to emerge from the British establishment. On 7 November, for example, Sir Algernon Rumbold (a veteran of the old India Office and now employed by the Commonwealth

Relations Office in London) drew up an elaborate plan for the holding of a plebiscite in which, once the various intruders from both India and Pakistan had withdrawn from the Srinagar region, British troops would be flown in to hold the ring while former British Indian Army officers supervised a poll in every District with a view to assigning it either to Pakistan or to India. The ruling British politicians were not impressed by this addition to the burdens of Empire in a region which they had already quit, and to which they were determined never to return.

Behind such proposals was much British study of the theory and practice of plebiscites and search for electoral alternatives. The Commonwealth Relations Office, for instance, first took a good look at the Jammu & Kashmir *Praja Sabha*, the Lower House of the State Legislative Assembly as established by the 1934 and 1939 Constitutions, with its 40 elected (on a communal basis) members out of 75 (1939 Constitution). Could a vote here serve in lieu of a plebiscite to decide the State's future? It was soon revealed that this Assembly was in fact based on a franchise of no more than six per cent of the total population. So, as Algernon Rumbold observed on 30 October, "the *Praja Sabha* is not a very suitable place to settle the future of Kashmir".

A Commonwealth Relations Office survey followed of those plebiscites which had been held elsewhere in the aftermath of World War I: Schleswig, Allenstein and Marienwerder, Klagenfurt, Upper Silesia, Sopron, as well as attempts at Teschen, Spisz and Orava, Vilna, were examples, as also Tacna and Arica in Latin America in 1925–26, and the Saarland in 1935. The main conclusion from this exhaustive investigation, greatly assisted by admirable research already carried out in 1943 by the Foreign Office, was that in practice it was only possible to hold a plebiscite in a region which had been put under the command of some strong neutral authority with adequate troops to establish and maintain order if need be. No such authority existed in the State of Jammu & Kashmir. As one very senior Commonwealth Relations Office official with vast experience on Indian affairs, Sir Paul Patrick, put it: "I do not believe a plebiscite is possible in Kashmir", and, he added, "in any case it could not be held during winter".

With this formidable array of precedents and opinions to hand, the Commonwealth Relations Office suspected that there might be better answers to the Kashmir conundrum that the classic plebiscite. A neutral commission could be formed, perhaps, to send officers (presumably

British) to the various Districts to ascertain the general state of public opinion. Actual voting might be confined to certain key areas, like the cities of Srinagar and Jammu. Here, of course, the old electoral rolls, with all their defects, would probably, lacking time to prepare anything better and more democratic, have to be used as a basis for the poll. The result would presumably have to be ratified in some way. The Commonwealth Relations Office was prepared to consider seeking a confirming vote by the 40 elected members of the *Praja Sabha* who were as near representatives of the will of the State's people as one could find (and among whom after the January 1947 elections the Muslim Conference held a powerful position). Any initiative for a plebiscite, of course, would have to emerge from the existing structure of Indo-Pakistani relations; there was no way that the British could impose it even if they wished to do so, which they certainly did not.

At a meeting of the Joint Defence Council in New Delhi on 8 November, the plebiscite question was discussed by V.P. Menon for India and Chaudhri Muhammad Ali for Pakistan, with Ismay holding a watching brief for Mountbatten. This appears to have been the most realistic Indo-Pakistani negotiation ever conducted on the vexed Kashmir problem. Attention was first paid to troop withdrawals. Chaudhri Muhammad Ali wanted simultaneous withdrawals by both sides. Menon thought this might be difficult for a variety of weighty, and wordy, reasons. Eventually he produced the following compromise:

> both Governments agree that all forces whether regular or irregular must be withdrawn from Kashmir at the earliest possible moment. The withdrawal will commence on the 12th November and will be concluded by the 26th November. The Government of Pakistan solemnly pledge themselves to do their utmost to ensure that the tribesmen are withdrawn according to this programme and that they make no further incursions. The Government of India undertake to withdraw their forces according to programme.

During these talks Chaudhri Muhammad Ali at one point asked whether a plebiscite was really called for at all as the entire State of Jammu & Kashmir (the plebiscite under consideration being for the whole State as a unit) must go to Pakistan in any case by virtue of its overwhelming Muslim majority. V.P. Menon replied that "he entirely agreed that Kashmir would go to Pakistan", but "emphasised that in view of what had passed, a formal plebiscite was essential". As for the actual plebiscite, it was agreed that

> a plebiscite will be held under the aegis of two persons nominated by the Governments of India and Pakistan with a person nominated by the Kashmir Government... [under Sheikh Abdullah] ... as observer. The plebiscite will be conducted by a British officer.

And, finally, the draft agreement contained

> a paragraph to the effect that neither Government would accept the accession of a State whose ruler was of a different religion to the majority of his subjects without resorting to a plebiscite.

This was, of course, a way of settling the Junagadh question as well (with a Muslim ruler wanting to join Pakistan despite the fact that a majority of his subjects were Hindu); and it seems probable that just such an exchange of Junagadh for Jammu & Kashmir had been contemplated by M.A. Jinnah and Liaquat Ali Khan since September. It was also, of course, laying down a distinctive marker for the possible solution of the looming problem of Hyderabad.

There is some evidence to suggest that such a surprisingly conciliatory attitude on the Indian side was inspired by V.P. Menon's mentor, Vallabhbhai Patel, the Deputy Prime Minister and in many respects Nehru's rival, who in his pragmatic way had been inclining towards the view that some sort of settlement with Pakistan was better than continued, and possibly escalating, war. Patel had no love for Jinnah and was no devotee of the idea of Pakistan. He was, however, a realist and, moreover, he did not, unlike Nehru, have a particular emotional attachment to Kashmir: his own roots were in Western India. He also, it seems, was still toying at this stage with some kind of bargain in which India's concessions over the State of Jammu & Kashmir might be exchanged for Pakistan's condonation of India's position over the future of Hyderabad (upon which, far more than Kashmir, depended the survival of India as the residual legatee to the British Raj). This was, at any rate, Chaudhri Muhammad Ali's interpretation of the situation.

For a very brief moment, then, the broad trend of Indian policy seemed clear: Kashmir would be settled by a truly fair plebiscite arranged by methods to be agreed bilaterally between India and Pakistan. There might be neutral supervision of the actual ballot; but there would be no external mediation.

TO THE UNITED NATIONS, OCTOBER 1947 TO 1 JANUARY 1948

In the event, it was Nehru's obsession with Kashmir which proved decisive in defeating this highly promising bilateral initiative. Patel's pragmatism, if it indeed had ever manifested itself, receded into the background, and soon it was replaced by his own brand of jingoism. V.P. Menon's efforts were rejected out of hand by Nehru, so Chaudhri Muhammad Ali told Ismay in a note dated 9 November in which he declared that "I am so sorry to have wasted so much of your time and I see no use in the further meetings that you suggested between yourself, Menon and myself". What seems to have happened, Ismay concluded, was that following the Indian reoccupation of Baramula (with all that was then said to have been revealed about Pathan tribal atrocities), Nehru was convinced that victory over the "raiders" and the man whom he believed was their arch-supporter, Jinnah, was at last in sight. He assumed, in other words, that the war was as good as won and that, thankfully, no direct negotiations with Pakistan about his beloved ancestral land were called for. India would obtain, and retain, control of the lion's share of the old State of Jammu & Kashmir. Instead, as we shall see, Nehru's thoughts turned increasingly towards a reference to the United Nations, which, even if undertaken jointly with Pakistan, yet somehow held out the possibility of a solution in India's favour without concessions to Mr. Jinnah. Already by 7 November 1947, Nehru was inclined to believe that his own country's case *vis à vis* Kashmir was so good that any objective external body like the United Nations could not fail to accept it. Ismay thought Nehru was being unduly optimistic. "They have got a frontier sore", he wrote prophetically, "which will last them for a very long time".

By the beginning of the second week of November, therefore, it was evident to British observers in both India and Pakistan that direct Indo-Pakistani discussions over a Kashmir plebiscite, or, indeed, over any other solution to the problem, whatever the officials on both sides might propose or negotiate, would probably be wrecked on the shoals of political obstinacy, particularly that of Jawaharlal Nehru. Sir Terence Shone in New Delhi began to wonder if the British could take a more active part in attempting to break the logjam. Perhaps the Secretary of State for Commonwealth Relations, Philip Noel-Baker, might preside over a committee consisting of Jawaharlal Nehru and Liaquat Ali Khan or representatives named by them. A "flying visit" by Noel-Baker to the Subcontinent had, after all, just (5 November) been requested by Liaquat Ali Khan. The scheme met with qualified approval by Mountbatten, who discussed it with Attlee on 12 November while he was briefly in England for the Royal Wedding (between his nephew Prince Philip and Princess Elizabeth).

A week or so later the Commonwealth Relations Office had concluded that this Noel-Baker committee would probably be futile. In any case, the British could not propose it; the request would have to come from the Subcontinent. It might be better, perhaps, to arrange for Attlee himself to play a role, possibly presiding over a Nehru-Liaquat Ali Khan meeting when next the two Dominion Prime Ministers were in London. By 19 November both Ismay and Sir Terence Shone had concluded that even this would not work. "The matter is so important", Shone reported to London, "that a visit ... [to the Subcontinent] ... by the Prime Minister himself would be justified and have the greatest chance of success". Attlee, however, did not have the slightest intention of going to India or Kashmir on what he clearly saw was a hopeless mission from which he could not possibly return with credit.

The Commonwealth Relations Office now came up with yet another idea. Maybe the President of the International Court of Justice at the Hague could be asked to nominate some suitably neutral person to preside over a joint Indo-Pakistani Commission "charged with the duty of making recommendations as to the procedure for ascertaining the will of the people of Kashmir regarding their future". For a moment Noel-Baker's enthusiasm was aroused. "Would you like me", he cabled both Nehru and Liaquat Ali Khan on 20 November,

> to take private soundings from the President of the International Court of Justice to discover whether he is of the opinion that it would be practicable and would be willing to try to get together a small team of international experts, not connected with India, Pakistan or the United Kingdom, in the event of a joint request being proffered by the Governments of India and Pakistan for this to be done?

The short answer, at least in the opinion of Sir Terence Shone, was "no". Jawaharlal Nehru, increasingly convinced that India would win the war outright and recover all of the State of Jammu & Kashmir, seemed for the moment to have once more lost his enthusiasm for any kind of mediation to arrange a plebiscite.

Moreover, there had been ever since the beginning of the month a growing irritation among the Indian leadership at the very idea of mediation. What was there to mediate? The Indian case was just. The State of Jammu & Kashmir, by virtue of the Instrument of Accession, rightfully belonged to India. There was nothing to be said in favour of Pakistan. What to some appeared to be even-handed, in New Delhi was interpreted as pro-Pakistani bias. All these "international experts" about whom Noel-Baker talked would probably be viewed in New Delhi as both unwanted and inherently anti-Indian. In any case, as one member of the British delegation to the United Nations pointed out to the Commonwealth Relations Office, Nehru had a particular antipathy to the International Court of Justice because he believed it had been unduly sympathetic to South Africa in another issue close to Indian hearts. To mention the Court to Nehru, therefore, "can only have the effect of the proverbial red rag".

Finally, there was the United Nations itself, an organisation which had, after all, been expressly designed to sort out disputes between sovereign states. The United Nations had, as we have seen, been considered at the time of the Transfer of Power as a possible agent in supervising the partition of the Punjab and Bengal; but the use of its services had been rejected for a variety of reasons. In his broadcast of 2 November, as has already been noted, Nehru pointed to the possibility of the conduct of a Kashmir plebiscite "under international auspices like the United Nations", thus formally bringing that body into the Kashmir equation, albeit in a tentative way. Neither Jinnah nor Liaquat Ali Khan were then interested; they still stood by the bilateral approach of Jinnah's proposals to Mountbatten of 1 November. In his formal reply to those proposals, however, Nehru declared on 7 November (at the very moment when, as we have seen, subordinate officials were negotiating a bilaterally arranged plebiscite) that after Pakistan had withdrawn all its tribesmen, India, once law and order had been restored in the State, would also begin withdrawing its own men; and next, he suggested, India and Pakistan might make a joint approach to the United Nations for help in the supervision of a plebiscite. By 12 November he had worked out a fairly detailed statement of policy along these lines which was explained to U.S. State Department officials in New York by his sister, Mrs. Vijaya Lakshmi Pandit. She

> expressed India's desire for Kashmir plebiscite on basis of adult suffrage to be held next spring [1948] under UN supervision. She mentioned plan

under which India and Pakistan would agree beforehand to take case [to] Se[curity] C[ouncil] with joint request that commission of small and disinterested countries be sent supervise and observe Kashmir elections and definitely indicate desire that Great Powers including USSR not participate in plebiscite commission. [*FRUS 1947, III*, Washington 1972, p. 184].

This plebiscite, election, or reference to the will of the Kashmiri people, of course, was intended to involve in a single operation the whole State of Jammu & Kashmir, all the territory that had once formed part, or the Indian side argued had once formed part, of the dominions of Maharaja Sir Hari Singh including both Azad Kashmir and those territories in the Gilgit region which had been leased to the British in 1935.

From the Pakistan point of view an apparently cooperative offer along these lines was fraught with problems. Even if the Indian troops did eventually withdraw, who would take their place in that part of the State of Jammu & Kashmir which had been under Indian occupation? Would it be a force nominally subject to Sheikh Abdullah's administration, and in reality an Indian army by another name? This Pakistan could not accept. In any case, on what franchise would the plebiscite be conducted and who would draw up the electoral rolls? If Sheikh Abdullah and his Indian friends had a direct hand here, Jinnah was not interested. As the British High Commission in Karachi noted on 9 November, unless a host of procedural matters were first "agreed between the two Dominions, the efforts of any team from UNO or elsewhere will be futile and more harm than good will have been done".

When Mountbatten was in England for the Royal Wedding and had his talk with Attlee on 12 November, the Commonwealth Relations Office was asked to comment on the merits of United Nations involvement in Kashmir. It was, on the whole, rather lukewarm about it for two main reasons. First: it might be hard to avoid the inclusion of some representative of the "Slav Bloc", that is to say the Soviet Union and its friends, in any United Nations commission deputed to the Subcontinent. Second: it still hoped to secure some kind of general Indo-Pakistani settlement over not only Jammu & Kashmir but also Junagadh and Hyderabad. The United Nations presence in but one of these issues, Kashmir, could greatly complicate discussions on the other two outstanding questions.

By 16 November the Pakistan attitude seems to have changed. It was clear that nothing would come of Jinnah's 1 November proposals. Perhaps a reference to the United Nations, though in quite what form was yet to be decided, might yield results where everything else appeared to offer no bright prospects. Pakistan would naturally wish to seek mediation on all possible aspects of the Kashmir question, which presumably meant in addition a wide range of issues, social, political and economic, arising out of the mechanics of Partition and the subsequent shape of Indo-Pakistani relations. The Indians were fully aware of the thinking in Karachi, and were, accordingly, contemplating a United Nations reference of their own. They would confine themselves to the narrowest possible agenda relating to the conduct of a plebiscite under clearly defined conditions which they considered would favour their cause, notably the removal of all military forces which might be deemed favourable to Pakistan. Given these divergent attitudes, Sir Terence Shone in New Delhi argued that the British might be well advised to consider making their own approach to the United Nations and thereby at least obtain some terms of reference which would not immediately be swamped by Indo-Pakistani acrimony. This was an interesting idea. It was not, however, followed up by London.

On 23 November, Nehru in a telegram to Attlee explained precisely what he had in mind with respect to the United Nations. He noted that

the appropriate authority to provide the machinery ... [for a plebiscite] ... would be the Security Council or Secretary General of the United Nations. But necessary approach can only be made when normal conditions have been restored in Kashmir.

Pakistan could help restore such conditions, Nehru went on, by ceasing to aid the "raiders"; it should deny them both supplies and safe passage across Pakistani territory. Under whatever circumstances, in Nehru's view at this moment a possible United Nations reference must still lie in the fairly distant future; there was no hurry.

Pakistan, however, now applied some surprisingly effective, if oblique, pressure to modify Indian attitudes. On 24 November its Representative at the United Nations, Zafrullah Khan, approached Hector McNeill, Minister of State at the Foreign Office then in New York with the British Delegation, to announce that Karachi had just asked him for advice on how the United Nations could take part in a Kashmir plebiscite, and in what way and to whom in the United Nations Pakistan could appeal. Zafrullah Khan also indicated to McNeill another possibility, a direct appeal to the British Government to mediate between India and Pakistan through the nomination of a very senior judge, a Law Lord no less, a super-Radcliffe (one wonders if Zafrullah Khan, who did not lack a sense of humour, was entirely serious here). In London this would not be welcome, as Zafrullah Khan was immediately advised. On the following day Zafrullah Khan told McNeill that he was now definitely in favour of seeking some form of plebiscite administered under direct United Nations supervision. No attempt was made to conceal any of this dialogue from the Indian Delegation at Lake Success.

Faced with the prospect of Pakistan's suddenly appealing to the United Nations, the Indian side became much more receptive to the idea of some kind of reference there of its own long before Nehru's ideal conditions of a Pakistani-induced total withdrawal of the "raiders" had been met. On 27 November Indian and Pakistani officials in New Delhi, following a meeting of the Joint Defence Council the previous day, produced an extremely conciliatory document. Hostilities in Kashmir would cease on the basis of Pakistan using its influence to get the "Azad Kashmir" forces (not "raiders" as hitherto) to withdraw as quickly as possible, and then, fighting having stopped, India "would withdraw the bulk of their forces, leaving only small contingents at certain points". Next, India and Pakistan would ask the United Nations to send a commission to the Subcontinent to seek recommendations from not only the two Dominions but also the Government of Jammu & Kashmir (which was here evidently considered as an entity in its own right, presumably with Sheikh Abdullah as its political head) as to how best to set about organising a free and unfettered plebiscite. Discussion of details by Nehru and Liaquat Ali Khan would be postponed until the next Joint Defence Council meeting, due to be held at Lahore on 8 (originally planned for 6) December, when there would be time to give them the consideration which they merited. Ismay, who was present throughout, noted that while the gulf between the two Prime Ministers was still wide, "the atmosphere in which the discussions were conducted was more friendly than he had known".

Unfortunately, this euphoria did not last. For various reasons, including a visit to the Kashmir front by Vallabhbhai Patel and Baldev Singh on 2 December and some alarming intelligence reaching Nehru about alleged Pakistani "aggressive" intentions, the Indian leaders, so Shone reported, "have started once more to think in terms of fighting out the issue and not holding a plebiscite". At the same time, Liaquat Ali Khan had visited the Pakistan-Jammu border near Sialkot, where he heard more horror tales about of what was happening over in Jammu

District on the Indian controlled side. All the Muslim males, without exception, he believed, had been butchered and "Muslim girls had been abducted and a large number were being kept naked in a camp by Sikhs and were being permanently raped" (and there was much truth, it is to be regretted, in these accounts of the Jammu atrocities in late November and early December 1947). The result was that the 8 December Joint Defence Council meeting achieved nothing on Kashmir. As Shone reported to London on 10 December, "so far as Kashmir was concerned I understand that an almost complete impasse was reached". All thought of a joint Indo-Pakistani approach to the United Nations was abandoned.

The impasse arose formally from the old question of troop withdrawals prior to the holding of the plebiscite. India was insisting on the total departure of the "raiders" (by which it meant all forces, Azad Kashmiri and Pathan) before it made any move. Pakistan refused to contemplate a plebiscite with Sheikh Abdullah in a position of power and called for an Indian agreement for the establishment of an impartial interim administration, according to Shone, to

> be set up in Kashmir before the plebiscite to take the place of Sheikh Abdullah's administration which they [Pakistan] accuse of persecuting all Pakistan supporters in the State and by its very existence in authority of ensuring that the voting in the plebiscite will go in favour of India.

India did in fact agree in principle that at some fairly remote future date it might accept the establishment of some kind of Indo-Pakistani influenced coalition regime in the State of Jammu & Kashmir for purposes of a plebiscite. Even to consider this now, however, would undermine the authority of Sheikh Abdullah, which was quite out of the question. In other words, India would not for a long time to come accept a plebiscite on terms with which Pakistan would be at all comfortable.

It was at this juncture (8 December), so Sir Terence Shone, who was singularly well informed about what was going on in the highest levels of government in New Delhi, maintained, that Mountbatten came up with a proposal (this was to be confirmed by Mountbatten's own account now preserved among his papers) which seemed to offer an escape from the current doldrums into which the talks had drifted. Mountbatten explained to both Nehru and Liaquat Ali Khan that it looked as if the only way out was to find some acceptable (if not of necessity entirely, or equally, congenial to both sides) formula or device by which to introduce the

United Nations into the discussions as a neutral third party. He put it to Liaquat Ali Khan that to this end he might have to accept on behalf of his country a process which was initiated through a complaint of some kind by India in the United Nations against Pakistan for "having helped the raiders". It was probably only on this basis that Nehru would actually bring himself in the end, however much the matter might be discussed in theory, to accept in practice any form whatsoever of United Nations presence. He asked Liaquat Ali Khan, therefore, in the interest of peace in the Subcontinent, to show restraint while this "indictment" mechanism was set in motion. Pakistan would always have the right of reply once matters were being discussed at Lake Success.

Liaquat Ali Khan, in a hitherto unacknowledged attitude of altruism, accepted the full implications of Mountbatten's proposal. He said he would agree, if need be, that the reference to the United Nations should take the "form of an accusation by India that Pakistan was assisting the raiders". And so the final Indo-Pakistani discussions of December 1947 took place in the shadow of what can only be described as a projected collusive arrangement, rather like some divorce proceedings where Pakistan had accepted the role of, if not the guilty party, at least the party which would not at the outset protest its innocence too loudly.

Evidently with Mountbatten's scheme in mind, at the 22 December Joint Defence Council meeting Nehru solemnly handed over to Liaquat Ali Khan a letter accusing Pakistan of assisting the "raiders" in Kashmir and requesting that Pakistan refrain forthwith from aiding them in any way. Unless Pakistan promised in writing in the very near future to give up this unpleasant habit of meddling in the State of Jammu & Kashmir, the Government of India

> will be compelled to take such action, consistently with provisions of the United Nations Charter, as they may consider necessary to protect their interests and discharge their obligations to the government and people of Kashmir.

While the Pakistani diplomats were still digesting the implications of this document, which was only just within the parameters of "indictment" indicated by Mountbatten, the Indians sent a reminder on 26 December. Liaquat Ali Khan, having finally resolved to stick with the Mountbatten scheme, replied on 30 December in a quite conciliatory tone, although surrendering none of the points of grievance against India in all their various disputes, and, indeed, outlining them in prodigious detail. Referring to Nehru's letter of 22 December, Liaquat Ali Khan said that

> I trust that I am right in assuming that your letter is not an "ultimatum" but a fore-runner of a formal reference of the matter to the UNO. If so, nothing could be more welcome, for you will recollect, this is exactly what the Pakistan Government has been suggesting throughout as the most effective method of ironing out our mutual differences. I am sincerely glad that you propose at last to adopt this particular line of approach.

The Indians have said that before Liaquat Ali Khan's letter of 30 December was to hand they had concluded that, as no reply seemed to be forthcoming to Nehru's letter of 22 December, they might as well go ahead anyway and approach the Security Council. Accordingly, they drafted a letter to this end, a version of which was ready by 28 December. The text was at once sent to the British Cabinet in London by way of Sir Terence Shone, with an explanatory telegram direct from Nehru to Attlee. It was also sent to the Government of Pakistan in a memorandum which, however, owing to some extremely convenient cryptographic muddle, did not actually get read in Karachi until 3 January 1948. Thus on 31 December the Indian appeal to the United Nations was transmitted to the Indian Embassy in Washington without having been seen or commented on by the Pakistan side. On the following day, 1 January 1948, the Indian Representative at the United Nations, P.P. Pillai, passed it along to the President of the Security Council, F. van Langenhove of Belgium. It is possible that the contents had already been communicated to Trygve Lie, the Secretary General of the United Nations, on 30 December 1947.

This is an extremely revealing, as well as important, document. A unilateral complaint by India was lodged under Article 35 of the Charter of United Nations, where, so India observed,

> any member may bring any situation, whose continuance is likely to endanger the maintenance of the international peace and security, to the attention of the Security Council.

The major point here was that under Article 35 any action by the Security Council, or indeed the General Assembly, would be essentially of an advisory nature. The Council could, in the interests of international peace, look into the matter and suggest ways in which tempers could be cooled down and tensions eased. The sanctions available were severely limited, relating to recommendations for international co-operation and the like. Anything decided under Article 35 alone could never turn into something mandatory. The contrast must be made with other routes provided for by the United Nations Charter which could even lead to the unleashing of a fearful panoply of United Nations military might (such as was soon to be seen in the case of Korea and, more recently, against Iraq).

The use of Article 35 was in the spirit of the Mountbatten proposal for Pakistan to submit to some tolerable form of indictment by India in order to persuade Nehru to go to the United Nations at all. Rather less in this spirit were the actual contents of the document which P.P. Pillai, the full nature of which apparently still unknown to the Pakistani side, sent up to the President of the Security Council on 1 January 1948. While technically it was merely drawing the Council's attention to the disturbances then going on in Kashmir, and soliciting suggestions as to how the risks to the general peace could be reduced, probably (there was a clear implication) by arrangements for some kind of plebiscite, yet in fact it was a stark indictment of Pakistan as an aggressor and the sponsor of violence. Interestingly, while the suggestion is evident that the State of Jammu & Kashmir, the site of the crisis, was sovereign Indian territory, yet the Indian charge (para 5) did not say that the Maharaja of Kashmir actually *did* accede to the Indian Union on 26 October (and prior to the Indian intervention), merely that he had requested that he be allowed to do so. Perhaps the Indian diplomatic draughtsman were still being careful lest unwelcome facts about the chronology of accession might come to light during the course of United Nations debate.

Although relating to the relatively mild climate of Article 35, the Indian presentation of 1 January 1948 contained a sting in its tail (para 13) which was anything but mild (and which certainly alarmed Attlee when he saw it outlined in Nehru's telegram of 28 December). Declared India:

> in order that the objective of expelling the invader from Indian territory and preventing him from launching fresh attacks should be quickly achieved, Indian troops would have to enter Pakistan territory; only thus could the invader be denied the use of bases and cut off from his sources of supplies and reinforcements in Pakistan. Since the aid which the invaders are receiving from Pakistan is an act of aggression against India, the Government of India are entitled, under international law, to send their armed forces across Pakistan territory for dealing effectively with the invaders.

However:

> as such might involve armed conflict with Pakistan, the Government of India, ever anxious to proceed according to the principles and aims of the Charter of the United Nations, desire to report the situation to the Security Council under Article 35 of the Charter.

On this basis, India continued, the Security Council was asked to prevent the Pakistan Government from participating in any way in what was then going on in the State of Jammu & Kashmir, and to ensure that no tribesmen were able to continue to use Pakistan as a base for their depredations in territory for the security of which India was now responsible. Of course, such requests far exceeded the scope of Article 35. The Indian letter, however, was an effective vehicle for issuing a threat of direct intervention in Pakistan, a threat which, perhaps surprisingly, does not seem to have emerged in so unambiguous a form during the Indo-Pakistani discussions which had been in progress since 1 November.

Had such a specific threat been made to M.A. Jinnah and Liaquat Ali Khan by Nehru outside the parameters of the United Nations, the Pakistan leadership would certainly have responded with like for like, and it might well be that the situation would have escalated out of control into open inter-Dominion war. Having accepted, however, the Mountbatten proposal that Pakistan put up with a bit of Indian indictment in order to get to the United Nations and away from the existing impasse, the Pakistan leadership felt itself morally obliged to try to ignore Indian menaces and persist in the processes of negotiation covered by Article 35. But it is likely that had Jinnah or Liaquat Ali Khan been able to study the Indian letter to the Security Council *before* it had been presented, they might have reacted in a somewhat different way. They might, for example, have immediately introduced their own complaint against India, invoking not Article 35 but some alternative procedure which carried far more forceful sanctions. They could thus have denied India the valuable advantage, in diplomacy as in war, of firing the first salvo.

In the event, there can be no doubt that the tone of the Indian letter failed to calm the language of Indo-Pakistani relations. Jinnah and Liaquat Ali Khan felt they had yet again been deceived by Mountbatten. The terms of the Indian reference to the United Nations, as we have already noted, went far beyond the spirit of "collusion" which Mountbatten had urged the Pakistan side to adopt on 8 December; and it was widely believed in Karachi that Mountbatten, the Governor-General of India, knew all along that this is what would transpire. Here, then, was a real turning point in the Kashmir story. Both Jinnah and Liaquat Ali Khan (and generations of Pakistani statesmen in years to come) could not avoid suspecting that Mountbatten was in some way reflecting the inner councils of the Government in London. It was probably significant to them that they had received no advance warning of the contents of the Indian reference from British diplomats who hitherto had been only too willing to keep each side informed as to what the other was up to. British credibility suffered accordingly, and from the initial stages of the United Nations involvement British mediation lost much of the value it had once possessed in Pakistan.

Nehru and his colleagues had never showed great enthusiasm for British mediation. What they wanted was British approval of the absolute rightness of their case, and from the British media at least, notably after the visit to Kashmir in February 1948 by Kingsley Martin, the influential editor of the left wing *New Statesman*, there were to be some gratifying developments. Meanwhile, the war in the State of Jammu & Kashmir during the course of 1948 did indeed become overt conflict between Indian and Pakistani regular forces. The United Nations debates and negotiations from the outset took place against a background of extreme acrimony which contributed nothing towards a durable settlement of the problem (though they certainly helped bring about the cease-fire which came into effect on 1 January 1949). Little has changed over the next four decades and more.

In later years the Indian side was increasingly to dismiss the idea of a Kashmir plebiscite as something an outside world, unfamiliar with the realities of the Subcontinent and all too often hostile to the moral values which India proclaimed, was endeavouring to impose upon it. It is an indisputable fact, moreover, that in the Indian reference of 1 January 1948 the Security Council were not asked specifically to do anything about a Kashmir plebiscite. The Indian request was that the Security Council would somehow stop the Pakistan authorities from aiding and abetting the "raiders" in the State of Jammu & Kashmir, though in quite what way, under Article 35, it is hard to specify.

It is quite clear, however, from the narrative outlined above that Jawaharlal Nehru, when he authorised a reference to the United Nations, was knowingly approaching a forum which would inevitably turn to the possibility of a plebiscite as a solution to the problem presented to it. Even though the Indians did not ask the Security Council to devise the terms and conditions for a plebiscite, they did make the following argument.

> The grave threat to the life and property of innocent people in the Kashmir Valley and to the security of the State of Jammu and Kashmir that had developed as a result of the invasion of the Valley demanded immediate decision by the Government of India.... It was imperative on account of the emergency that the responsibility for the defence of the Jammu and Kashmir State should be taken over by a government capable of discharging it. But, in order to avoid any suggestion that India had utilized the State's immediate peril for her own advantage, the Government of India made it clear that once the soil of the State had been cleared of the invader and normal conditions restored, the people would be free to decide their future by the recognized democratic method of plebiscite or referendum which, in order to ensure complete impartiality, might be held under international auspices.
> [*United Nations Security Council Official Records Supplement*, November 1948].

Thus, once the "aggression" had been stopped, India wanted a "plebiscite or referendum" under "international auspices", which meant in effect the United Nations. Obliquely, therefore, the Indian reference of 1 January 1948 did indeed put a Kashmir plebiscite on the agenda.

The idea of a Kashmir plebiscite, of course, came as no surprise to the British, one of the permanent members of the Security Council; and the Americans, also permanent members, after Mrs. Pandit's statement of 12 November, understood that something along these lines was what India was seeking. All this would have been communicated to the other members of the Council. The only problem, it must have seemed, was how to devise a set of suitable circumstances for the holding of a plebiscite. This surely appeared to be the major question posed to the Security Council by the Indian reference. The emphasis, however, had to be on the word "suitable". There were ways of holding plebiscites which in Indian eyes were definitely "unsuitable"; and it was highly unlikely that India and Pakistan would see eye to eye on what was equable and reasonable.

All this having been said, however, there is no escaping the fact that it was India which through its initial reference to the United Nations effectively, if not directly, first asked that body to help in bringing about a Kashmir plebiscite. The United Nations in its various plebiscite proposals which emerged during 1948 (and subsequently) was only doing what the evidence indicated India had wished it to do.

It must be asked, as a concluding speculation, whether the kind of plebiscite contemplated by the Security Council of the United Nations as a result of the Indian reference actually promised to be the best solution to the Kashmir problem. In treating Jammu & Kashmir as a whole, this type of plebiscite would inevitably raise problems arising from the essentially fragmented nature of the State. The Northern Areas, that is to say the former Gilgit leased tracts and adjacent territory acquired by Pakistan during the course of the first Indo-Pakistani Kashmir war, was something quite different from the Vale of Kashmir, the old Kashmir Province, which, again, was culturally, communally and ethnically distinct from Buddhist Ladakh or those parts of Jammu with majority Hindu and Sikh populations. It may be, as many British observers noted during the first days of the Kashmir dispute in late 1947 and early 1948, that some form of partition of the State by one means or another (including "regional plebiscites" as Sir Owen Dixon was to propose to the United Nations in 1950) would be more conducive to the restoration of peace. We will, of course, never know since "regional plebiscite" schemes failed in the first days of the Kashmir dispute, as they have subsequently, to arouse much Subcontinental enthusiasm.

In the context of the United Nations it may well be that the Kashmir question must be examined in parallel with that of Palestine, another region under British control from which the Attlee Government resolved to withdraw in February 1947. On 29 November 1947 the United Nations General Assembly approved a plan for the partition of Palestine between Arabs and Jews. The result was not peace but escalating war, the consequences of which were already all too apparent during the final days of 1947. In January 1948 the war spread beyond the limits of the former British Mandate with the entry of Syrian troops on the Arab side. It could well be that some observers in late 1947 and early 1948 anticipated that a partition plan for the State of Jammu & Kashmir would have had a similar outcome, an extension of the area of open hostilities: far better explore the possibilities of plebiscites.

VI

The Birth of a Tragedy

On 1 January 1948, when the issue was first referred to the Security Council of the United Nations, the Kashmir cancer in the international relations of South Asia (if one may be permitted an unpleasant but by no means inapt medical analogy) was already well established. In that such malignancies are best cured if detected and treated early, by the beginning of 1948 time was fast running out. In the event the involvement of the United Nations yielded no cure: indeed, to persevere with our medical analogy a moment longer, it produced some equivalent of metastasis, an increase in complexity and gravity of the problem, which probably guaranteed that therapy would fail. So, at any rate, one might conclude from an examination of the case history of the more than four decades of conflict and polemic which have followed.

Could earlier treatment, some decisive action before 1 January 1948, have avoided a process which has evolved inexorably into the Kashmir tragedy that is with us today? The story which we have examined here does suggest a number of possibilities which certainly merit examination.

The immediate roots of the Kashmir tragedy lie in the mechanics of Partition, in the way in which the British surrendered their imperial role in South Asia. While it is true that the British had no option (confronted with a lack of both funds and will) but to terminate their Indian Empire shortly after the end of World War II, yet there were then available to them a number of ways of achieving this end. The Attlee Government, for example, originally planned, once the decision to leave India had been made (in February 1947), to depart on or about June 1948 (and it could well, in practice, have turned out to be a bit later). It was Mountbatten, apparently on his own responsibility, without prior consultation with London, and for reasons which have never been satisfactorily explained, who advanced the date of the Transfer of Power to 15 August 1947. The result was that a great many things which might have been done within the original timetable now had to be ignored and left to chance.

It is hard to escape the conclusion that Mountbatten's self-inflicted haste contributed enormously to the ghastly consequences of the partition of the Punjab, the Punjabi holocaust in which many millions of people were obliged to move and more than half a million were slaughtered, for all of which the last Viceroy must bear his considerable share of the responsibility. Perhaps a slower process of British withdrawal would still have been accompanied by its quota of atrocities, but it is easy to argue that the scale might well have been reduced very considerably had the two successor Dominions been better able to establish the authority of their local administrations in the crucial new frontier zone before the final act of Transfer of Power had been completed. Less haste might have meant the generation of less ill will. The explosion of animosity between Muslims on the one hand and Sikhs and Hindus on the other which accompanied the process of Partition in the Punjab guaranteed that the subsequent course of Indo-Pakistani relations would be dominated by sentiments of communal hostility founded upon the undisputed fact of all too real atrocities. Here was the psychological backdrop against which the opening scenes of the Kashmir tragedy were enacted.

The speed with which the process of the Transfer of Power was executed ensured that some of the more complex administrative problems of the Indian Empire involving the redistribution of territory, spheres of influence, resources and assets, problems which the successor states would inevitably inherit come what may, were left unresolved. No problem, in the Kashmir context, was of greater significance than that arising from the existence of the Princely States.

It was really rather absurd, as had indeed already been recognised by those responsible for the 1935 Government of India Act, to consider a process of Transfer of Power in the Indian Subcontinent which did not deal explicitly with the States. These States constituted more than one third of the total area of the old British Indian Empire, and it was certain that they would not on any account be left to their own devices by the successor regimes. In practice, of course, the vast majority of the States were to all intents and purposes incorporated into the two new Dominions either on the eve of the final Transfer of Power or shortly after it, though the implications for the States' future of the 1947 arrangements would take some time to be revealed in full. The doctrine of Paramountcy was used, as the Nawab of Bhopal put it so clearly in the memorandum quoted in Chapter I above, to justify what amounted to the abolition of the State system. Paramountcy, in other words, was a charade. If the States really were in the process of abolition, then it would have been better if that process had been so managed as to bring the maximum benefit to both India and Pakistan; and it was undoubtedly foolish to permit the creation of situation which would poison the subsequent shape of Indo-Pakistani relations.

One can point to many features of recent South Asian political history which might have had a happier aspect if the States problem had been tackled more systematically prior to the Transfer of Power. It might, for example, have been possible (as indeed some in 1947 hoped for in the creation of PEPSU, Patiala and East Punjab States Union) to bring about a form of political entity which would have satisfied Sikh aspirations to a degree that would have prevented their current disaffection and alienation. But we must concentrate here on Jammu & Kashmir.

A glance at a map of the proposed 1947 Partition line in the Punjab would have revealed that it by no means represented the totality of the contemplated border between India and West Pakistan: it was merely the portion of that border which ran through what was directly administered British Indian territory in a single Province. On the Indian side, both to its south and its north, lay Princely States, to the south some States of the Rajputana group and of Kutch in Western India, and the State of Jammu & Kashmir to the north. On the Pakistani side, to the south of the Punjab was the unquestionably Muslim State of Bahawalpur and the undoubted Muslim-majority Province of Sind (one of the core elements of Pakistan), and to the north, as in the Indian case, there was the State of Jammu & Kashmir. Southward of the Punjab the Indo-Pakistani border effectively, and logically, followed the Hindu-Muslim divide along the established limits of these States which were on the whole well enough understood (though the border between Kutch State and Sind was to present some problems in later years). Northward of the Punjab, however, there was no such conveniently obvious line (based essentially on communal criteria) since the State of Jammu & Kashmir, according to the strict and formal interpretation of the doctrine of Paramountcy which the Mountbatten Viceroyalty adopted, could actually produce three theoretical Indo-Pakistani border alignments with staggeringly different geopolitical implications.

First: if the State of Jammu & Kashmir (taken in its entirety) opted to join Pakistan, then the new inter-Dominion boundary would be that which today separates Ladakh from Himachal Pradesh, with Pakistan extending eastward right up to the western border of Tibet where it crossed the Indus. Second: if the State of Jammu & Kashmir (again taken in its entirety) went to India, one consequence would be that the new border would be removed far to the west, following the line of the River Jhelum to the east of Rawalpindi and then extending along the edge of the old North-West Frontier Province all the way to Afghanistan, with which country India would be in direct territorial contact. Finally: if the entire State of Jammu & Kashmir remained independent, then along these two border lines both India and Pakistan would march with a newly established sovereign polity in a part of the Subcontinent which since at least 1890 had been fairly strictly controlled by the British. Unlike the British, the two new Dominions would now be cut off from direct contact with a crucial point in Central Asia where both China and Russia either touched or closely approached the Indian Subcontinent.

The differences between these possibilities were far from minor. There could be a severely truncated West Pakistan, or an India excluded from all contact with "the pivot of Asia", Sinkiang, or, finally, the creation of a new independent state along the Subcontinent's northern border to add to the geopolitical problems posed by Nepal, Bhutan and Sikkim. Had there been more time in which to organise the partition of the British Indian Empire, there can be no doubt that the problem of the State of Jammu & Kashmir in the context of Indo-Pakistani boundary policy would have received a great deal of attention. As it was, despite various attempts to bring Jammu & Kashmir into the Indian orbit before 15 August 1947 (which have been examined above), the State emerged from the moment of Transfer of Power in a strange limbo, notionally independent, actively sought after by India, and menaced by no less than two internal civil conflicts, in Gilgit and Poonch, in which one party would inevitably call upon Pakistan for help. It is hard to escape the conclusion that a more detached examination of the prospects for the State of Jammu & Kashmir than that provided by the Mountbatten Viceroyalty would have resulted in a serious consideration of the possibility of a partition of the State along with the partition of the Punjab.

There were two powerful arguments for such an approach. First: the State was situated right over the fault line, so to say, in north-western India which separated Muslim-majority areas from those which were in the language of the 1946 Cabinet Mission plan called "General" (that is to say not Muslim-majority, a euphemism for Hindu adopted out of deference to Congress's secularist pretensions). This line was the product of a long process of historical evolution, and it was well understood by those experienced in Indian affairs. Had the Radcliffe Award border been extended northwards through the State of Jammu & Kashmir it would in fact have roughly followed such a divide, with Hindu Jammu and Buddhist Ladakh on one side, and Muslim Poonch and Mirpur, Kashmir Province and the Gilgit region and (perhaps) Baltistan on the other.

The merits of following this fault line, which appear quite to have escaped Mountbatten's notice, became all too obvious by October 1947. To British observers of the Kashmir crisis in its opening stages it was evident that partition along this line provided the obvious (and, probably, the only) geopolitical solution to the problem. If it were right, politically and morally, to partition British India on the basis of contiguous Muslim-majority areas, then it was absurd to ignore the communal divide in the State of Jammu & Kashmir.

Second: there was also, as Professor Michel has pointed out in his classic study of the Indus rivers, an argument of economic geography. What we have called a communal fault line also represented a natural divide of sorts between the major sources of irrigation vital to the two halves of the partitioned Punjab and adjacent territory. As we have seen, virtually all the water flowing into the west Punjab, and much flowing into the east Punjab as well, came from or through the State of Jammu & Kashmir. For either India or Pakistan to hold all of the State was to create a threat to the water supply, and thus to the economic viability and chances of prosperity, of whichever side did not control the State. As has already been noted, the fact was that in the event the State of Jammu & Kashmir was *de facto* partitioned as a result of the October 1947 crisis and its sequel, not of course in the best possible way, but efficiently enough to give Pakistan some control over Kashmiri waters, which surely contributed enormously to Pakistan's viability in the critical first years of its life.

What about Paramountcy? This constitutional doctrine, as has been noted in Chapter I above, was always rather artificial, and there were many British experts who doubted its validity or relevance (a careful reading of W. Lee-Warner's *The Protected Princes of India*, London 1894, can provide much food for thought). In any case, its strict application could well have left the State of Jammu & Kashmir in a somewhat uncertain position after the Transfer of Power in 1947. At this moment, so the doctrine had it, the State would have reverted to a what it had been prior to the treaties (which now lapsed) between its Ruler and the British Crown.

On the basis of this argument it could be maintained easily enough that what now remained in these circumstances was the core of the State, Jammu, Ladakh and Baltistan, which had been Gulab Singh's territories before the 1846 Treaty of Amritsar. Other territories which were included within the limits of the State in 1947, such as the Vale (Kashmir Province) and the Gilgit region, came by way of the British either through the Treaty of Amritsar or after it. The Vale of Kashmir, for example, had been transferred by the British to Gulab Singh in 1846 on terms which certainly possessed a conditional aspect, capable even of being interpreted as if it implied an element of leasehold. Again, the Gilgit region had been acquired very largely under British direction and as a product of British policy, and in 1935 the bulk of this region had been leased to the Government of India for sixty years. Finally, it would not have been too difficult to cast doubt on the Maharaja's title to Poonch, as we have seen in Chapter II: this could have been treated easily enough as a State in its own right with a good prospect of the Poonch dynasty opting for a close association with Pakistan.

Thus it would have been perfectly possible, had the will been there, for the Government of India in the final days of the Indian Empire to maintain that Gulab Singh's descendent, Hari Singh, must now lose title over territories such as these which would revert to British India (or in the case of Poonch to a separate existence in its own right): he would have to content himself with the old Jammu and its pre-1846 dependencies in Ladakh and (perhaps) Baltistan.

If the term Jammu were understood to refer to the territory under that name in 1846, that is to say without the Bhimber district (in 1947 included for administrative purposes in a unit under the name Mirpur and deeply involved in the Poonch revolt) which had formed part of Dhian Singh's legacy to his two sons and remained a quite separate entity until well after the Treaty of Amritsar (as we have seen in Chapter II), then Jammu and its dependencies (even with overwhelmingly Muslim Baltistan) would have possessed a comfortable non-Muslim (Hindu, Sikh and Buddhist) majority. Its future, presumably in association with India, would have presented no major problems. Evidence from 1948 suggests that both the Buddhists of Ladakh and the Hindus and Sikhs of Jammu would have welcomed incorporation, lock, stock and barrel, in the Indian Union.

Those territories (such as Gilgit, Kashmir Province and Poonch) which on this basis would have reverted to British India, or have been detached from the State of Jammu & Kashmir, were all Muslim-majority areas contiguous to the Pakistani core. They, too, would have presented no problems. With the Transfer of Power they would have become part of the new Dominion of Pakistan. While Sheikh Abdullah might not have been too happy, other players on the Srinagar political stage would have welcomed such an outcome, which certainly would not have been resisted in the way that Indian control has been contested since 1989.

This is not the place to speculate further upon such alternative interpretations of the doctrine of Paramountcy. A variety of arguments can be advanced for Poonch and Bhimber (Mirpur), the Valley (Kashmir Province), and Gilgit and its hinterland including Hunza and Nagar. In the event, the Mountbatten Viceroyalty at an early stage went out of its way to exclude such an approach. The crucial decision, taken in April 1947, was over the future of the Gilgit lease. As we have seen, despite the opposite interpretation of Paramountcy in the case of Berar (leased by the British from Hyderabad), Mountbatten determined to return (interestingly, in the face of objections from Jawaharlal Nehru) the Gilgit leased territories to the direct control of the State of Jammu & Kashmir before the Transfer of Power. Here was a lost opportunity to initiate the process of partitioning the State, and it may indeed have been the result of a deliberate attempt to frustrate such a process. Other possibilities, such as the explicit separation of Poonch from the dominions of Hari Singh, totally escaped British notice in the hectic last days of the Raj.

If the State of Jammu & Kashmir were not to be partitioned (following one possible interpretation of Paramountcy), then it might well have been wise for the British in the final stage of the Transfer of Power to ensure that it were recognised as an independent entity with formal guarantees from both Pakistan and India. It is clear that Pandit Kak wanted something like this; and, given the importance of the State to its two neighbouring Dominions, only by some such formula could the economic and psychological requirements of both be satisfied without conflict. British policy under Mountbatten, however, was explicitly opposed to the idea of an independent Jammu & Kashmir, not only because there was a general antipathy to the proliferation of South Asian sovereignties but also because the Viceroy was clearly convinced by his friend Nehru that the proper place for this particular State was, on democratic and geopolitical grounds, in India (if only because that was what he was told Sheikh Abdullah wanted). Mountbatten, therefore, as we have seen, abetted the overthrow of Pandit Kak on 11 August 1947 which ended all realistic prospects for the State's independence (though ironically, as has already been noted, this may really have been what Sheikh Abdullah, in his heart of heart's, wished for all along, if we accept what he wrote in his 1944 *New Kashmir* manifesto).

After the Transfer of Power solutions for the Kashmir problem became far more difficult to define, let alone implement, if only because there was no longer a single supreme authority in the Subcontinent. Everything required Indo-Pakistani agreement at a time when feelings on both sides were being increasingly aroused by reports of the progress of the Punjabi holocaust. It was just not possible for the two Dominions, even had the leaders on both sides been in full possession of the facts (which was certainly not the case), to talk realistically with each other about the civil conflicts which were developing within the State of Jammu & Kashmir, in Poonch and in the Gilgit region. Thus the Kashmir crisis of October 1947 developed in a total absence of Indo-Pakistani consultation.

It may well be, even against this particular background, that some useful Indo-Pakistani dialogue might have emerged in late October 1947 had it not been for the strange story of the alleged accession of the State of Jammu & Kashmir to India (related in Chapter III). Some official British observers at the time were convinced that the emphasis by Mountbatten upon the State's accession to India was a serious mistake in policy. Accession was not essential to justify Indian intervention. Once claimed, however, accession could not so easily be ignored. There would always be those Indians of legalistic bent who would argue that the State of Jammu & Kashmir was now a permanent part of the Indian Union, from which no force could detach it. This emphasis was all the more unfortunate given the way in which the Indian side deliberately distorted, even fabricated, the facts of accession, as we have seen. The Indian claim that India only intervened in Kashmir *after* the Maharaja had acceded to India was false, as Nehru, and in all probability Mountbatten too, knew full well at the time even though they allowed it to be enshrined in formal communications to M.A. Jinnah and in the Indian *White Paper* of March 1948.

THE BIRTH OF A TRAGEDY

Accession after intervention, if indeed it took place at all, could all too well be accession under duress and, as such, of dubious validity.

One immediate effect of the accession story was that it provided grounds for the British to resist, in the first hours of the crisis, the direct involvement of the Pakistan Army in Kashmir as a counter to the intervention by the Indians. If the Pakistani leadership had known on the morning of October 27 1947, as the Indians started landing at Srinagar, that the State of Jammu & Kashmir had *not* yet acceded to India, it would have been hard indeed to justify British opposition to Pakistani overt involvement in the crisis (Pakistan, after all, had as legitimate an interest in the internal affairs of an *independent* adjacent State of Jammu & Kashmir as India). The Pakistani side had much easier access to Srinagar (along the Jhelum Valley Road) than did India; and, doubtless there would shortly have been a meeting of Pakistani and Indian troops, perhaps in the region of Baramula. It has been argued that such an encounter would surely have precipitated a general inter-Dominion war. In fact, it is more likely that it would have resulted, at a critical early stage, in the opening of realistic inter-Dominion discussions which might well have produced an acceptable compromise solution. This could well have taken the form of some kind of partition along communal lines. The involvement at this stage of regular Pakistani forces, of course, would also have helped keep the tribesmen in order.

Accession, whatever the facts might have been, has over the years become the central element in India's argument for possession of the State of Jammu & Kashmir. As Krishna Menon put it to the Security Council of the United Nations during an address of prodigious length during its 762nd, 763rd and 764th meetings on 23–24 January 1957:

> On 26 October 1947 ... [in 1962, in another address to the Security Council, Menon changed the date to 27 October] ... the Maharaja of Kashmir ... submitted to the Governor-General of India an instrument of accession.... That instrument was sent over on 26 October and on the 26th Lord Mountbatten, Governor-General of India, accepted the accession.... The accession is complete.
>
> This is a very serious matter for us.... We are a federation; we are not a confederation, and the units that accede to federation stay in once they have acceded. There is no provision in our Constitution, there is no contemplation in our Constitution for secession.... It is well known to international law that in a federation of our kind there is no right of secession. ...

Therefore, the Government of India, out of considerations of security, out of considerations of international law and the law of India, and the law that has been given to it by the British Parliament, cannot ever accept the idea that accession is anything but an indissoluble bond. When Kashmir acceded, that matter was finished. Therefore, there is no such thing as going out. [*Official Records of the United Nations Security Council*, Year 12].

This line of argument, while basically false within the context of the actual course of events in late 1947, is very powerful, particularly in India. As long as it persists, however, the Kashmir problem is incapable of any solution involving Indian compromise (difficult to secure at the best of times). It would have been much better if, when India decided in late October 1947 to intervene in Kashmir, Mountbatten had not been so obstinate on the question of accession. By so doing, he effectively guaranteed the Kashmir tragedy.

Why this obsession with accession by Mountbatten at this crucial period, 25–27 October 1947? While accession was not in itself an essential prerequisite to intervention, it did ensure, as we have just observed, that Pakistan would be greatly hindered in countering the Indian initiative with comparable measures. Accession technically made the State of Jammu & Kashmir Indian sovereign territory, even if it was intended to be so temporarily, pending ratification by some reference to the people. India could do what it liked there. Pakistan, by the same token, could only cross onto Kashmiri territory at the risk of being labelled an aggressor. Accession, moreover, could also be argued to imply permanence despite talk about plebiscites and referenda. It would ensure that, come what may, India possessed a powerful argument (such a Krishna Menon was to wield, as we have seen) for staying in the State for ever. There is a great deal of evidence to suggest that some of the leading figures behind the overt Indian intervention in Kashmir on 27 October 1947 intended a permanent Indian occupation.

The introduction of the accession issue, then, made the Kashmir question virtually insoluble through any compromise. It took some time, however, for the full effects of the accession dogma to be felt in India, and up to the moment of the Indian reference to the United Nations on 1 January 1948 it was probably still of lesser importance than the various Indian commitments to a reference to the will of the Kashmiri people.

During the course of November and December 1947 there took place a series of Indo-Pakistani bilateral discussions (with British observers in the wings) which from time to time promised to yield at least the theoretical basis for a solution to the Kashmir problem. As we have seen in Chapter V, Indian and Pakistani officials (notably in the discussions of 8 November 1947) came very close to securing agreement on the terms for their mutual disengagement from Kashmiri territory such that would make the holding of a plebiscite acceptable to both parties. In the event, these efforts all aborted. Why?

The complex of animosities and suspicions between the leaders of the two new Dominions which had contributed so much towards precipitating the crisis of 22–27 October 1947 continued, naturally enough, to add to the difficulty of securing a settlement. A solution of some kind, however, might still have been agreed (a number of civil and military officials on both sides soon perceiving the essential futility of the first Kashmir war) had it not been for the profound emotional involvement of the Indian Prime Minister, Jawaharlal Nehru, with his ancestral land. Nehru (as was to become evident again in 1953, another near miss in the sad history of Indo-Pakistani compromise) could never quite bring himself to agree to any proposal which involved a significant risk that the Vale of Kashmir, and its capital city of Srinagar, might pass from Indian to Pakistani hands. In that any settlement involving the criteria of a Pakistani possession of contiguous Muslim-majority areas, be it explicit or implicit, involved just this, Nehru was determined to block the application in any shape or form to his beloved Kashmir of those principles which had brought Pakistan into being. Rather than be caught up in bilateral discussions in which he might have in person to make proposals to the Pakistani leadership which put the Indian title to the Vale at risk, he chose a reference to the United Nations. Somebody else would have to take on the hated task of talking to the Pakistanis; and he would retain (as, indeed, proved to be the case) the option of repudiating any suggestions which were not to his taste.

There was, as we have seen, a collusive element in this proceeding. Pakistan was persuaded by British mediators to put up with a bit of Indian condemnation in order to get India not only to agree in principle to the United Nations reference but also to its practical initiation. What Pakistan clearly imagined was that the United Nations would preside over discussions not all that different in nature from those bilateral Indo-Pakistani talks which had been going on for the last two months: these were very largely concerned in one way or another with practical issues arising from

THE BIRTH OF A TRAGEDY

the plebiscite concept. What could not be agreed bilaterally might perhaps, the Pakistan side hoped, be accepted in the moderating presence of third parties provided by the United Nations.

In the event Pakistan found something very different. While the United Nations appreciated the underlying terms of reference and concentrated upon practicable methods of bringing about a plebiscite to settle Kashmir once and for all according to the wishes of the people, the Indian side increasingly interpreted the main object of the exercise to be the international condemnation of Pakistan as an aggressor. Only if Pakistan "vacated its aggression" under international pressure would India contemplate a plebiscite which, conducted under the umbrella of the Indian Army and dominated by the presence of Sheikh Abdullah, ought (at least in the first year or two) to assure a result entirely to India's taste. Pakistan was presented with terms which it could not possibly accept. In these circumstances the efforts of the United Nations were doomed to failure. The eventual tragedy of Kashmir was now inevitable.

The United Nations in 1948 offered the last chance for a peaceful settlement of the Kashmir question. It was lost for many reasons, but paramount must rank the Indian attitude. Nehru, as we have already observed, just could not bring himself to stand by and permit his ancestral homeland, the Vale of Kashmir, pass into the hands of Pakistan. Indian public opinion, increasingly convinced of the merits of the accession argument, supported him to the full. Nehru has now gone. Over the years, however, the force of accession has grown ever stronger, not least in the face of attempts by other portions of the Indian Union to secede. It is certainly far harder to demolish this dogma today than it would have been in 1948, let alone late 1947.

The tragedy of Kashmir is twofold, human and geopolitical.

First the human tragedy. In March 1947, as we have seen, the leaders of Congress, Jawaharlal Nehru and Vallabhbhai Patel above all, concluded that it was impossible for that body to control all of the Punjab, a Province with powerful Muslim-majority areas: hence, at the risk of considerable over-simplification, there came about Partition. Congress, whatever its leaders have said since, accepted a definition of the limits of its authority in which communal criteria played a vital part. In Kashmir since 1989 it has become abundantly clear that this conclusion was correct. India under a system of government which is essentially the Congress legacy cannot rule a Muslim-majority State. In an effort to do so India has had to abandon

THE BIRTH OF A TRAGEDY

those high moral principles, the message of Mahatma Gandhi, in which it used to take such pride, and resort to methods of repression which rival, indeed probably exceed, anything the British ever wrought against their Indian colonial subjects since 1858. The result has been appalling for the people of Kashmir. Tens of thousands have now been slaughtered. There have been assassinations, rapes, tortures, arson, all exceedingly well documented not only in the media outside India but also within that country. It has been horrible for the Vale of Kashmir, a land so often equated with an earthly paradise. It has also been singularly unpleasant for Indians of goodwill throughout the Subcontinent who have taken little pleasure in being associated with such atrocities.

Second, the geopolitical consequences. These have been catastrophic. India and Pakistan ought to have evolved, if not as firm friends, at least as symbiotic cohabitants of the Subcontinent. Instead, from the outset they have lived as enemies, thrice engaged in overt war and generally in a state of confrontation which has dominated both their economies and their foreign policies. Two essentially very poor countries have turned themselves into military powers of the first magnitude, complete with the full panoply of arms (particularly in the case of India) including nuclear devices and missile delivery systems. A zone of instability has been created which has expanded its influence far beyond the limits of Indo-Pakistani territory, to China, to the States of the former Soviet Union, to Afghanistan and the Middle East, into the Indian Ocean.

The tragedy of Kashmir, and all its ramifications and consequences, must stop. No person with the modicum of concern for human rights can contest this proposition. What is disputed, of course, is how the horror can be ended.

The dominant conclusion from the study of the events presented here is that any realistic settlement of the Kashmir dispute must take into account how the dispute started, in fact rather than in myth, and what were the essential issues at the beginning, arising as they did from the same circumstances which brought about the end of the British Indian Empire, the partition of the Subcontinent and the creation of a new Islamic polity, Pakistan.